PROJECT BASED

SOLIDWORKS 2020

Kirstie Plantenberg

University of Detroit Mercy

Publications

SDC Publications
P.O. Box 1334
Mission, KS 66222
913-262-2664
www.SDCpublications.com
Publisher: Stephen Schroff

ISBN-13: 978-1-63057-320-1
ISBN-10: 1-63057-320-5

Printed and bound in the United States of America.

PROJECT BASED SOLIDWORKS®

PREFACE

Overview

Project Based SOLIDWORKS® is specifically designed to complement an engineering graphics course. It covers how to apply engineering graphics concepts such as part prints, section views, assembly drawings, tolerancing and fasteners. It also extends these topics into the world of design.

Project Based SOLIDWORKS® takes a specific part or assembly and teaches you how to model each part and its configurations, create part prints including assembly drawings if appropriate, and takes it one step further and teaches concepts such as FEA, tolerancing, and parametric design.

Many students prefer learning software through video instruction. Therefore, this book comes with instructional videos showing how to perform each of the tutorials. It also comes with instructional videos showing how to complete each problem in the book. The exceptions are when a problem is open ended and each student will get different results or if the problem is a quiz problem.

After completing all the tutorials in this book, you will be able to design moderately difficult parts and assemblies in a realistic manner. This book is perfect for a Freshman design class that wishes to include realistic design problems within their curriculum.

Structure

Project Based SOLIDWORKS® is arranged in projects. For example, Chapter 2 deals with the modeling of a Connecting Rod, Chapter 3 continues with the connecting rod to introduce the concept of configurations, Chapter 4 creates a part print of the connecting rod, and Chapter 5 wraps up the project by performing a static FEA on the connecting rod. At the beginning of each chapter a list of pre-requisite tutorials or knowledge is listed. You do not necessarily need to complete the tutorials within the book in order, but make sure that you have the pre-requisite knowledge before you begin.

Topics covered

The following topics are covered in this book.

- Part modeling
- Part configurations
- Assembly
- Static FEA
- Part Prints
- Assembly drawings
- Fasteners
- Tolerancing
- Parametric Modeling
- 3D-sketches

Student Supplements

      Project Based SOLIDWORKS® comes with video help and tutorial files. Videos of each tutorial and problem are given for those students that need extra help or are visual learners. Additional videos on specific difficult topics are also included. Also included are all the tutorials files that a student will need to complete the assignments.

Instructor Supplements

      Quiz files will be provided to instructors. These are the files that students will need in order to complete some of the quizzes presented in the book.

Have questions? E-mail: plantenk@udmercy.edu
                  Please include the book and edition that the question refers to.

Found a mistake? Please e-mail a detailed description of the errata to:
                  plantenk@udmercy.edu
                  Please include the book and edition that the errata refers to.

This book is dedicated to my family for their support and help.

I would also like to thank Joseph Jessop, Paul Dellock, and Job Gumma for the use of their models as quiz problems in the book.

PROJECT BASED SOLIDWORKS®

TABLE OF CONTENTS

<u>NOTES:</u>

CHAPTER 1

INTRODUCTION TO SOLIDWORKS®

CHAPTER OUTLINE

1.1) PREREQUISITES

To complete this tutorial, you are not expected to have any prior experience with solid modeling programs. The following topics are prerequisites for this tutorial.

- Familiarity with computer navigation (e.g. how to open a program, what is a pull-down menu.)

1.2) WHAT YOU WILL LEARN

The objective of this tutorial is to introduce you to SOLIDWORKS® and its user interface. You will be modeling the very basic part shown in Figure 1.2-1.

<u>File setup and User interface</u>

- New
- Save
- Help
- Resources
- Pull-down menu
- Units
- View (heads-up) toolbar

<u>Sketcher</u>

- Sketching on a plane or face
- Circle
- Line

<u>Features</u>

- Extrude Base/Boss
- Extrude Cut

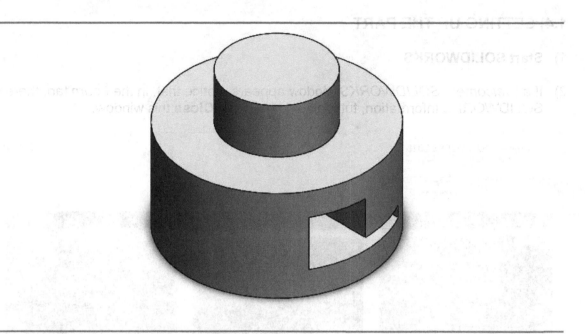

Figure 1.2-1: Basic part model

1.3) TUTORIAL LAYOUT

Each tutorial in this book consists of a series of steps that will ultimately produce a part, assembly or drawing and blocks. If an operation or step is new (e.g. this is the first time this particular operation is presented), an informational block will accompany the step explaining the different options of the operation and possibly some related commands/operations. An abbreviated index at the back of the book lists the commands covered in this book and the chapter where its informational block can be found.

Each command, in SOLIDWORKS®, can be accessed through the *Command Manager*, *toolbars*, or the *pull-down menu*. If a command is accessed through the *Command Manager* or *toolbar*, a command in bold will be listed next to its associated icon (e.g. **Line**). If a command is accessed through the *pull-down menu*, it will be listed in a series of bolded commands (e.g. **View – Toolbars – Dimensions/Relations**) as shown below. If more explicit information about an icon's location is needed, the tab location or window name will be given in italics (e.g. *Command Manager*).

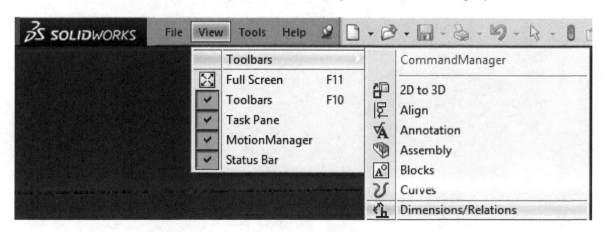

1.4) SETTING UP THE PART

1) **Start SOLIDWORKS**

2) If a *Welcome – SOLIDWORKS* window appears, notice that, in the *Learn* tab, there is SOLIDWORKS information, tutorials and training. **Close** this window.

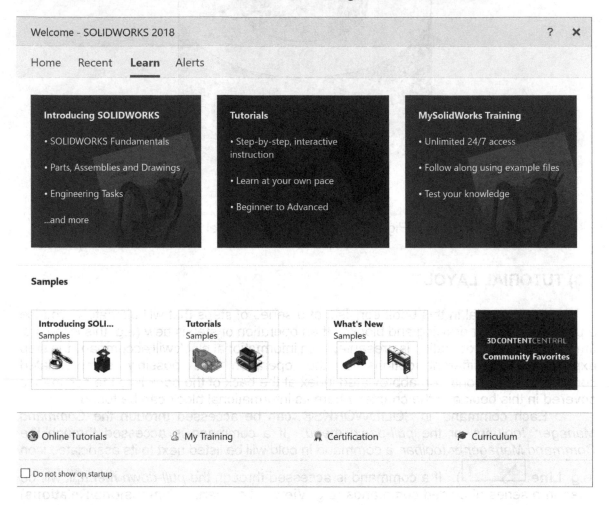

3) Look at the informational block on the *SOLIDWORKS® User Interface* to get familiar with the different areas of the interface.

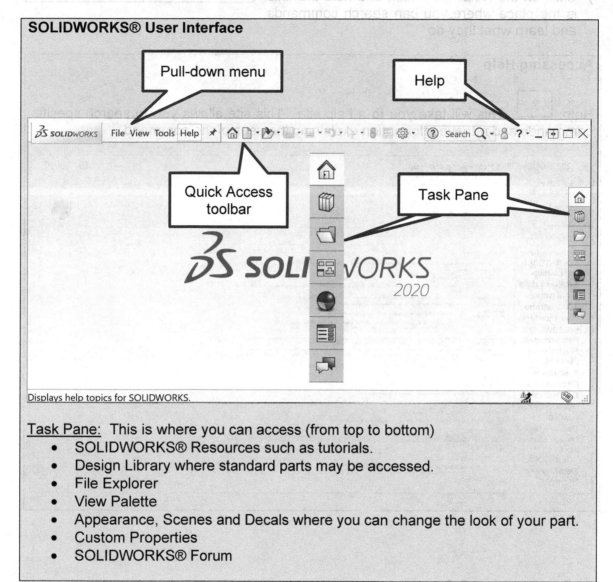

Task Pane: This is where you can access (from top to bottom)
- SOLIDWORKS® Resources such as tutorials.
- Design Library where standard parts may be accessed.
- File Explorer
- View Palette
- Appearance, Scenes and Decals where you can change the look of your part.
- Custom Properties
- SOLIDWORKS® Forum

4) Click on the Help 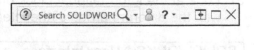 icon and note that this is the place where you can search commands and learn what they do.

Accessing Help

Help: ?   This will take you to a help site. This site allows you to search specific commands and retrieve information explaining the uses of the command.

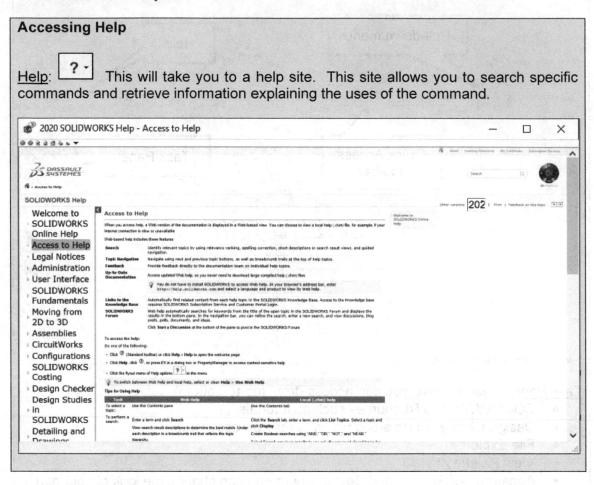

5) Pin the pull-down menu. (See the informational block on **Accessing the Pull-down menu**.)

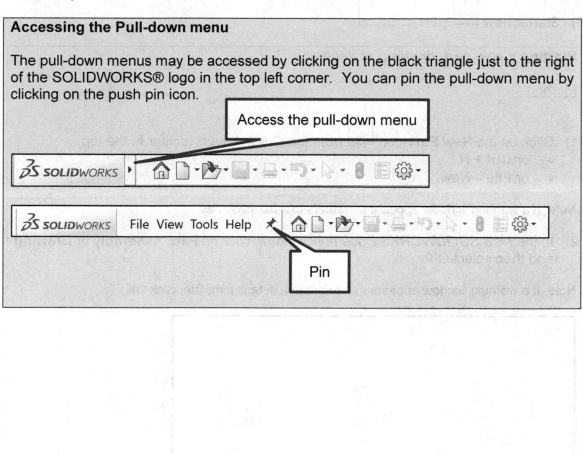

Accessing the Pull-down menu

The pull-down menus may be accessed by clicking on the black triangle just to the right of the SOLIDWORKS® logo in the top left corner. You can pin the pull-down menu by clicking on the push pin icon.

Access the pull-down menu

Pin

6) Start a **new**  **part** .

Starting a new part, drawing or assembly

<u>Method 1</u>

1) Click on the **New Part** icon from the *Quick Access* toolbar at the top.
   - or **Ctrl + N**
   - or **File – New…**

Note: If a warning window appears that refers to a file, click **Yes**.

2) In the *New SOLIDWORKS Document* window, click on **Part, Assembly** or **Drawing** and then select **OK**.

Note: If a warning window appears that refers to a default template, click **OK**.

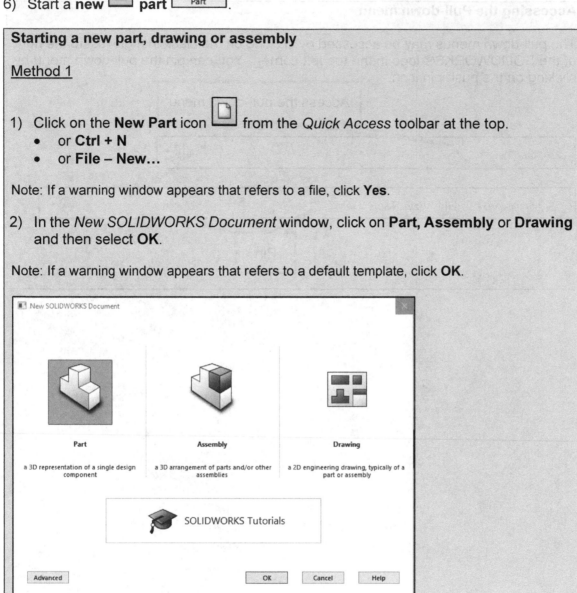

7) Notice the user interface of your new part. See the information block on **Part User Interface**.

Part User Interface

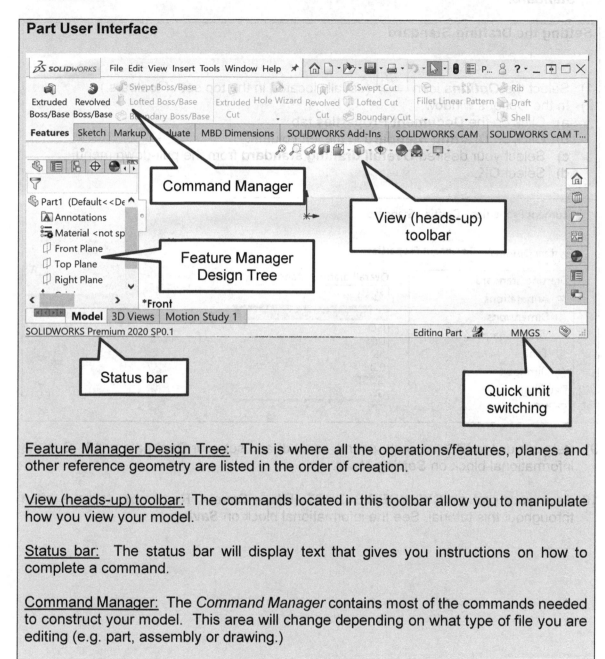

Feature Manager Design Tree: This is where all the operations/features, planes and other reference geometry are listed in the order of creation.

View (heads-up) toolbar: The commands located in this toolbar allow you to manipulate how you view your model.

Status bar: The status bar will display text that gives you instructions on how to complete a command.

Command Manager: The *Command Manager* contains most of the commands needed to construct your model. This area will change depending on what type of file you are editing (e.g. part, assembly or drawing.)

8) Set your drafting standard to **ANSI**. See the informational block on *Setting Drafting Standard*.

Setting the Drafting Standard

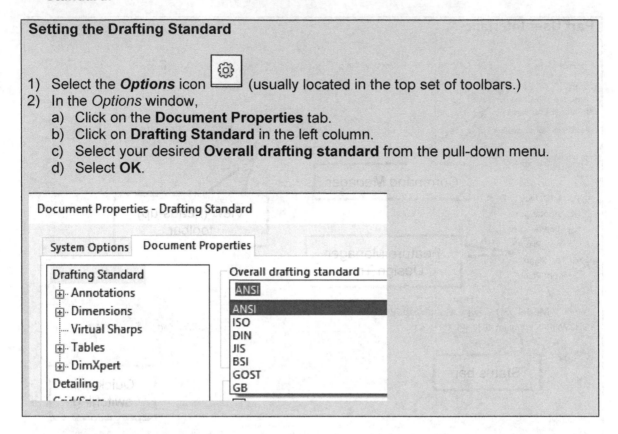

1) Select the *Options* icon 　 (usually located in the top set of toolbars.)
2) In the *Options* window,
   a) Click on the **Document Properties** tab.
   b) Click on **Drafting Standard** in the left column.
   c) Select your desired **Overall drafting standard** from the pull-down menu.
   d) Select **OK**.

Document Properties - Drafting Standard

System Options | Document Properties

Drafting Standard
  ⊞ Annotations
  ⊞ Dimensions
  ─ Virtual Sharps
  ⊞ Tables
  ⊞ DimXpert
Detailing

Overall drafting standard

ANSI
ANSI
ISO
DIN
JIS
BSI
GOST
GB

---

9) Set your unit to **IPS** (i.e. inch, pound, second) and set your **Decimals = .12**. See the informational block on *Setting Units*.

10) Save your part as **CYLINDER.SLDPRT** (**File – Save**). Remember to save often throughout this tutorial. See the informational block on *Saving*.

Setting Units

Method 1

1) Select the **Options** icon ⚙ (usually located in the top set of toolbars.)
2) In the *Options* window,
   a. Click on the **Document Properties** tab.
   b. Click on **Units** in the left column.
   c. Select your desired **Unit system**.
   d. Set your **Decimals**.
   e. Select **OK**.

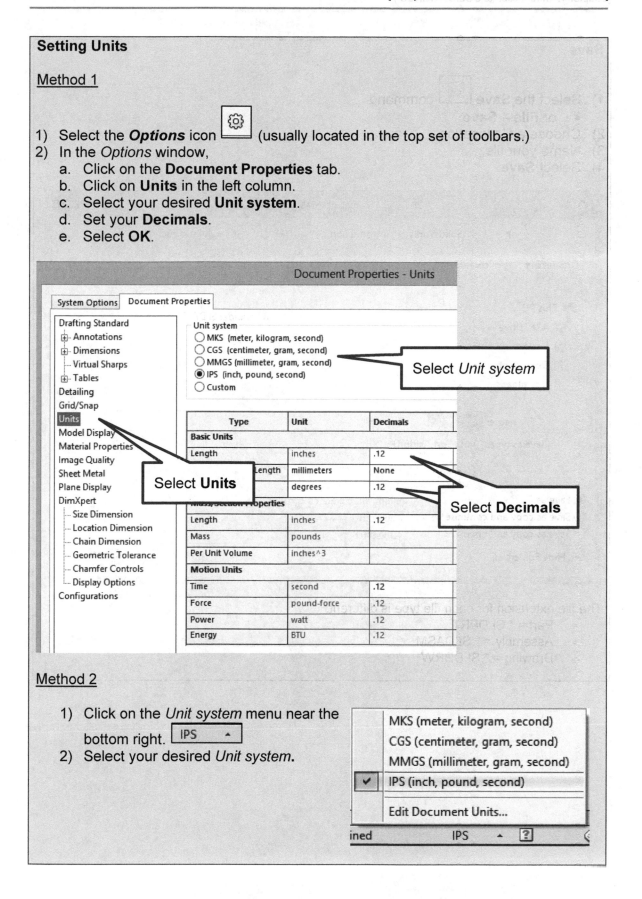

Method 2

1) Click on the *Unit system* menu near the bottom right. `IPS ▲`
2) Select your desired *Unit system*.

Save

1) Select the **Save** 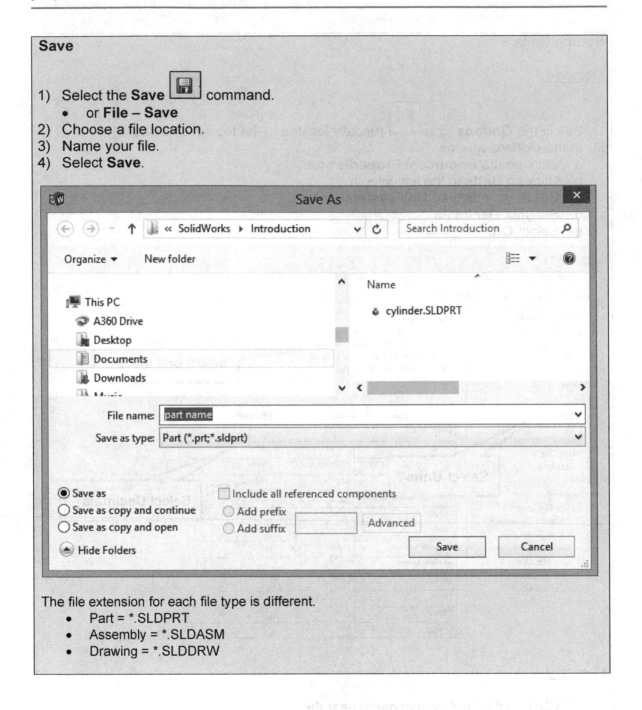 command.
   - or **File – Save**
2) Choose a file location.
3) Name your file.
4) Select **Save**.

The file extension for each file type is different.
- Part = *.SLDPRT
- Assembly = *.SLDASM
- Drawing = *.SLDDRW

1.5) SKETCHING AND EXTRUDE BOSS/BASE

1) **Sketch** 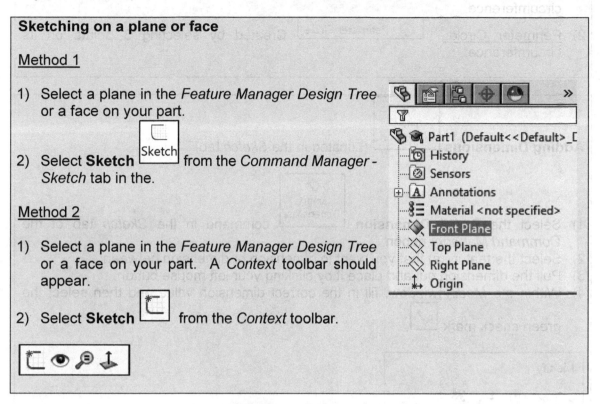 on the **Top Plane**. (See the informational block on **Sketching on a plane or face**.)

Sketching on a plane or face

Method 1

1) Select a plane in the *Feature Manager Design Tree* or a face on your part.

2) Select **Sketch** from the *Command Manager - Sketch* tab in the.

Method 2

1) Select a plane in the *Feature Manager Design Tree* or a face on your part. A *Context* toolbar should appear.

2) Select **Sketch** from the *Context* toolbar.

2) Sketch and **Dimension** a **Circle** whose center is **Coincident** with the origin and diameter is **2 inches**. Note that your cursor will snap to the origin making the center of the circle coincident with the origin. To do this, move your cursor near the origin and a small circle should appear when you have snapped to it. If the circle is too large to see its entirety, select the **F** key to fit all. (See informational block on **Drawing a Circle** and **Adding Dimensions**.)

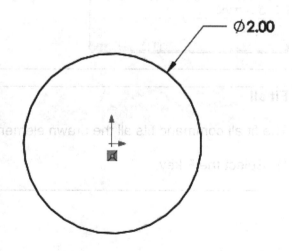

Ø**2.00**

Drawing a Circle (Located in the *Sketch* tab)

There are two ways to draw a circle:

1) Circle: ⊙ Circle Created by selecting a center point and then a point on its circumference.

2) Perimeter Circle: ⊕ Perimeter Circle Created by selecting 3 points on its circumference.

Adding Dimensions ◇ Smart Dimension (Located in the *Sketch* tab)

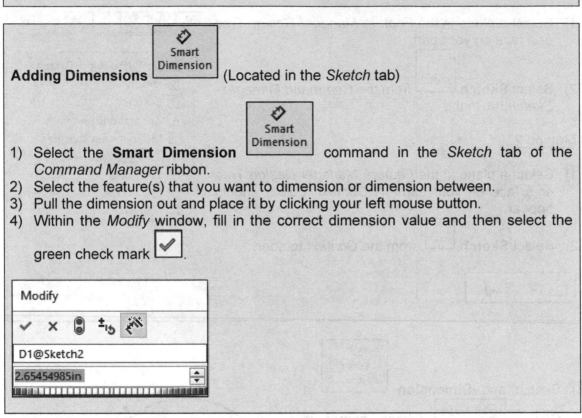

1) Select the **Smart Dimension** ◇ Smart Dimension command in the *Sketch* tab of the *Command Manager* ribbon.
2) Select the feature(s) that you want to dimension or dimension between.
3) Pull the dimension out and place it by clicking your left mouse button.
4) Within the *Modify* window, fill in the correct dimension value and then select the green check mark ✓.

Modify
✓ ✕ 🔘 ±₅ 📐
D1@Sketch2
2.65454985in

Fit all

The fit all command fits all the drawn elements with the visible area.

1) Select the **F** key.

---

3) Select the *Feature* tab and then use the **Extrude**

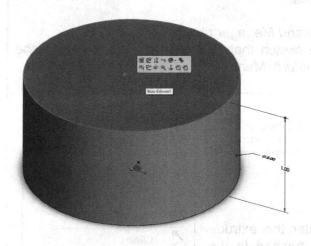

command to extrude the circle to a distance of **1.00 inch**. (See informational block on *Extrude Boss/Base*.)

4) **Sketch** and **Dimension** a **1.00 inch** diameter **Circle** on the top face of the cylinder. Make the center of the circle **Coincident** with the origin. Select **Ctrl + 8** to see the normal view. (See the informational block on *Sketching on a plane or face*.)

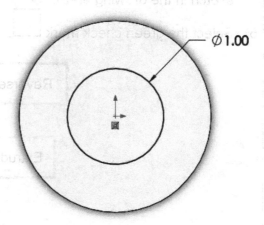

Extrude Boss/Base 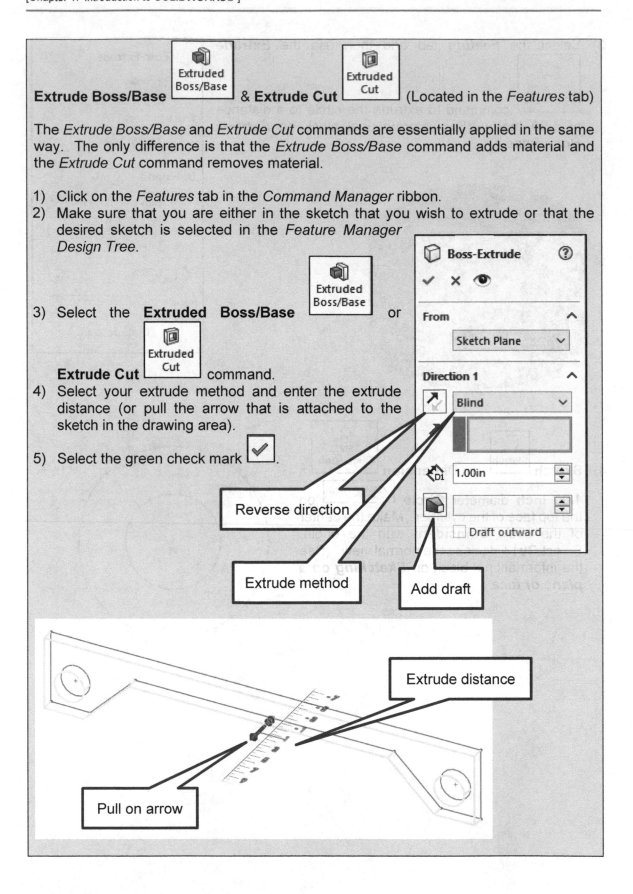 & **Extrude Cut** (Located in the *Features* tab)

The *Extrude Boss/Base* and *Extrude Cut* commands are essentially applied in the same way. The only difference is that the *Extrude Boss/Base* command adds material and the *Extrude Cut* command removes material.

1) Click on the *Features* tab in the *Command Manager* ribbon.
2) Make sure that you are either in the sketch that you wish to extrude or that the desired sketch is selected in the *Feature Manager Design Tree*.

3) Select the **Extruded Boss/Base** or

Extrude Cut command.
4) Select your extrude method and enter the extrude distance (or pull the arrow that is attached to the sketch in the drawing area).

5) Select the green check mark.

Reverse direction

Extrude method

Add draft

Extrude distance

Pull on arrow

Extrude Methods

The *Extrude Boss/Base* and *Extrude Cut* commands allow you to select between several different extrude methods.

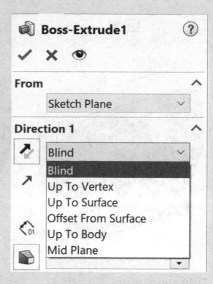

- Blind: Input a specific distance.
- Up to Vertex: Select a vertex you wish to extrude up to.
- Up to Surface: Select a surface you wish to extrude up to.
- Offset from Surface: Select a surface that you wish to extrude up to and then an offset from that surface.
- Up to Body: Select a body you wish to extrude up to.
- Mid Plane: Extrude about the mid plane. The extrude distance is the total distance. Half of the distance on each side of the mid plane.

The *Extrude Cut* has the additional methods of:

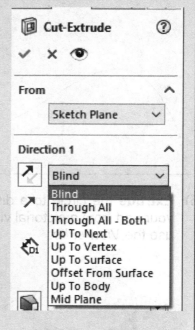

- Through All: Extrude through all material.
- Through – Both: Extrude through all material in both directions.

There is also an option to create a **Thin** extrude. This may be done with an open or closed profile.

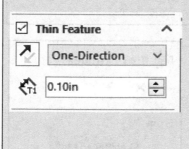

Examples of *Extrude* methods

<u>Blind</u>   <u>Mid Plane</u>   <u>Offset from Surface</u>

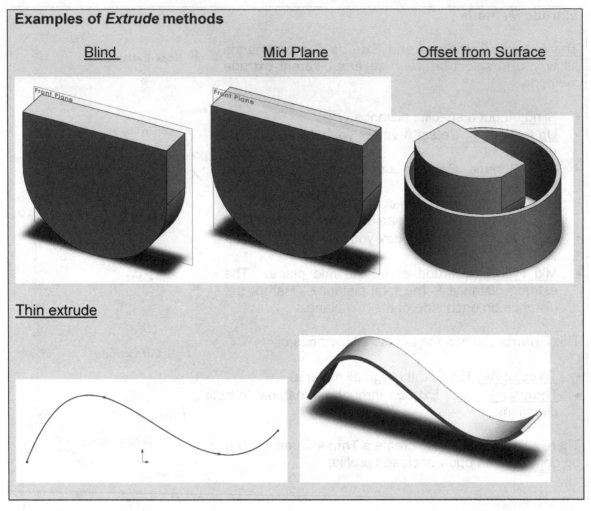

<u>Thin extrude</u>

5) **Extrude** the circle to a distance of **0.50 inch**. To see your part from a pictorial view, select the **Space bar** and use the *View cube*.

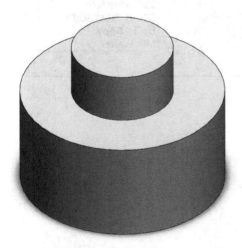

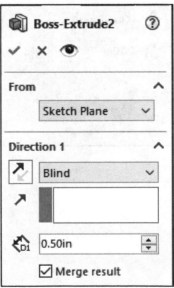

Viewing your part

Ctrl + 8 = Normal view
Ctrl + 7 = Isometric view

<u>Method 1</u>

1) Hit the **Space** bar.
2) A *View Selector* and *Orientation* window will appear.
3) The *View Selector* may be activated by selecting the **View Selector** icon 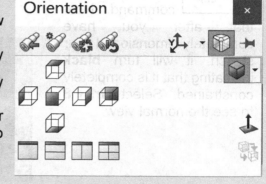 or by selecting **Ctrl + Space**.
4) Select the view, using the *View Selector* or *Orientation* window, from which you wish to view your part.

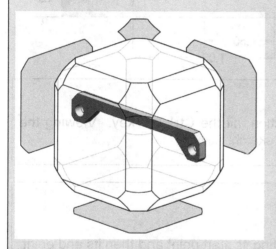

<u>Method 2</u>

1) View orientations may also be accessed from the *Heads-up* toolbar. You can also access the **pan** and **zoom** commands here.

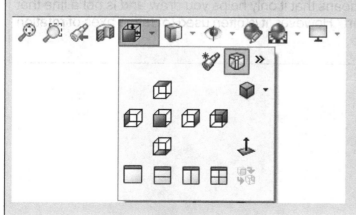

1.6) SKETCHING AND EXTRUDE CUT

1) **Sketch** on the **Right Plane**. Hit **Ctrl + 8** to see the normal view.

2) **Sketch** and **Dimension** the profile shown using the **Line**

   [/ Line] command. Note that after you have completely dimensioned your sketch, it will turn **black** indicating that it is completely constrained. Select **Ctrl + 8** to see the normal view.

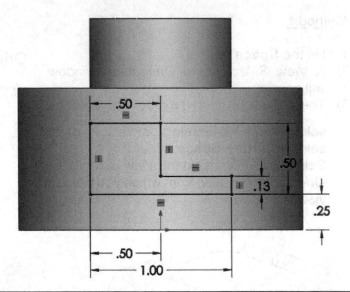

Viewing the Sketch plane

To view your sketch plane in the normal direction, hit the **Ctrl + 8** key. Viewing the sketch plane in this direction makes it easier to sketch.

Drawing a Line (Located in the *Sketch* tab)

1) Line: [/ Line] A *Line* is created by selecting its start point and then its end point.
   - Single line: Click (start point) – Hold – Drag – Release (end point)
   - Connected lines: Click (Start point) – Release – Click (end point)

2) Centerline: [Centerline] A *Centerline* is created exactly like a line, but it is a *Construction Geometry*. This means that it only helps you draw and is not a line that defines an edge of your solid part. However, it is often used to define axes of rotation for commands such as *Revolve*.

3) **Extrude Cut**  the sketch using the **Through All – Both** method. See the previous informational block on *Extrude Cut*.

4) **Save** your part.

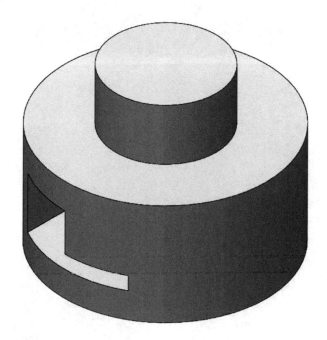

<u>NOTES:</u>

<u>NOTES:</u>

SOLIDWORKS® INTRODUCTION PROBLEMS

P1-1) Model the following object. Note that the dimensions are given in inches.

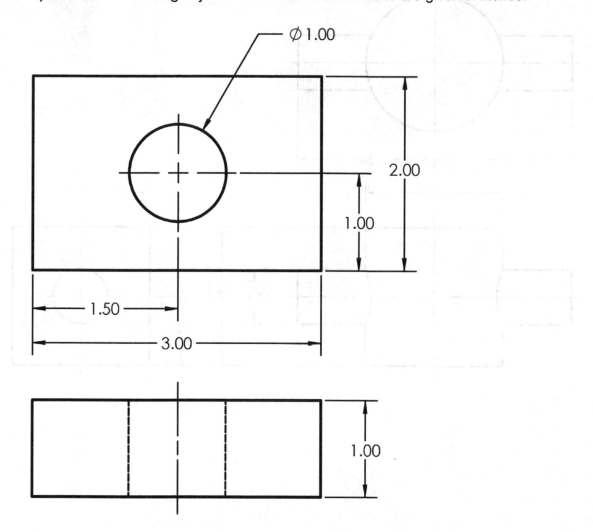

P1-2) Model the following object. Note that the dimensions are given in millimeters.

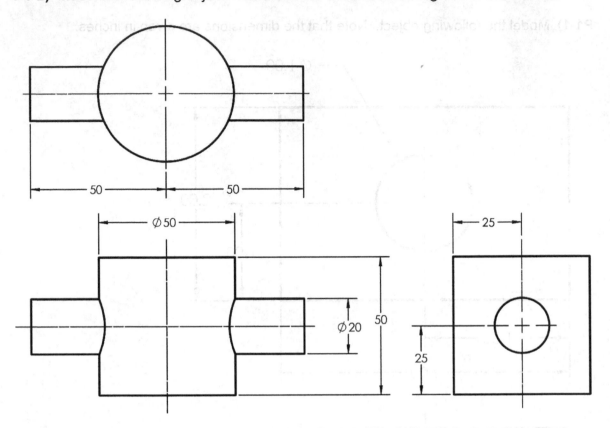

SOLIDWORKS® INTRODUCTION QUIZ PROBLEMS

Q1-1) Model the following 1020 Steel object and note the mass of your part. Note that the dimensions are given in millimeters. Directions on how to apply material and calculate the mass of your part are given on the next page.

	Group 1	Group 2	Group 3
A = Extrude Distance	90	100	110

Mass = _____ grams

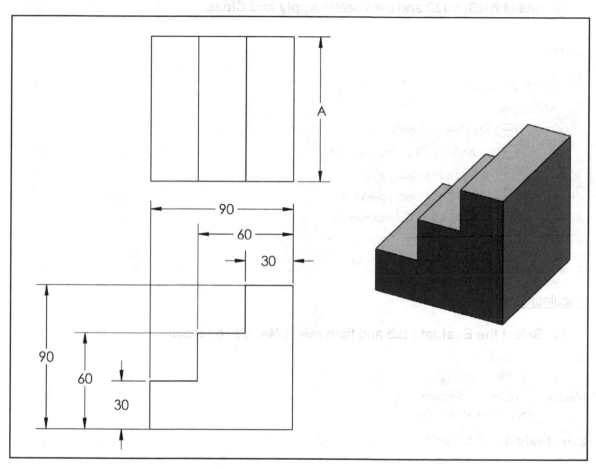

Applying Material

1) Right-click on **Material** in the *Feature Design Tree* and select **Edit Material**.

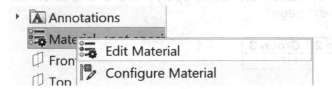

2) Select **ANSI 1020** and then select **Apply** and **Close**.

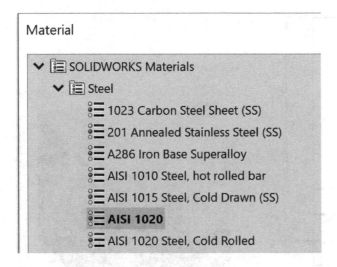

Calculating Mass

1) Select the **Evaluate** tab and then select **Mass Properties**.

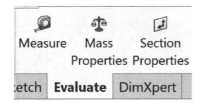

CHAPTER 2

CONNECTING ROD PROJECT
Model

CHAPTER OUTLINE

2.1) PREREQUISITES

Before completing this tutorial, you should have completed the following tutorial and be familiar with the following topics.

Pre-requisite Tutorial

- Chapter 1 – Introduction to SOLIDWORKS®

Pre-requisite Topics

- Computer navigation.
- Passing familiarity with orthographic projection.
- Ability to read dimensions.

2.2) WHAT YOU WILL LEARN

The objective of this tutorial is to introduce you to creating simple *Sketches*, *Extrudes* and *Cuts*. You will be modeling the connecting rod shown in Figure 2.2-1. Specifically, you will learn the following commands and concepts.

Sketching

- Sketch relations
- Editing dimensions
- Editing sketches
- Sketch chamfers
- Sketch fillet
- Rectangle

Features

- Chamfer
- Fillets
- Editing a feature

Material and properties

- Applying material
- Mass properties

View

- Panning
- Rotating

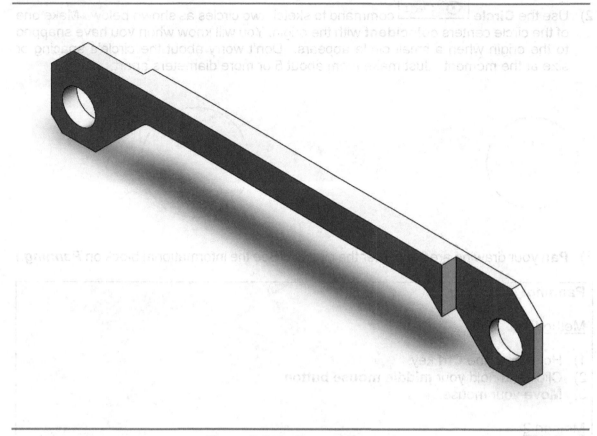

Figure 2.2-1: Connecting rod

2.3) SETTING UP THE PROJECT

1) **Start SOLIDWORKS** and then start a **new** ☐ **part** ⬚ .

2) Set your unit to **IPS** (i.e. inch, pound, second) and set your **Decimals = .12** and your

standard to **ANSI** (*Options* ⚙ – *Document Properties – Units*)

3) Save your part as **CONNECTING ROD.SLDPRT** (**File – Save**). Remember to save often throughout this project.

2.4) BASE EXTRUDE

1) **Sketch** ⬚ on the **Front Plane**.

2) Use the **Circle** 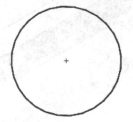 command to sketch two circles as shown below. Make one of the circle centers **coincident** with the origin. You will know when you have snapped to the origin when a small circle appears. Don't worry about the circle's spacing or size at the moment. Just make them about 5 or more diameters apart.

3) **Pan** your drawing area to center the circles. (See the informational block on **Panning**.)

Panning

Method 1

1) Hold down the **Ctrl** key.
2) Click and hold your **middle mouse button**.
3) **Move** your mouse.

Method 2

1) Select **View – Modify - Pan** commands.
2) Click your **left mouse button** and move the mouse.

4) Use the **Line** command to sketch the following profile. Be approximate. Don't worry about getting it exact. Notice that when you are drawing the lines that dashed lines will appear occasionally. These dashed lines allow you to snap to geometric features of the object that have already been drawn or to the origin.

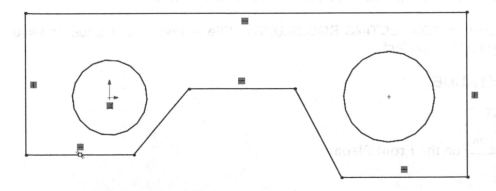

5) Add the following sketch relations. Don't worry if your drawing goes wonky. Just click and drag the elements into position. (See the informational block on *Applying Sketch Relations*.)

    a) If any of the **horizontal** or **vertical** lines are not perfectly horizontal or vertical, add those relations.

    b) Make the two circle diameters **Equal**.

    c) Make the circle centers **Horizontal**.

    d) Make the two bottom horizontal lines **Collinear**.

    e) Make the two bottom horizontal line lengths **Equal**.

    f) Make the two angled line lengths **Equal**.

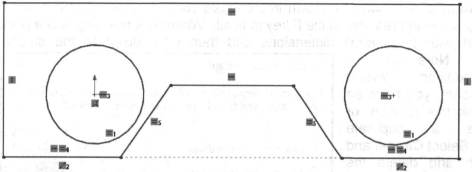

Applying sketch relations

Sketch relations add geometric constraints between two or more entities. For example, we can make two lines parallel, or two circles concentric.

1) Select one of the elements that you want to apply the relation to.
2) Hold the **Ctrl** key and then select the next element that you want to apply the relation to.
3) Continue selecting elements if you want to apply the relation to more than two elements.
4) In the *Properties* window, select the relation that you wish to apply.

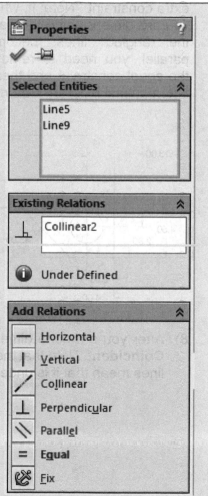

6) **View** your **Sketch Relations**. Your geometric relations will show up as symbols inside a green box. (See the informational block on *Viewing Relations*.)

Viewing relations

1) From the pull-down menu at the top, select **View – Hide/Show - Sketch Relations**.

---

7) Add the **Dimensions** [Smart Dimension] shown in the figure shown below. If your drawing exceeds your viewing area, select the **F** key to fit all. When dimensioning, it is a good idea to start with the overall dimensions and then work down to the smaller dimensions. Note that if a *Make Dimension Driven?* window appears, you have an unwanted sketch relation or you have a duplicate dimension. Select **Cancel** and then search and delete the extra constraint. Note: If, while you are dimensioning the part, the angled lines become parallel, you need to remove the equal constraint and then reapply it after you have adjusted the lines. (See the informational block on *Editing Dimensions*.)

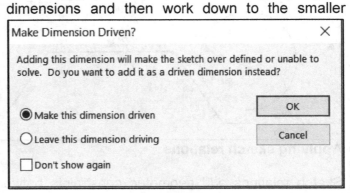

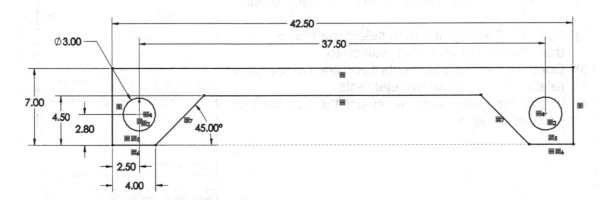

8) After you are done dimensioning, you should make the left circle and the origin **Coincident**. Note that there should be **no blue lines** when you are finished. Blue lines mean that it is under-constrained.

Editing a dimension

<u>Method 1</u>

1) Double click the dimension that you wish to edit.
2) Within the *Modify* window, fill in the correct dimension value and then select the

   green check mark ☑.

<u>Method 2</u>

1) Select the dimension that you wish to edit.
2) Features of the dimension may be changed within the *Dimension* window that appears on the left.

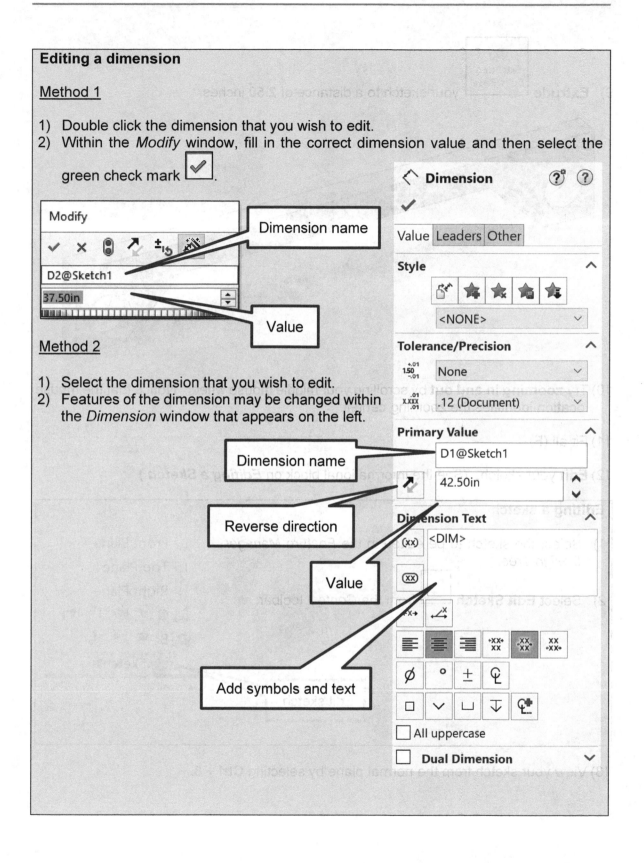

Dimension name

Value

Dimension name

Reverse direction

Value

Add symbols and text

9) **Extrude** 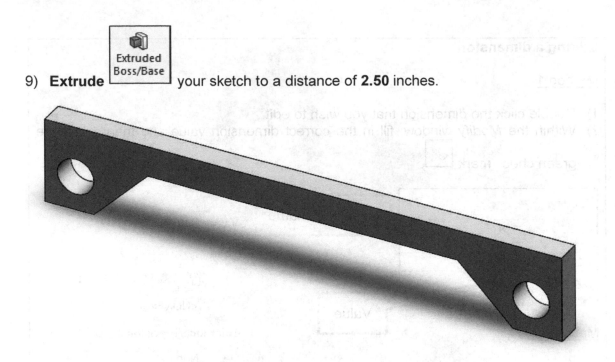 your sketch to a distance of **2.50** inches.

10) Try **zooming in and out** by scrolling your middle mouse wheel. Notice that the mouse location identifies the zooming center.

11) Fit all (**F**).

12) **Edit** your sketch. (See the informational block on *Editing a Sketch*.)

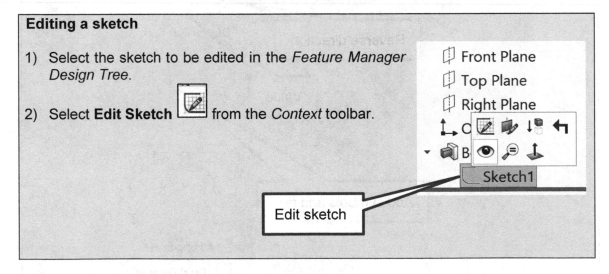

Editing a sketch

1) Select the sketch to be edited in the *Feature Manager Design Tree*.

2) Select **Edit Sketch** from the *Context* toolbar.

13) View your sketch from the normal plane by selecting **Ctrl + 8**.

14) Add two **2 x 45°** **Chamfers** ⟍ Sketch Chamfer to the top outside corners and two **1 x 45° Chamfers** to the bottom outside corners. The *Chamfer* command is located under the *Fillet* ⌐ Sketch Fillet command. When applying the 1 x 45°, select **Yes** in the warning window. Note that this will delete the *Equal* relation between the two bottom horizontal lines. Reapply the **Equal** relation after you have applied the chamfer. (See the information block on ***Sketch Chamfers & Sketch Fillets*.**) After you reapply the Equal relation, you may be asked to **Rebuild and Save**.

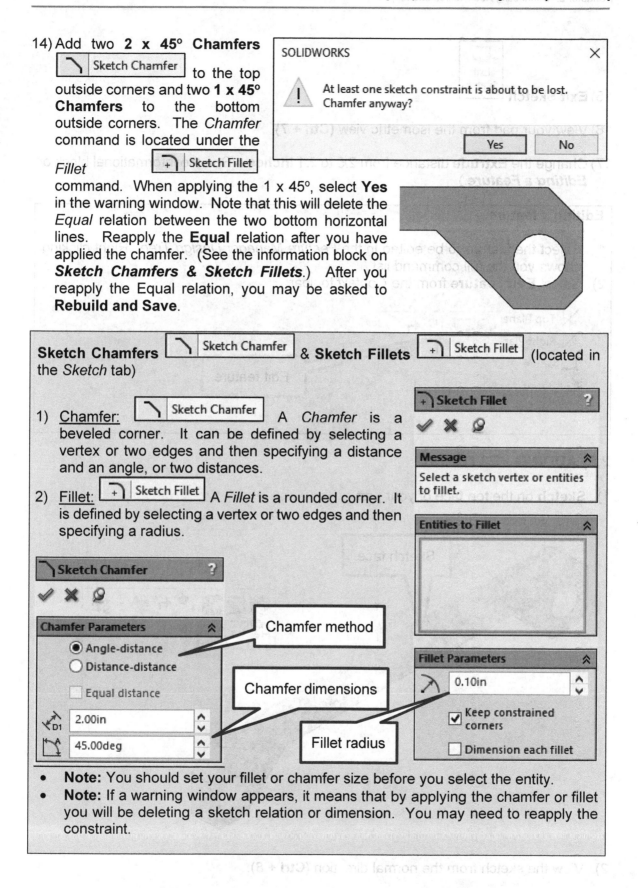

Sketch Chamfers ⟍ Sketch Chamfer **& Sketch Fillets** ⌐ Sketch Fillet (located in the *Sketch* tab)

1) <u>Chamfer:</u> ⟍ Sketch Chamfer A *Chamfer* is a beveled corner. It can be defined by selecting a vertex or two edges and then specifying a distance and an angle, or two distances.

2) <u>Fillet:</u> ⌐ Sketch Fillet A *Fillet* is a rounded corner. It is defined by selecting a vertex or two edges and then specifying a radius.

Chamfer method

Chamfer dimensions

Fillet radius

- **Note:** You should set your fillet or chamfer size before you select the entity.
- **Note:** If a warning window appears, it means that by applying the chamfer or fillet you will be deleting a sketch relation or dimension. You may need to reapply the constraint.

15) **Exit Sketch** .

16) View your part from the isometric view **(Ctrl + 7)**.

17) Change the **Extrude** distance from 2.5 to **2.1 inches**. (See the informational block on *Editing a Feature*.)

Editing a feature

1) Select the feature to be edited in the *Feature Manager Design Tree*. Right clicking shows you the full command list.
2) Select **Edit Feature** from the *Context* toolbar.

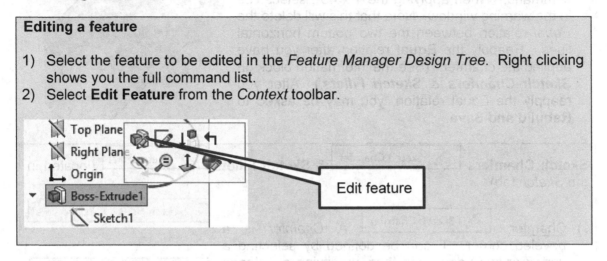

Edit feature

2.5) ADDING FEATURES

1) **Sketch** on the top face of your part.

Sketch face

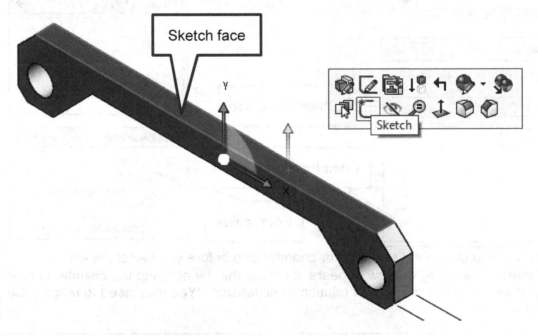

Sketch

2) View the sketch from the normal direction (**Ctrl + 8**).

3) Sketch and dimension the following two **Rectangles** 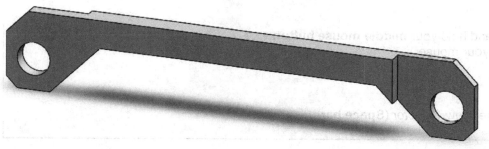 (See the informational block on *Rectangles*.)

4) **Extrude Cut** the rectangles **Through All**.

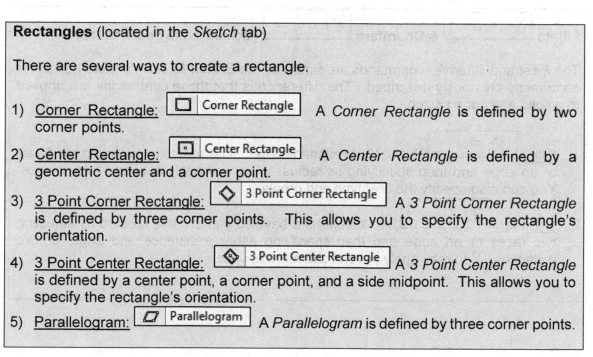

Rectangles (located in the *Sketch* tab)

There are several ways to create a rectangle.

1) Corner Rectangle: □ Corner Rectangle   A *Corner Rectangle* is defined by two corner points.

2) Center Rectangle: ▣ Center Rectangle   A *Center Rectangle* is defined by a geometric center and a corner point.

3) 3 Point Corner Rectangle: ◇ 3 Point Corner Rectangle   A *3 Point Corner Rectangle* is defined by three corner points. This allows you to specify the rectangle's orientation.

4) 3 Point Center Rectangle: ◈ 3 Point Center Rectangle A *3 Point Center Rectangle* is defined by a center point, a corner point, and a side midpoint. This allows you to specify the rectangle's orientation.

5) Parallelogram: ▱ Parallelogram   A *Parallelogram* is defined by three corner points.

5) Add **R1.00 Fillets** to the area where the angled lines meet the main body of the rod. You may need to **rotate** your part to view the underside of the part. (See the informational blocks on *Rotating your part* and *Fillets & Chamfers*.)

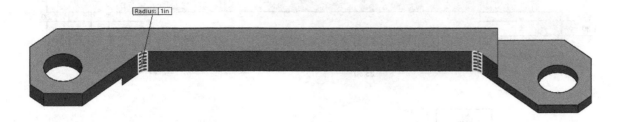

Rotating your part

Method 1

   1) Click and hold your **middle mouse button**.
   2) Move your mouse.

Method 2

   1) Use the *View Selector* (**Space bar**).

Fillets 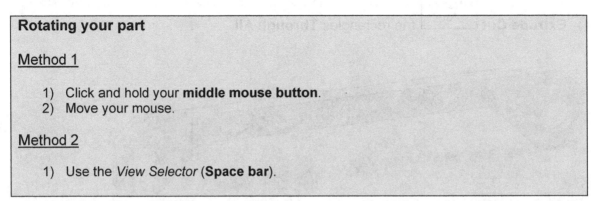 **& Chamfers** (located in the *Features* tab)

The *Fillet* and *Chamfer* commands are similar to the *Sketch Fillet* and *Sketch Chamfer* commands previously described. The difference is that these commands are applied to a solid and not a sketch.

1) Fillet: 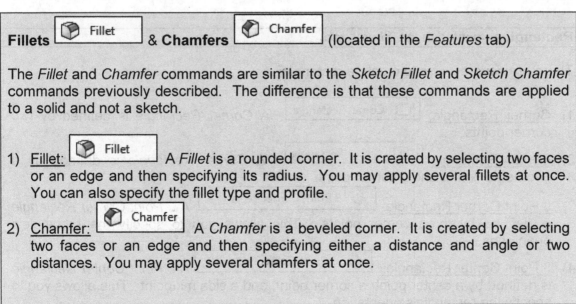 A *Fillet* is a rounded corner. It is created by selecting two faces or an edge and then specifying its radius. You may apply several fillets at once. You can also specify the fillet type and profile.

2) Chamfer: A *Chamfer* is a beveled corner. It is created by selecting two faces or an edge and then specifying either a distance and angle or two distances. You may apply several chamfers at once.

Fillets 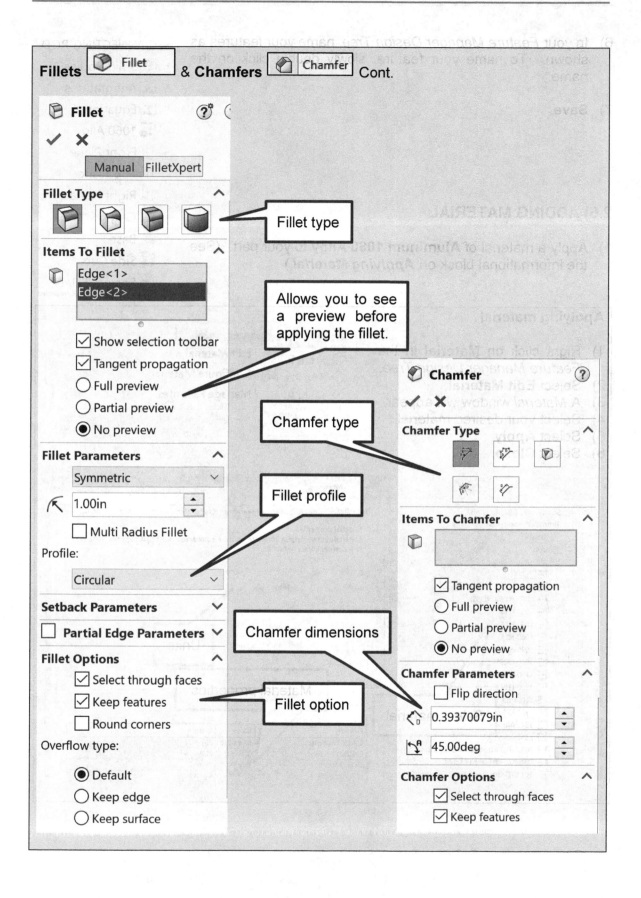 **& Chamfers** Cont.

Fillet type

Allows you to see a preview before applying the fillet.

Chamfer type

Fillet profile

Chamfer dimensions

Fillet option

6) In your *Feature Manager Design Tree*, name your features as shown. To name your feature, slowly double click on the name.

7) **Save**.

CONNECTING ROD
▸ 🗍 Solid Bodies(1)
▸ 🅰 Annotations
▸ ∑ Equations
   🔧 1060 Alloy
   🗍 Front Plane
   🗍 Top Plane
   🗍 Right Plane
   ↳ Origin
▸ 🗍 Base
▸ 🗍 Side Cuts
   🗍 Bottom Fillets

2.6) ADDING MATERIAL

1) Apply a material of **Aluminum 1060 Alloy** to your part. (See the informational block on *Applying Material*.)

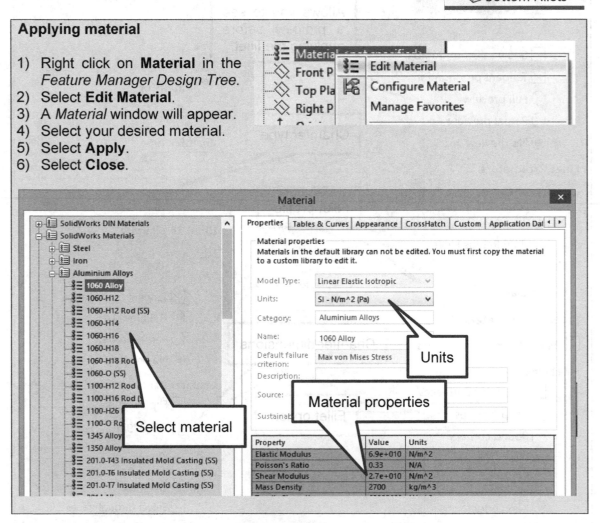

Applying material

1) Right click on **Material** in the *Feature Manager Design Tree*.
2) Select **Edit Material**.
3) A *Material* window will appear.
4) Select your desired material.
5) Select **Apply**.
6) Select **Close**.

Material[not specified]
Front P   — Edit Material
Top Pla   — Configure Material
Right P   — Manage Favorites

Material

SolidWorks DIN Materials	Properties	Tables & Curves	Appearance	CrossHatch	Custom	Application Dat

SolidWorks Materials
   Steel
   Iron
   Aluminium Alloys
      1060 Alloy
      1060-H12
      1060-H12 Rod (SS)
      1060-H14
      1060-H16
      1060-H18
      1060-H18 Rod
      1060-O (SS)
      1100-H12 Rod
      1100-H16 Rod (
      1100-H26
      1100-O Rod
      1345 Alloy
      1350 Alloy
      201.0-T43 Insulated Mold Casting (SS)
      201.0-T6 Insulated Mold Casting (SS)
      201.0-T7 Insulated Mold Casting (SS)

Material properties
Materials in the default library can not be edited. You must first copy the material to a custom library to edit it.

Model Type: Linear Elastic Isotropic
Units: SI - N/m^2 (Pa)
Category: Aluminium Alloys
Name: 1060 Alloy
Default failure criterion: Max von Mises Stress
Description:
Source:
Sustainab

Select material

Units

Material properties

Property	Value	Units
Elastic Modulus	6.9e+010	N/m^2
Poisson's Ratio	0.33	N/A
Shear Modulus	2.7e+010	N/m^2
Mass Density	2700	kg/m^3

2) Calculate the weight of your part. In the **Evaluate** tab, select **Mass Properties** 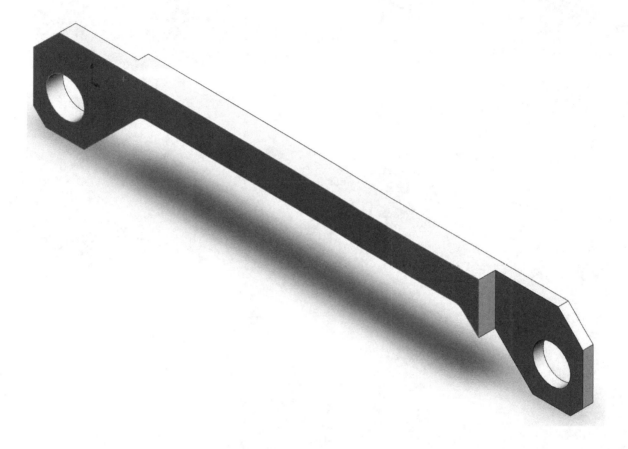. In the *Mass Properties* window note that the mass of your part is 22.22 lb. This is really the weight of your part because of the units. If your weight is not this value, your model is incorrect. This window also gives other physical properties.

<u>NOTES:</u>

<u>NOTES:</u>

CONNECTING ROD PROJECT (MODEL) PROBLEMS

P2-1) Create a solid model of the following 1345 Aluminum part and calculate the weight of the part. Dimensions are given in inches.

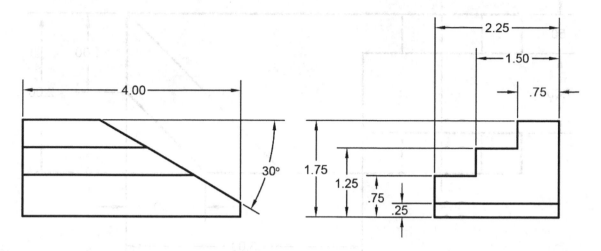

P2-2) Create a solid model of the following Gray Cast Iron part and calculate the weight of the part. Dimensions are given in inches.

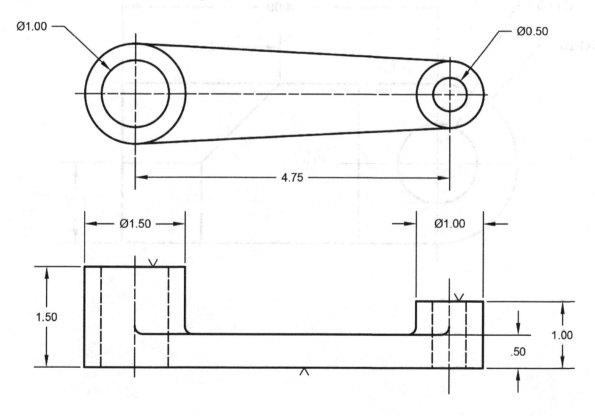

NOTE: ALL FILLETS AND ROUNDS R.12
UNLESS OTHERWISE SPECIFIED

P2-3) Create a solid model of the following 1020 Steel part and calculate the weight of the part. Dimensions are given in inches.

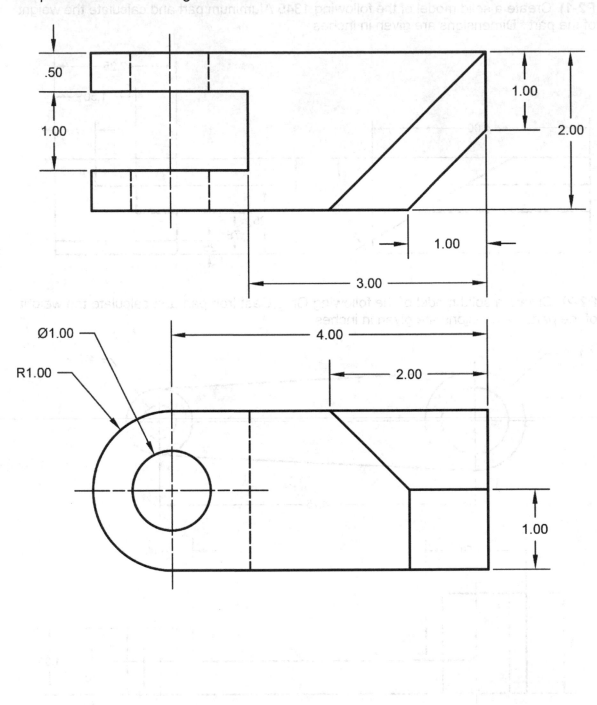

P2-4) Create a solid model of the following ABS plastic part and calculate the weight of the part. Dimensions are given in inches.

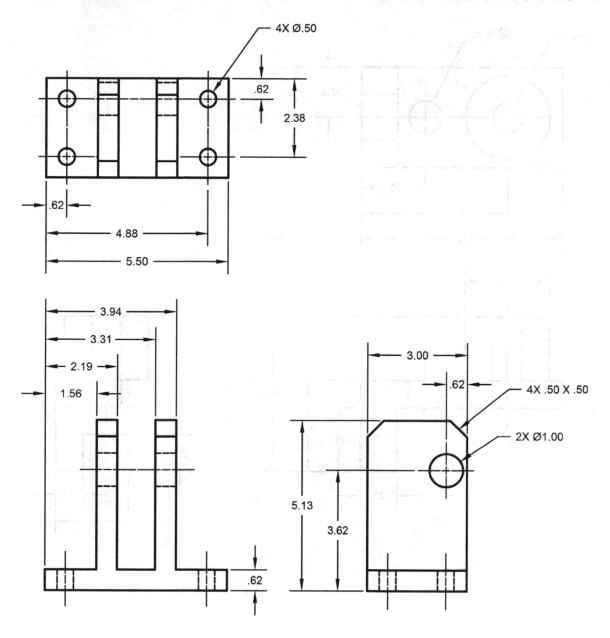

P2-5) Create a solid model of the following Brass part and calculate the mass of the part. Dimensions are given in millimeters.

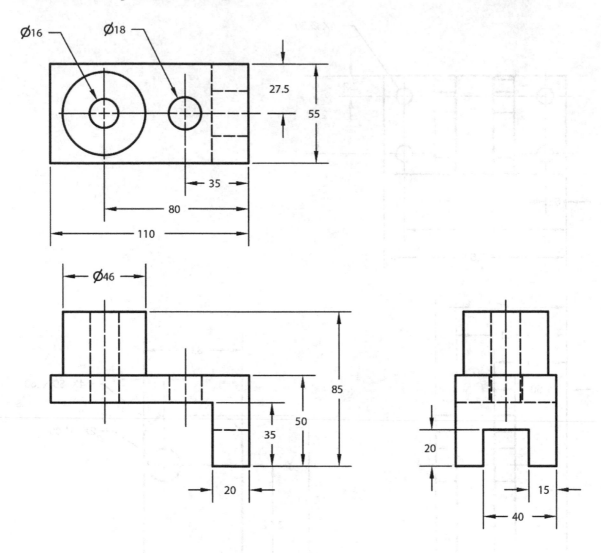

P2-6) Create a solid model of the following Oak part and calculate the weight of the part. Dimensions are given in inches.

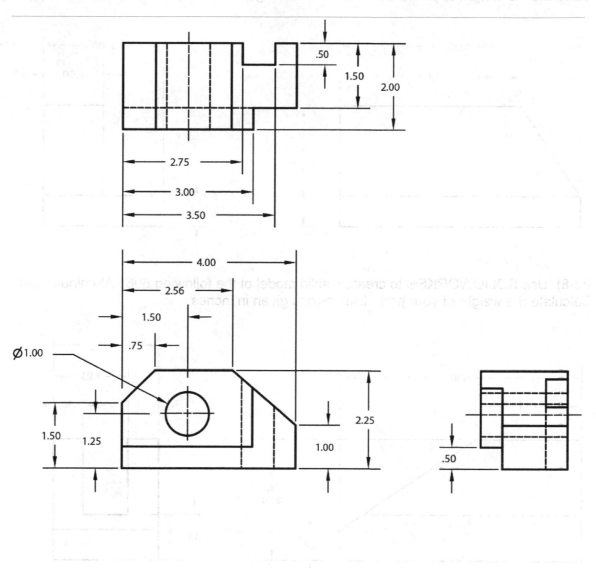

P2-7) Use SOLIDWORKS® to create a solid model of the following 1345 Aluminum part. Calculate the weight of your part. Dimensions are given in inches.

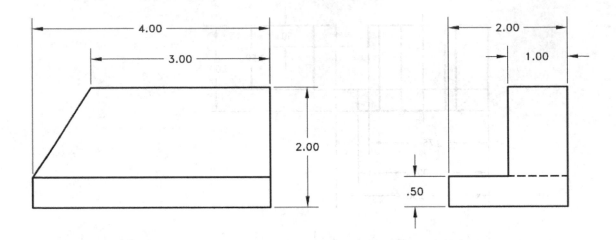

P2-8) Use SOLIDWORKS® to create a solid model of the following 6061 Aluminum part. Calculate the weight of your part. Dimensions given in inches.

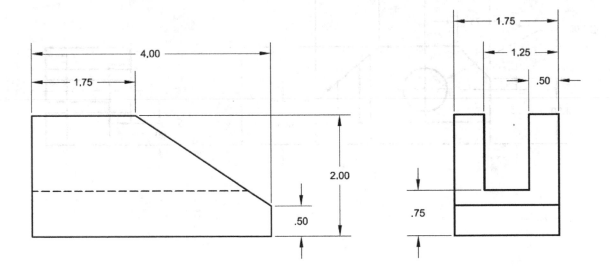

P2-9) Use SOLIDWORKS® to create a solid model of the following 1020 Steel part. Calculate the weight of your part. Dimensions given in inches.

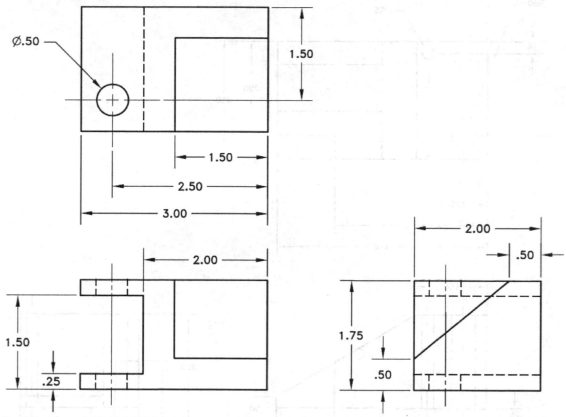

P2-10) Use SOLIDWORKS® to create a solid model of the following 1020 Steel part. Calculate the weight of your part. Dimensions given in inches.

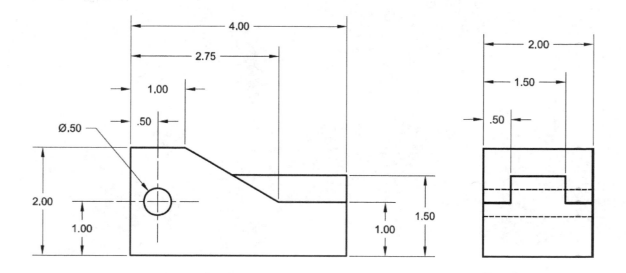

P2-11) Use SOLIDWORKS® to create a solid model of the following ABS plastic part. Calculate the weight of your part. Dimensions given in millimeters.

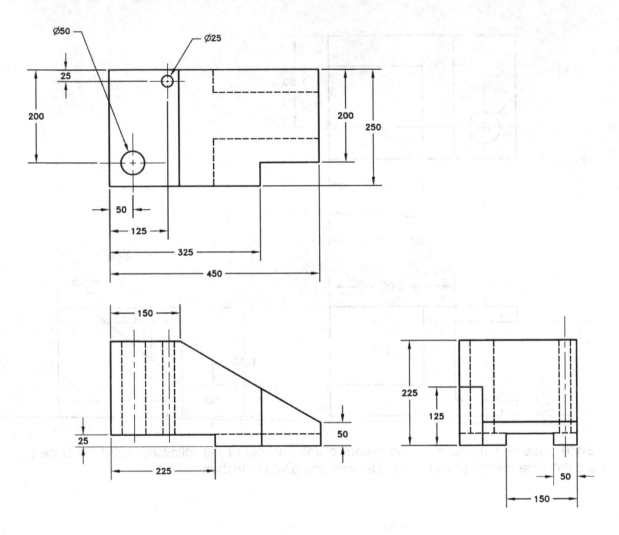

P2-12) Use SOLIDWORKS® to create a solid model of the following Oak part. Calculate the mass of your part. Dimensions given in millimeters.

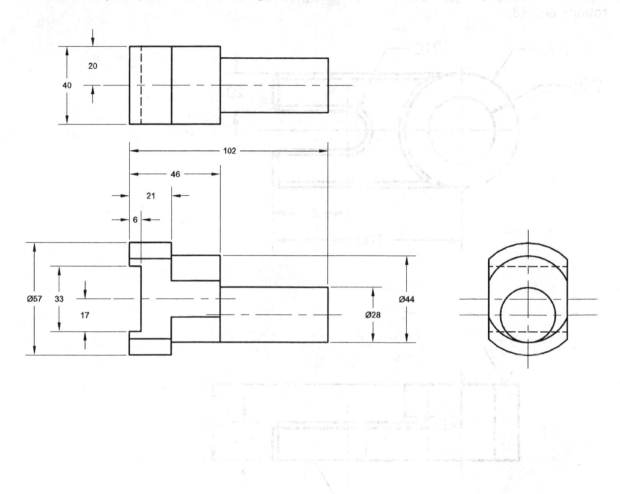

P2-13) Use SOLIDWORKS® to create a solid model of the following Grey Cast Iron. Calculate the mass of your part. Dimensions given in millimeters. Note that all fillets and rounds are R3.

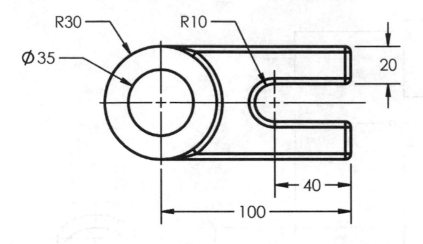

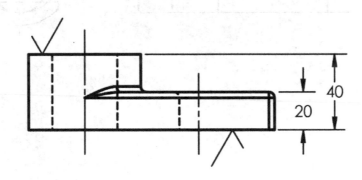

CONNECTING ROD PROJECT (MODEL) QUIZ PROBLEMS

Q2-1) Use SOLIDWORKS® to create a solid model of the following 1060 Aluminum Alloy part. Dimensions given in millimeters.

a) Calculate the mass of your part and circle the correct answer.

- 1835.02 grams
- 1724.08 grams
- 1040.73 grams
- 998.01 grams
- 783.99 grams
- 726.04 grams

Group 1	Group 2	Group 3
A = 100	A = 110	A = 90
B = 90	B = 100	B = 95
C = 50	C = 70	C = 40

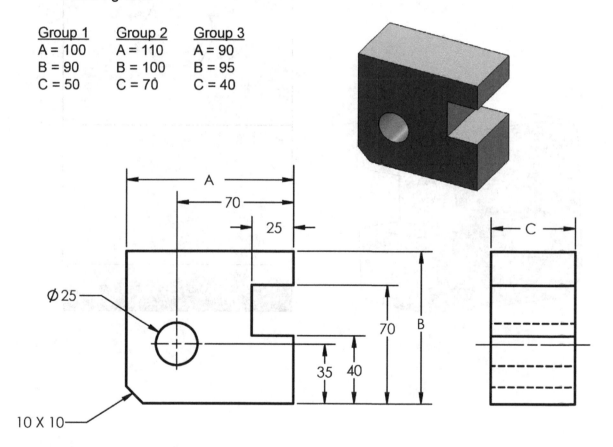

Ø 25

10 X 10

A

70

25

70

35   40

B

C

b) Make the following modifications to your part and calculate the mass.
   i.   Add three R10 fillets as shown.
   ii. Cut a hexagon through on the right side of the part as shown.

Mass = _____ grams

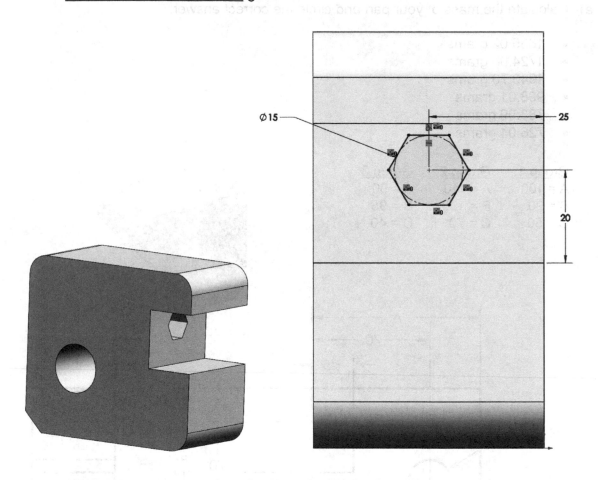

CHAPTER 3

CONNECTING ROD PROJECT
Configurations

CHAPTER OUTLINE

3.1) PREREQUISITES

Before starting this tutorial, you should have completed the following tutorial and be familiar with the following topics.

Prerequisite Tutorials

- Chapter 2 – Connecting Rod Project – Model

Prerequisite Topics

- Ability to read dimensions.

3.2) WHAT YOU WILL LEARN

The objective of this tutorial is to introduce you to SOLIDWORKS' ability to create configurations of a part. You will be creating configurations of the connecting rod shown in Figure 3.2-1. Specifically, you will be learning the following commands and concepts.

Features

- Configurations

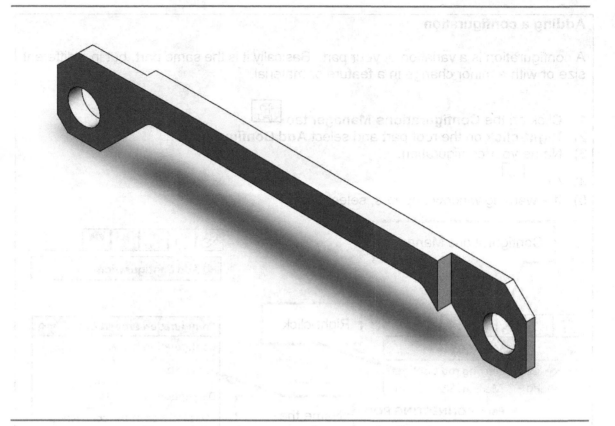

Figure 3.2-1: Connecting rod base configuration

3.3) CREATING CONFIGURATIONS

1) **Open** your **CONNECTING ROD.SLDPRT** file completed in *Chapter 2 – Connecting Rod Project - Model.*

2) Name the *Default* configuration **Medium**. Do this by entering the *Configuration Manager* (a tab found on the top of the *Feature Manager Design Tree*) and then slowly double clicking on the default name.

3) **Add** a **Configuration** for the *Connecting Rod* and call it **Short**. (See the informational block on ***Adding Configurations***.)

4) Add another configuration and name it **Long**.

5) **Double click** on **Short** to make this the active configuration.

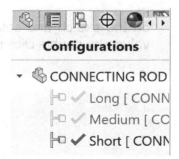

Configurations

▼ 🖏 CONNECTING ROD
  ├□ ✓ Long [CONN
  ├□ ✓ Medium [CC
  ├□ ✓ Short [CONN

Adding a configuration

A configuration is a variation of your part. Basically it is the same part, but in a different size or with a minor change in a feature or material.

1) Click on the **Configurations Manager** tab [icon].
2) **Right-click** on the root part and select **Add Configuration...**
3) Name your configuration.
4) Click [icon].
5) If a warning window appears, select **Yes**.

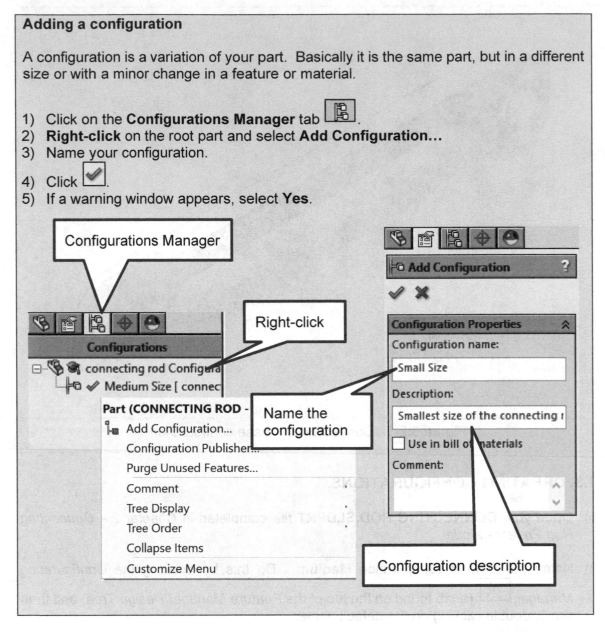

6) Get back into the **Feature Manager Design Tree** tab so that you can edit the *Short* configuration.

7) **Edit** the **sketch** attached to the **Base** extrude. Do this by expanding *Base* and click on the sketch and selecting **Edit Sketch** [icon]. Now you may edit the dimension values by double clicking on them.

8) Change the overall length to **25** and the distance between the holes to **20**. **IMPORTANT!!** Make sure that when you edit the dimensions that you apply it to only **This Configuration**. After you edit the dimension values, **Rebuild** 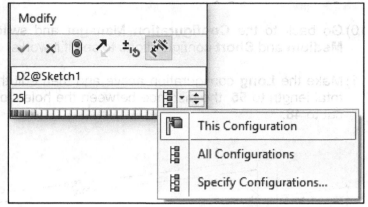 to see the effect. This icon is usually located at the top. If you get an error, you will have to look at your original configuration and figure out what is not constrained properly. If your sketch is not completely black, you will most likely have a problem applying configurations.

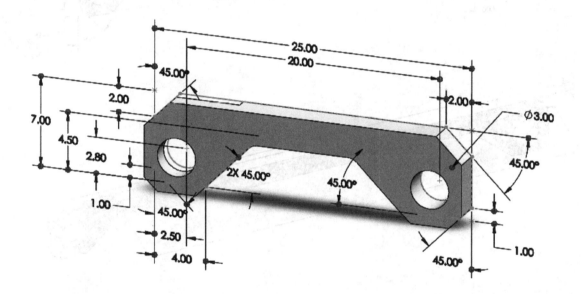

9) Notice that the side cut on the right side has disappeared. Change the dimension of the *Side cuts* as shown and then **Rebuild**. Remember to apply the dimension change to **This Configuration**.

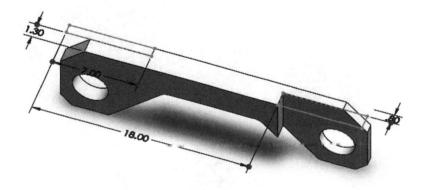

10) Go back to the **Configuration Manager** and switch back and forth between the **Medium** and **Short** configurations to see if it works.

11) Make the **Long** configuration active and then edit the sizes as shown. Change the total length to **55**, the distance between the holes to **50** and the distance to the side cut to **48**.

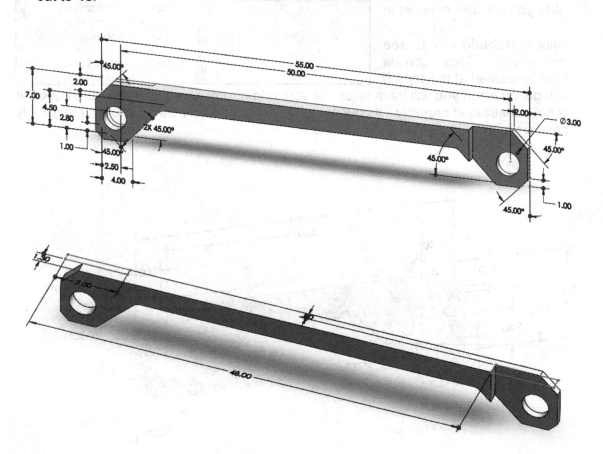

12) Go to the **Configuration Manager** tab and double click on the different configurations and see how the sizes change.

13) **Save**.

CONNECTING ROD PROJECT (CONFIGURATIONS) PROBLEMS

P3-1) Create a configuration of the part given in P2-1. Make the added configuration twice as long as the original part and determine the new configuration's weight.

P3-2) Create a configuration of the part given in P2-2. Make the added configuration have an increased diameter. Make the ∅1.50 diameter, ∅3.00 and determine the new configuration's weight.

P3-3) Create a configuration of the part given in P2-3. Suppress the holes in the new configuration and determine its weight.

P3-4) Create a configuration of the part given in P2-4. Create a configuration where the larger hole is half the size and the smaller holes are eliminated.

P3-5) Create a configuration of the part given in P2-5. Create a configuration where the solid cylinder on top is half the height/long and the material is Pine.

P3-6) Create a configuration of the part given in P2-6. Create a configuration where the hole is located 1.50 inches high (instead of 1.25) and the height of the part is 2.5 inches.

P3-7) Create a configuration of the part given in P2-7. Create a configuration where the base thickness is 1.00 inch (instead of 0.50 inch).

P3-8) Create a configuration of the part given in P2-8. Create a configuration where the thickness of the two upright walls is 0.25 inch (instead of 0.50 inch).

P3-9) Create a configuration of the part given in P2-9. Create a configuration where the holes are suppressed and the material part material is Brass.

P3-10) Create a configuration of the part given in P2-10. Create a configuration where the hole is suppressed and the thickness of the part is doubled. This includes the thickness of the tab.

P3-11) Create a configuration of the part given in P2-11. Create a configuration where the size of the large hole is changed to 25 mm (instead of 50 mm) and the height at which the angle face starts changes to 25 mm (instead of 50 mm).

P3-12) Create a configuration of the part given in P2-12. Create a configuration where the two larger cylinder diameters are doubled.

P3-13) Create a configuration of the part given in P2-13. Create a configuration where the 100 mm dimension changes to 150 mm.

NOTES:

CONNECTING ROD PROJECT (CONFIGURATIONS) QUIZ PROBLEMS

Q3-1) Model the following 1345 Aluminum part. Create three configurations as indicated in the table. Dimension are given in millimeters.

	Configuration 1	Configuration 2	Configuration 3
A	150	100	200
B	50	55	60
Mass			

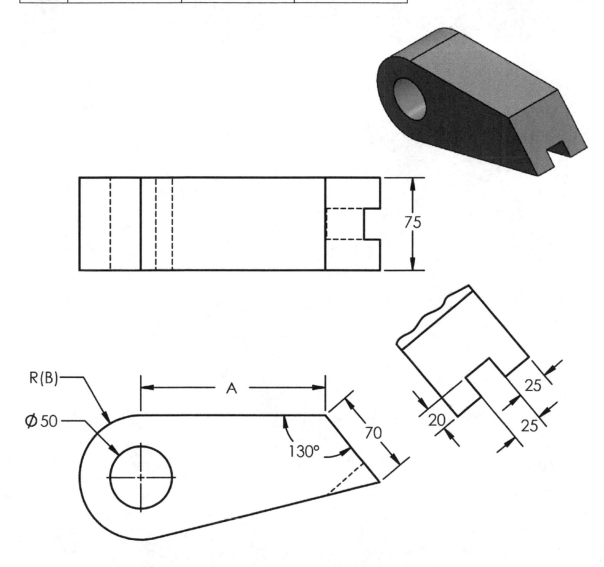

NOTES:

CHAPTER 4

CONNECTING ROD PROJECT
Part Print

CHAPTER OUTLINE

4.1) PREREQUISITES

To complete this tutorial, you should have completed the listed tutorial and be familiar with the listed topics.

- Chapter 2 – Connecting Rod – Part model tutorial
- Passing familiarity with orthographic projection.
- Ability to read dimensions.

4.2) WHAT YOU WILL LEARN

The objective of this tutorial is to introduce you to SOLIDWORKS' drawing capabilities (i.e. the ability to create orthographic projections.) In this tutorial, you will be creating a part print of the connecting rod that you modeled in Chapter 2. The part print is shown in Figure 4.2-1. Specifically, you will be learning the following commands and concepts.

Drawing

- New drawing
- Sheet size
- Projected view
- Standard 3 view
- Display style
- Center line
- Center mark
- Layer toolbar
- Detail view
- Model items
- Dimensions
- Leader Note
- Edit sheet format
- Edit sheet

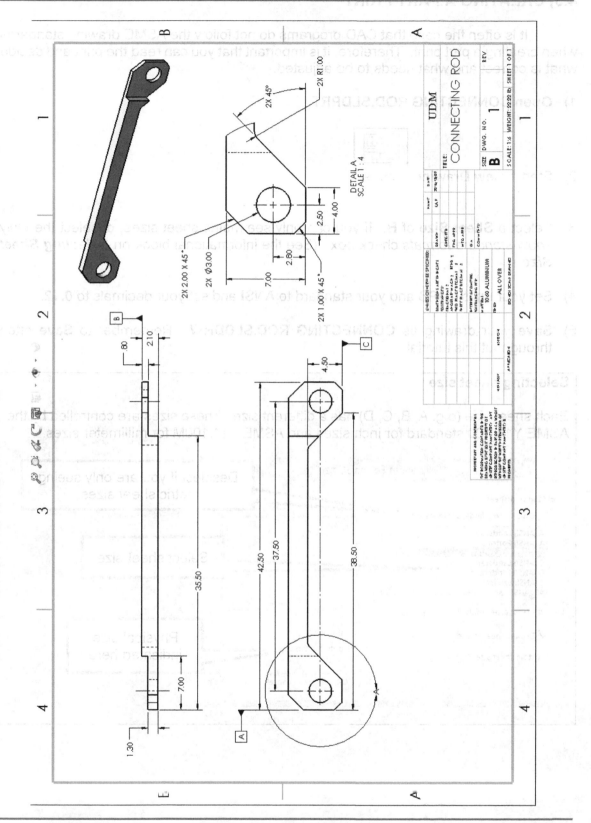

Figure 4.2-1: Detail drawing

4.3) CREATING A PART PRINT

It is often the case that CAD programs do not follow the ASME drawing standards when creating a part print. Therefore, it is important that you can read the print and decide what is correct and what needs to be adjusted.

1) **Open CONNECTING ROD.SLDPRT**.

2) Start a **New Drawing** .

3) Select a **Sheet Size** of **B**. If you can only see metric sheet sizes, deselect the *Only show standard formats* check box. (See the informational block on *Selecting Sheet Size*.)

4) Set your units to **IPS** and your standard to **ANSI** and set your decimals to **0.12**.

5) **Save** your drawing as **CONNECTING ROD.SLDDRW**. Remember to **Save** often throughout this tutorial.

Selecting sheet size

Each sheet size (e.g. A, B, C, D) has a different size. These sizes are controlled by the ASME Y14.100 standard for inch sizes and ASME Y14.100M for millimeter sizes.

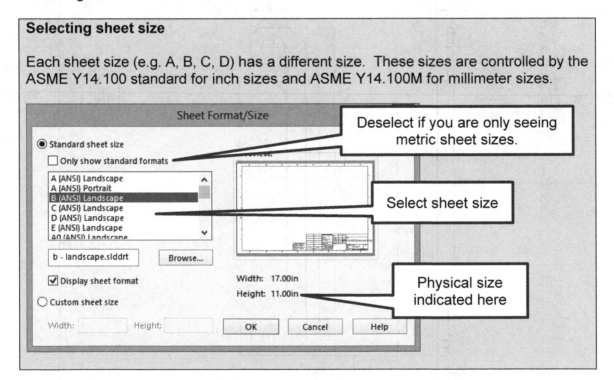

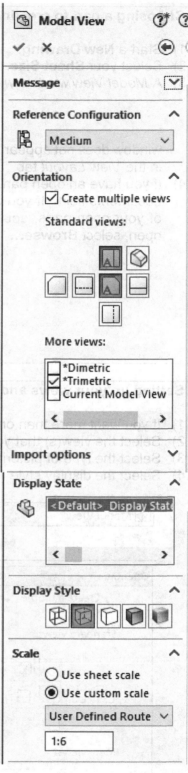

6) In the **View Layout** tab, select **Model View** [Model View]. (See the informational block on *Choosing a part to create a drawing from*, and *Setting up your views and view display style*.) In the *Model View* window, double click on your **CONNECTING ROD** part and then
   a. Select **Medium Size** as the *Reference Configuration*.
   b. Select **Create multiple views**.
   c. Choose to create a **Front** and **Top** view.
   d. Select **Trimetric** for the pictorial type.
   e. Select a display style = **Hidden Lines Visible**.
   f. Select the **Use custom scale** radio button and enter a scale of **1:6**.
   g. [✓]

Note that you can always add views using the *Projected View* command. (See the informational block on *Standard 3 View & Projected View*.)

7) Select the pictorial view and set its display style as **Shaded with Edges** and use a **1:8** scale.

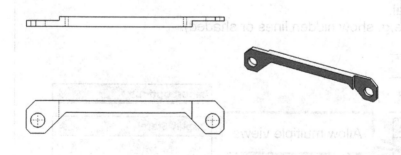

8) Move your views so that they are completely inside the drawing border. Do this by clicking and dragging on the view.

Choosing a part to creating a drawing from

1) Start a **New Drawing.**
2) Select your **Sheet Size**.
3) A *Model View* window will appear. If the model view window does not appear, select **Model View** in the *View Layout* tab.
4) If you have an open part, it will show up in the *Open documents* field. If you want to make a print of one of your open parts, double click on it. If no part is open, select **Browse...**

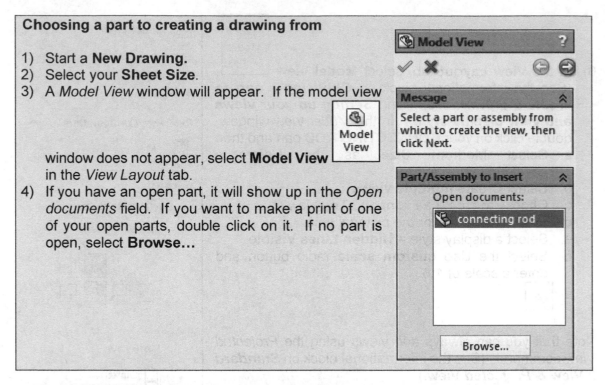

Setting up your views and view display style

1) If you want more than one view, activate the **Create multiple views** toggle.
2) Select the view(s) that you wish to create.
3) Select the type of pictorial.
4) Select the display style (e.g. show hidden lines or shaded).

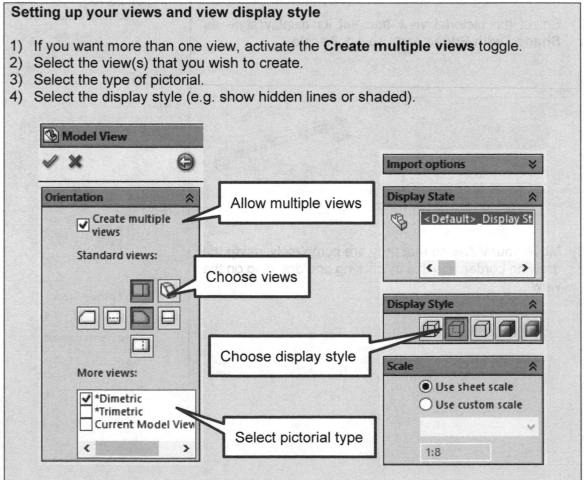

Standard 3 View 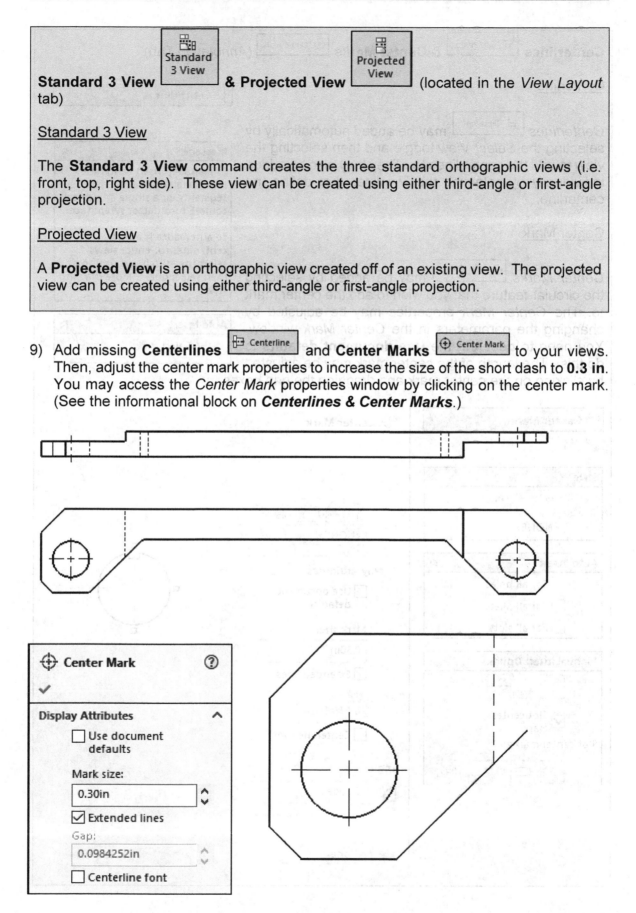 **& Projected View** (located in the *View Layout* tab)

Standard 3 View

The **Standard 3 View** command creates the three standard orthographic views (i.e. front, top, right side). These view can be created using either third-angle or first-angle projection.

Projected View

A **Projected View** is an orthographic view created off of an existing view. The projected view can be created using either third-angle or first-angle projection.

9) Add missing **Centerlines** and **Center Marks** to your views. Then, adjust the center mark properties to increase the size of the short dash to **0.3 in**. You may access the *Center Mark* properties window by clicking on the center mark. (See the informational block on **Centerlines & Center Marks**.)

Centerlines 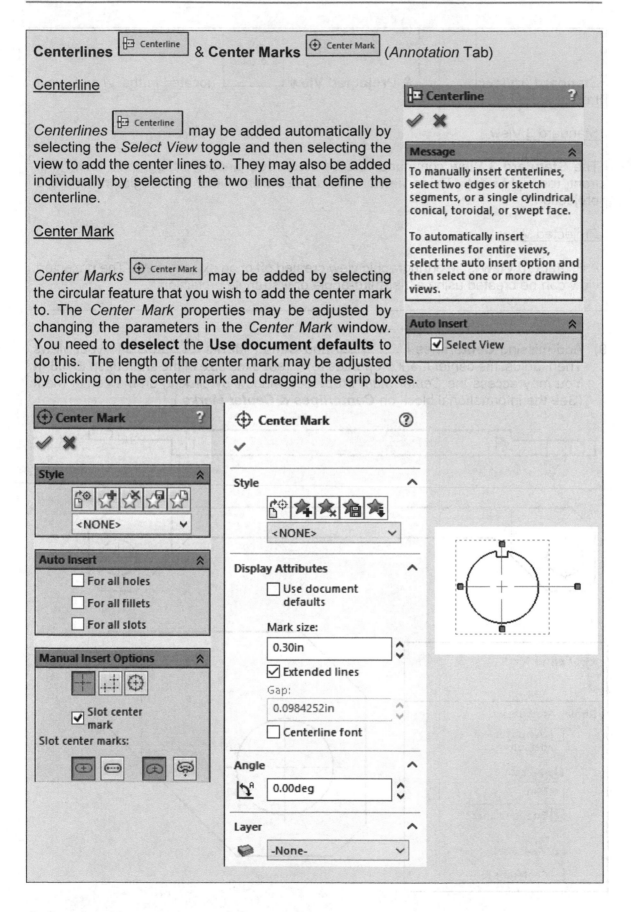 **& Center Marks** (*Annotation* Tab)

Centerline

Centerlines may be added automatically by selecting the *Select View* toggle and then selecting the view to add the center lines to. They may also be added individually by selecting the two lines that define the centerline.

Center Mark

Center Marks may be added by selecting the circular feature that you wish to add the center mark to. The *Center Mark* properties may be adjusted by changing the parameters in the *Center Mark* window. You need to **deselect** the **Use document defaults** to do this. The length of the center mark may be adjusted by clicking on the center mark and dragging the grip boxes.

10) If the *Layers* toolbar is not showing (it should be in the bottom left corner), activate it (**View – Toolbars – Layer**).

11) Create a **New** layer called **Centerline**. Set the line type to match the layer name. (See the informational block on ***Creating a new layer and setting its properties***.)

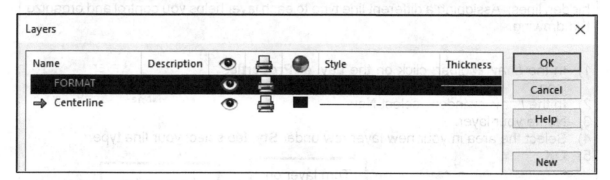

12) Set your current layer (i.e. the layer you will be drawing on) to **Centerline** and then *Sketch* a **Line** 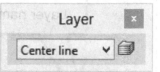 between the two center marks indicating that the holes are in line. To get an accurate line, snap to the quadrants of the circles.

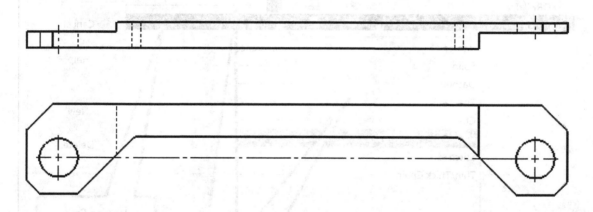

13) Notice the two hidden lines in the top view that indicate a change in surface direction. We want to hide these hidden lines. Right click on one of the inner hidden lines and select **Hide/Show Edges** . Repeat for the other inner hidden line.

Creating a new layer and setting its properties

Layers are like transparencies, one placed over the top of another. Each transparency/layer may contain a different line type or a different part of the drawing. One layer may be used to create visible lines, while another layer may be used to create hidden lines. Assigning a different line type to each layer helps you control and organize the drawing.

1) In the *Layer* toolbar, click on the **Layer Properties** icon.
2) In the *Layer* window, select **New**.
3) Name your layer.
4) Select the area in your new layer row under **Style** to select your line type.
5) **OK**

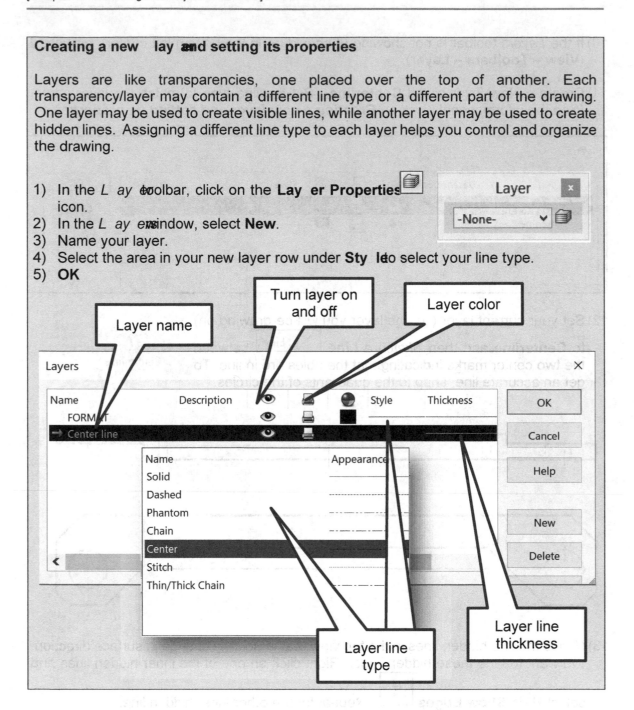

14) Phantom lines are used to show changes in surface directions. Right click on the remaining hidden lines and change their line type to **Phantom**. It may not look much different than the hidden line type. This is because it only traverses a short distance. If the lines were longer, they would look more like phantom lines.

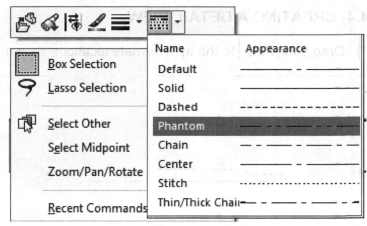

15) **Save**. A *Save* window may appear wanting you to save all models associated with this drawing. Select **Save All**.

4.4) CREATING A DETAIL VIEW

1) Drag your views to the approximate locations shown.

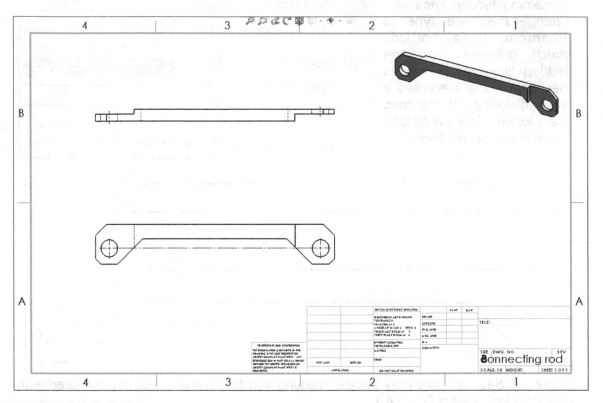

2) Change your current layer to **-None-** and then create a **1:4** scale **detail view** of the left end of the connecting rod. Adjust the *Center Mark* properties to increase the center dash length. (See the informational block on ***Detail views***.)

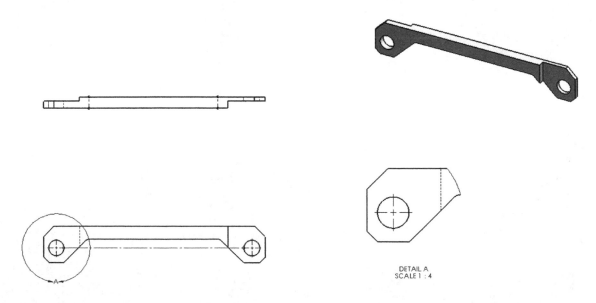

DETAIL A
SCALE 1 : 4

Detail view 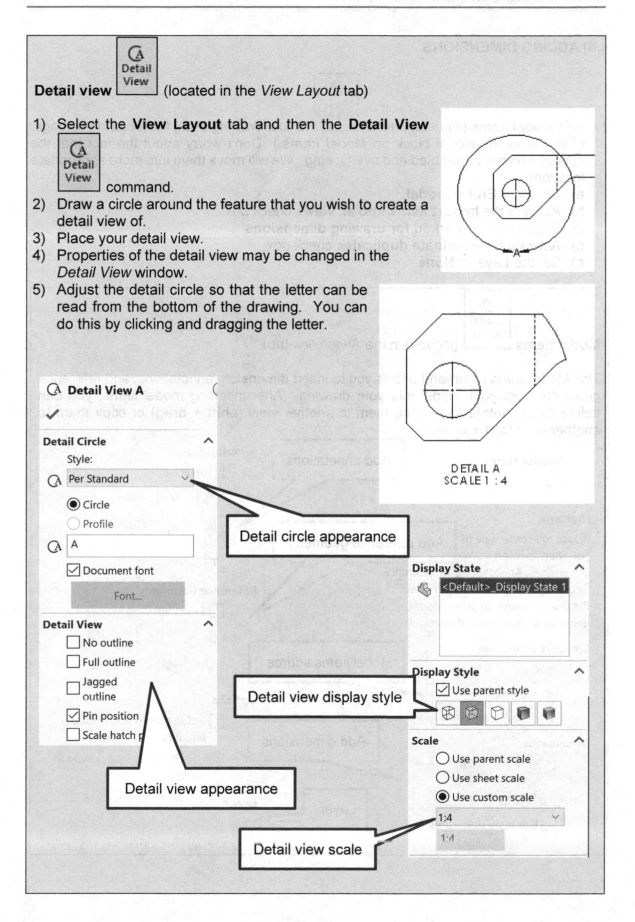 (located in the *View Layout* tab)

1) Select the **View Layout** tab and then the **Detail View** command.

2) Draw a circle around the feature that you wish to create a detail view of.

3) Place your detail view.

4) Properties of the detail view may be changed in the *Detail View* window.

5) Adjust the detail circle so that the letter can be read from the bottom of the drawing. You can do this by clicking and dragging the letter.

DETAIL A
SCALE 1 : 4

Detail View A

Detail Circle
Style:
Per Standard
● Circle
○ Profile
A
☑ Document font
Font...

Detail View
☐ No outline
☐ Full outline
☐ Jagged outline
☑ Pin position
☐ Scale hatch p...

Detail circle appearance

Detail view appearance

Display State
<Default>_Display State 1

Display Style
☑ Use parent style

Detail view display style

Scale
○ Use parent scale
○ Use sheet scale
● Use custom scale
1:4
1:4

Detail view scale

4.5) ADDING DIMENSIONS

1) Add **Model Items** (*Annotation* tab) to your drawing using the following settings. (See the informational block on *Model items*.) Don't worry about the fact that the dimensions are all jumbled and overlapping. We will move them into more appropriate locations.
    a) Source = **Entire model**
    b) Activate the **Import items into all views** check box.
    c) Dimensions = **Marked for drawing dimensions**
    d) Activate the **Eliminate duplicates** check box.
    e) Set the Layer = **None**

Model items (located in the *Annotation* tab)

The *Model items* command allows you to insert dimension, annotations, and reference geometry from your model into your drawing. After inserting model items, you can delete them (**delete** key), drag them to another view (**shift + drag**) or copy them to another view (**ctrl + drag**).

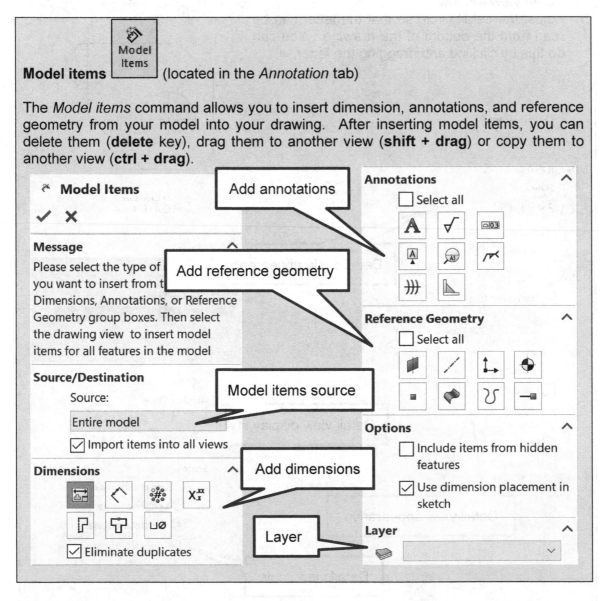

2) We want to make the top view look like the figure shown below.

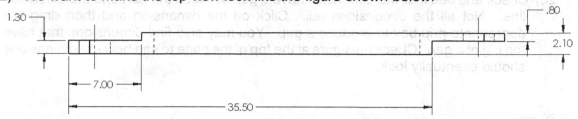

2a) This figure below shows how my top view ended up. Note that if any of your dimension text is vertical, you are in the ISO standard. Change that to the ANSI standard (**Options** icon – **Document Properties** tab – **Drafting Standard - ANSI**). If you are missing any dimension, try to locate it in another view. If you find it, hold the **SHIFT** key down and drag the dimension to the top view.

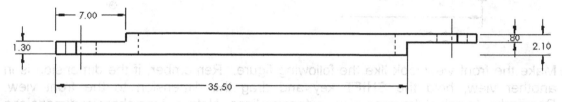

2b) Drag the dimensions and the dimension text into their correct locations. Holding the **ALT** key will produce a smooth drag.

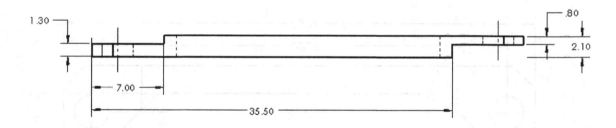

2c) Check and see if all the dimension have a gap between the part and the extension line. Not all the dimensions will. Click on the dimension and then drag the appropriate grip box to produce a gap. You may also find dimensions that have too big of a gap. Check the figure at the top of the page to see how the dimensions should eventually look.

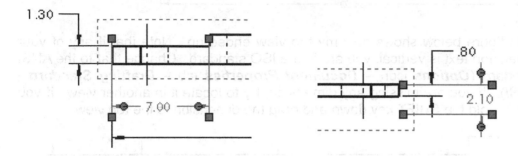

3) Make the front view look like the following figure. Remember, if the dimension is in another view, hold the **SHIFT** key and drag the dimension to the front view. Remember to adjust the gaps of the extension lines. Note that the chamfer dimensions are given using a linear dimension and an angle. Delete the dimensions associated with the following chamfer (1.00 x 45°, 2.00 x 45°). We will be adding those back using a leader line and note.

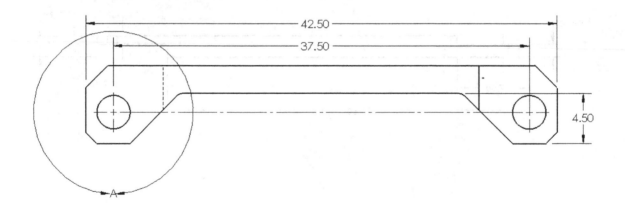

4) After making the appropriate adjustments, the detail view should look like the figure shown. Start by dragging the dimension away from the part.

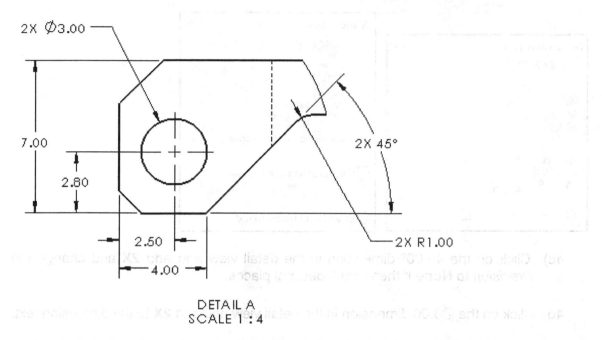

DETAIL A
SCALE 1 : 4

4a) **Delete** the dimensions associated with the (1.00 X 45°) and (2.00 X 45°) chamfer if they are included in the detail view. The following figure shows how the view should end up after adjusting the dimension positions. The radius dimension may look different. Don't worry about that now. Adjust the gaps as needed.

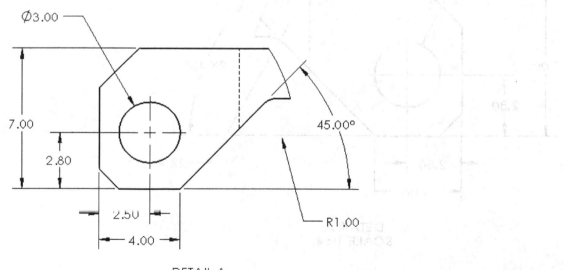

DETAIL A
SCALE 1 : 4

4b) Click on the R1.00 dimension in the detail view and add **2X** to the dimension text and then set the following leader properties by clicking on the **Leader** tab.

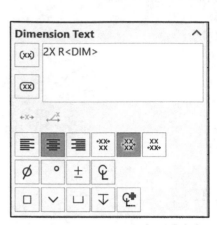
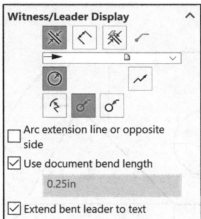

4c) Click on the 45.00° dimension in the detail view and add **2X** and change the *Precision* to **None** if there are 2 decimal places.

4d) Click on the ⌀3.00 dimension in the detail view and add **2X** to the dimension text.

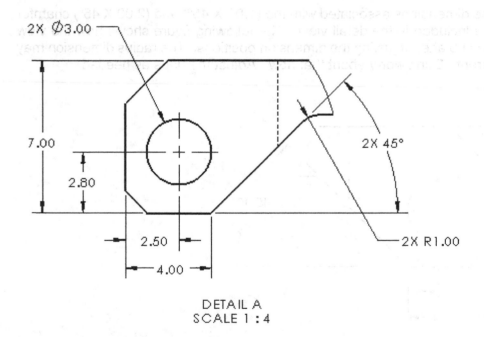

DETAIL A
SCALE 1 : 4

5) Create a **Dimension** layer with a **Solid** line type and set it to be the current layer.

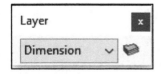

6) Add the following 38.50 dimensions to the front view using **Smart Dimension**. Make sure that they are on the **Dimension** layer. If your dimensions look gray, they are not on the correct layer.

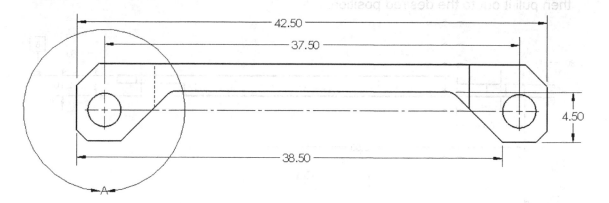

7) Add the chamfer dimensions to the detail view in the *Dimension* layer. Use the **Note**

 command to do this. (See the informational block on *Leader Notes*.)

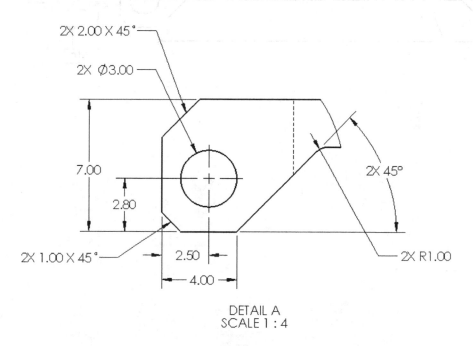

DETAIL A
SCALE 1 : 4

8) Add **Datum Feature** symbols 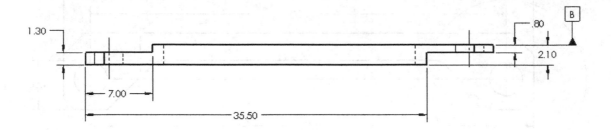 as shown in the figure. Do this by selecting the extension line that you wish to attach the datum feature symbol to and then pull it out to the desired position.

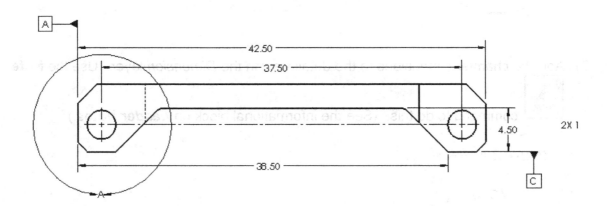

Leader notes 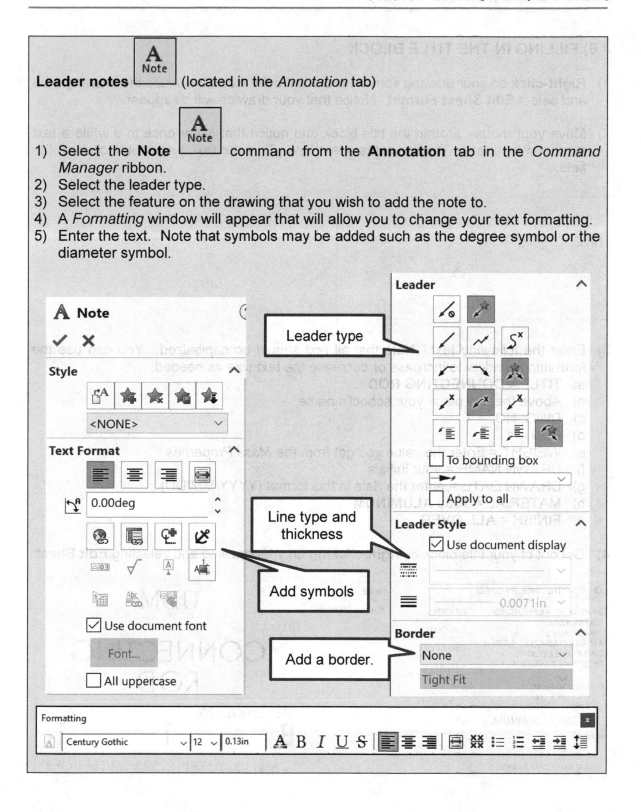 (located in the *Annotation* tab)

1) Select the **Note** command from the **Annotation** tab in the *Command Manager* ribbon.
2) Select the leader type.
3) Select the feature on the drawing that you wish to add the note to.
4) A *Formatting* window will appear that will allow you to change your text formatting.
5) Enter the text. Note that symbols may be added such as the degree symbol or the diameter symbol.

4.6) FILLING IN THE TITLE BLOCK

1) **Right-click** on your drawing somewhere outside the views but inside the drawing area and select **Edit Sheet Format**. Notice that your drawing will disappear.

2) Move your mouse around the title block and notice that every once in a while a text symbol will appear. This indicates a text field. To enter text, just double click on the field.

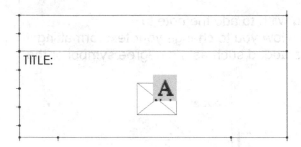

3) Enter the following text. Note that all text should be capitalized. You can use the formatting window to increase or decrease the text size as needed.
   a) TITLE = **CONNECTING ROD**
   b) Above the title place your school's name.
   c) DWG. NO. = **1**
   d) REV = **1**
   e) WEIGHT = Enter the value you got from the *Mass Properties*
   f) DRAWN NAME = your initials
   g) DRAWN DATE = enter the date in this format (YYYY/MM/DD)
   h) MATERIAL = **1060 ALUMINUM**
   i) FINISH = **ALL OVER**

4) Get out of your title block by **right-clicking** on your drawing and selecting **Edit Sheet**.

UNLESS OTHERWISE SPECIFIED:		NAME	DATE	UDM		
DIMENSIONS ARE IN INCHES	DRAWN	KAP	2016/09/18	TITLE:		
TOLERANCES: FRACTIONAL ±	CHECKED			CONNECTING ROD		
ANGULAR: MACH± BEND ± TWO PLACE DECIMAL ± THREE PLACE DECIMAL ±	ENG APPR.					
	MFG APPR.					
INTERPRET GEOMETRIC TOLERANCING PER:	Q.A.					
	COMMENTS:			SIZE **B**	DWG. NO. 1	REV 1
MATERIAL 1060 ALUMINUM						
FINISH ALL OVER						
DO NOT SCALE DRAWING				SCALE: 1:6	WEIGHT: 22,22 lb	SHEET 1 OF 1

CONNECTING ROD (PART PRINT) PROBLEMS

P4-1) Use SOLIDWORKS® to create the part print that looks exactly like the detailed drawing shown. Fill in the appropriate information into your title block. Enter the weight of your part into the title block of your drawing.

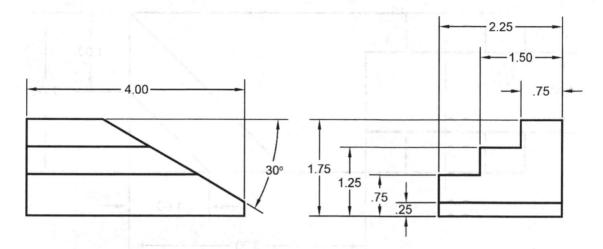

P4-2) Use SOLIDWORKS® to create the part print that looks exactly like the detailed drawing shown. Fill in the appropriate information into your title block. Enter the weight of your part into the title block of your drawing.

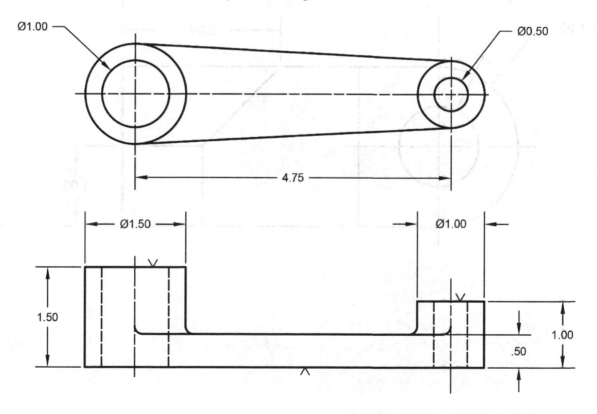

NOTE: ALL FILLETS AND ROUNDS R.12
UNLESS OTHERWISE SPECIFIED

P4-3) Use SOLIDWORKS® to create the part print that looks exactly like the detailed drawing shown. Fill in the appropriate information into your title block. Enter the weight of your part into the title block of your drawing.

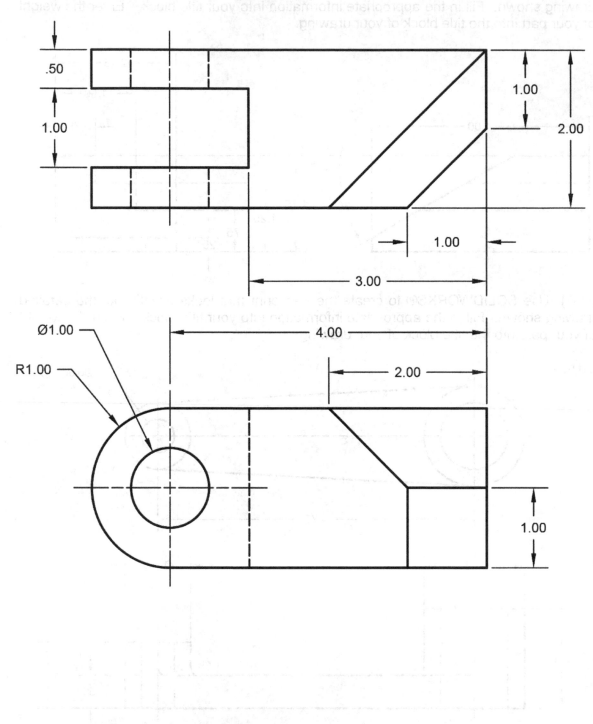

P4-4) Use SOLIDWORKS® to create the part print that looks exactly like the detailed drawing shown. Fill in the appropriate information into your title block. Enter the weight of your part into the title block of your drawing.

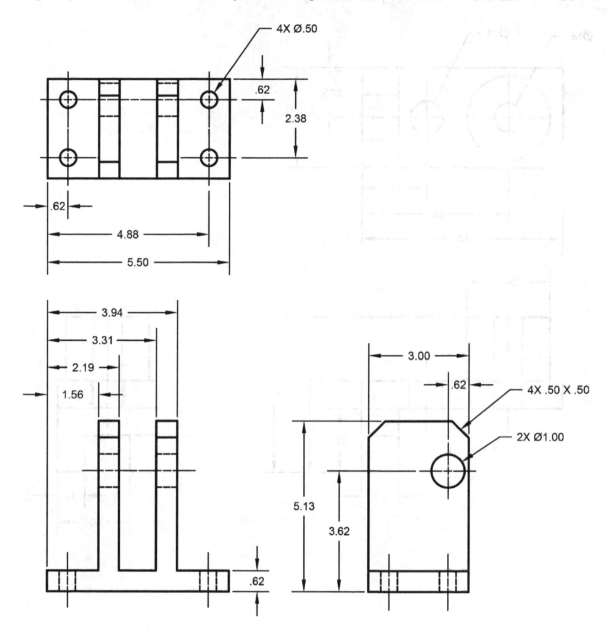

P4-5) Use SOLIDWORKS® to create the part print that looks exactly like the detailed drawing shown. Fill in the appropriate information into your title block.   Enter the weight of your part into the title block of your drawing.

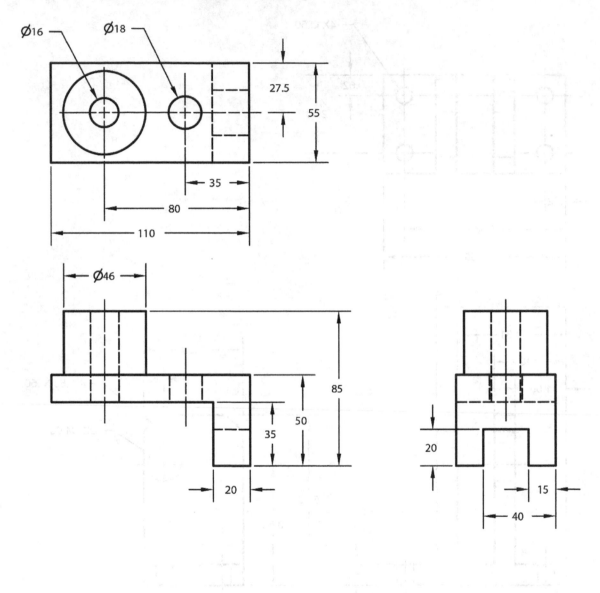

P4-6) Use SOLIDWORKS® to create the part print that looks exactly like the detailed drawing shown. Fill in the appropriate information into your title block. Enter the weight of your part into the title block of your drawing.

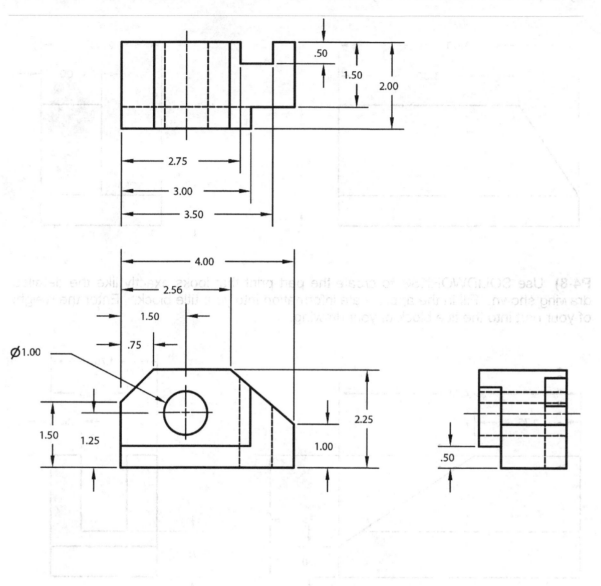

P4-7) Use SOLIDWORKS® to create the part print that looks exactly like the detailed drawing shown. Fill in the appropriate information into your title block.   Enter the weight of your part into the title block of your drawing.

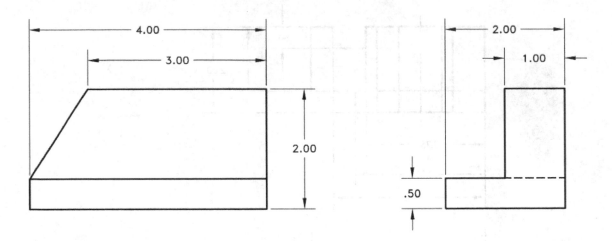

P4-8) Use SOLIDWORKS® to create the part print that looks exactly like the detailed drawing shown. Fill in the appropriate information into your title block.   Enter the weight of your part into the title block of your drawing.

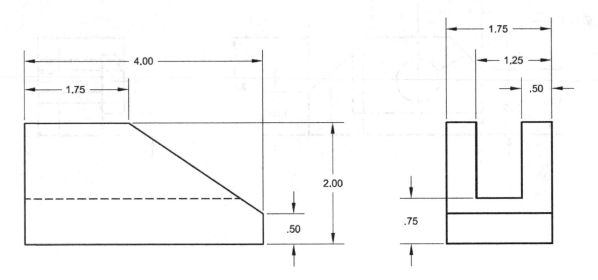

P4-9) Use SOLIDWORKS® to create the part print that looks exactly like the detailed drawing shown. Fill in the appropriate information into your title block. Enter the weight of your part into the title block of your drawing.

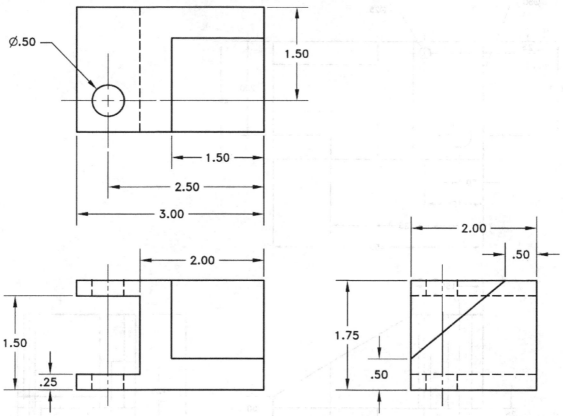

P4-10) Use SOLIDWORKS® to create the part print that looks exactly like the detailed drawing shown. Fill in the appropriate information into your title block. Enter the weight of your part into the title block of your drawing.

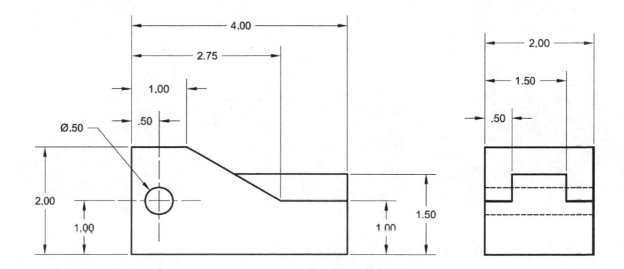

P4-11) Use SOLIDWORKS® to create the part print that looks exactly like the detailed drawing shown. Fill in the appropriate information into your title block.   Enter the weight of your part into the title block of your drawing.

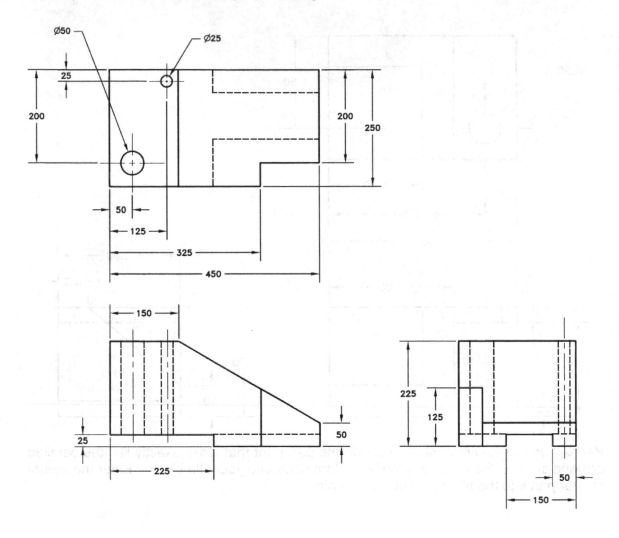

P4-12) Use SOLIDWORKS® to create the part print that looks exactly like the detailed drawing shown. Fill in the appropriate information into your title block.   Enter the weight of your part into the title block of your drawing.

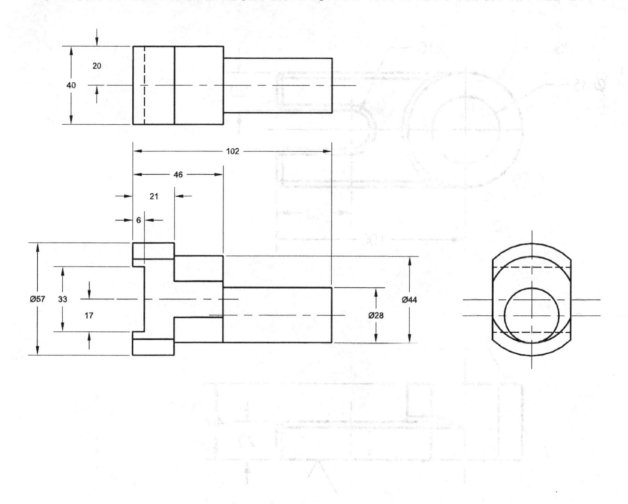

P4-13) Use SOLIDWORKS® to create the part print that looks exactly like the detailed drawing shown. Fill in the appropriate information into your title block.   Enter the weight of your part into the title block of your drawing. Note that all fillets and rounds are R3.

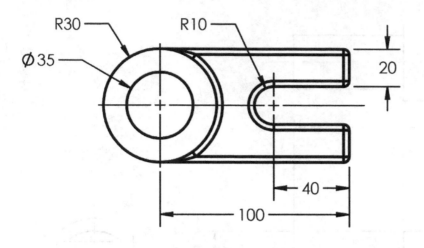

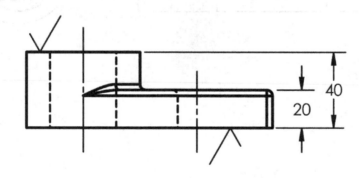

CONNECTING ROD (PART PRINT) QUIZ PROBLEMS

Q4-1) Model the following 1020 Steel *Step* and create a part print using proper dimensioning techniques. Fill in the title block with the appropriate information. Note that the dimensions are given in millimeters.

	Group 1	Group 2	Group 3
A = Extrude Distance	90	100	110

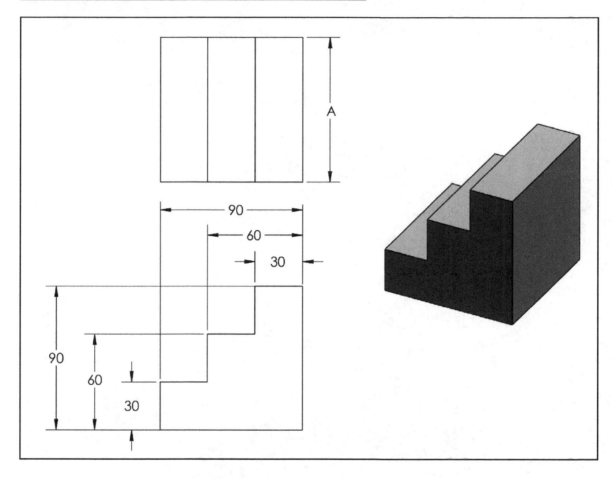

NOTES:

CHAPTER 5

CONNECTING ROD PROJECT
Static FEA

CHAPTER OUTLINE

5.1) PREREQUISITES

To complete this tutorial, you should have completed the listed tutorial. It would also be helpful if you were familiar with the listed topics.

- Chapter 2 – Connecting Rod – Part model tutorial
- Passing familiarity with the concepts of force, stress, and strain.

5.2) WHAT YOU WILL LEARN

The objective of this tutorial is to introduce you to SOLIDWORKS' static simulation capabilities. In this tutorial you will be analyzing the connecting rod model under load (modeled in Chapter 2). The part print of the connecting rod is shown in Figure 5.2-1. Specifically, you will be learning the following commands and concepts.

Simulation

- Add-Ins
- New study
- Static simulation
- Simulation study tree
- Stress
- Strain
- Generating a report

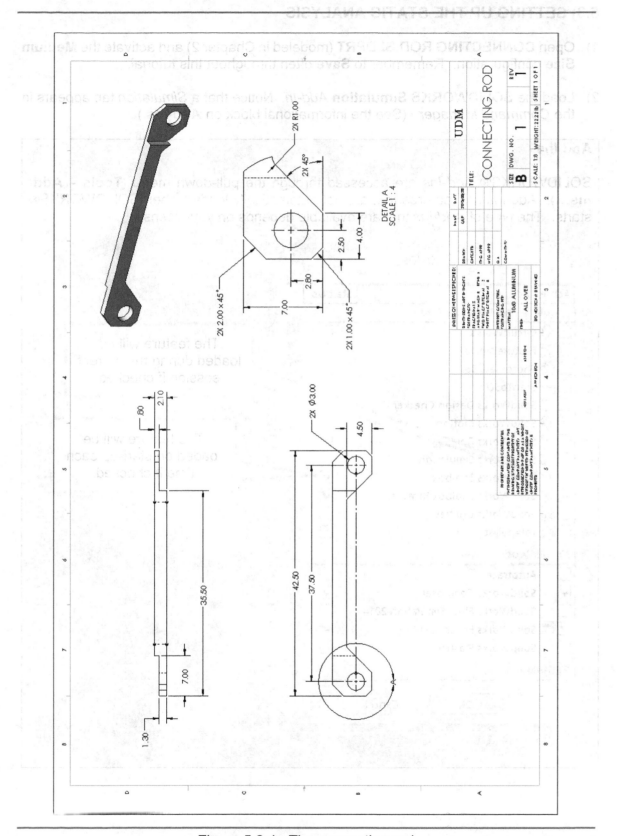

Figure 5.2-1: The connecting rod

5.3) SETTING UP THE STATIC ANALYSIS

1) Open **CONNECTING ROD.SLDPRT** (modeled in Chapter 2) and activate the **Medium Size** configuration. Remember to **Save** often throughout this tutorial.

2) Load the **SOLIDWORKS Simulation** *Add-In*. Notice that a *Simulation* tab appears in the *Command Manager*. (See the informational block on ***Add-Ins***.)

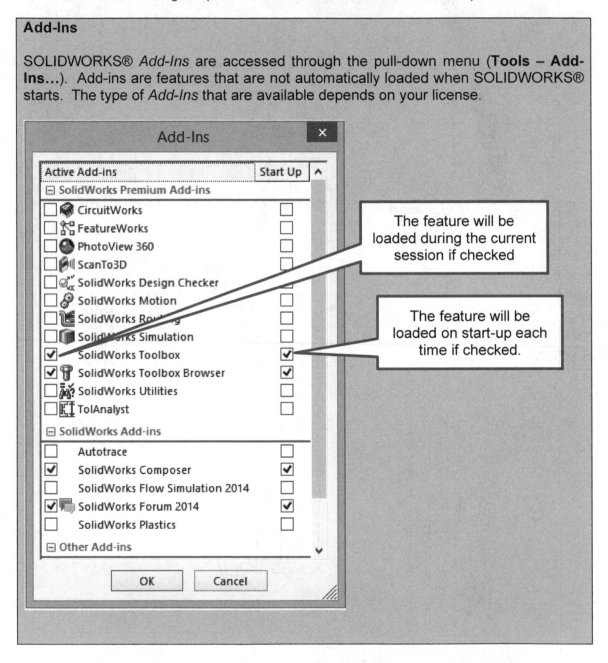

Add-Ins

SOLIDWORKS® *Add-Ins* are accessed through the pull-down menu (**Tools – Add-Ins...**). Add-ins are features that are not automatically loaded when SOLIDWORKS® starts. The type of *Add-Ins* that are available depends on your license.

The feature will be loaded during the current session if checked

The feature will be loaded on start-up each time if checked.

3) Click on the *Simulation tab* and select **New Study**

.

4) Create a new **Static Study** 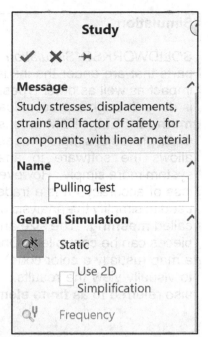 and name it **Pulling test**. (See the informational block on *Simulation*.)

5) A *Simulation Study Tree* should have appeared below the *Feature Manager Design Tree*. We need to complete the steps from top to bottom. The first step is to assign a **material** to the part. This should already be done since we assigned the material in our model. (See the informational block on *Simulation Study Tree*.)

6) Next, fix the left hole of the connecting rod. Do this by right clicking on **Fixtures** and selecting **Fixed Geometry…**. In the *Fixture* window, activate the **Fixed Geometry** option and then select the inside surface of the left hole. Green arrows should appear indicating which surface(s) are fixed.

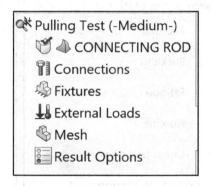

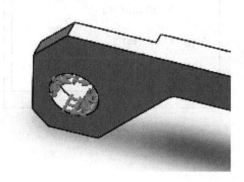

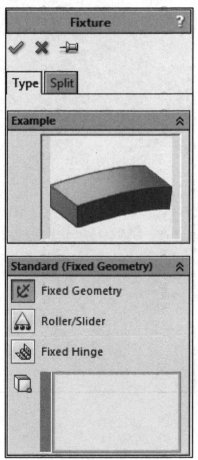

Simulation

SOLIDWORKS® *Simulation* is designed to analyze parts that are under the influence of forces, heat, or impact as well as other types of loads. This analysis is done through a process called the **finite element method** (FEM). FEM breaks up the part into many small pieces of simple shapes called **elements**. This allows the software to analyze a very complex system more simply. However, with simplicity comes loss of accuracy. It is a trade-off. The small pieces used to simplify the analysis are created by a process called **meshing**. The size and shape of the mesh or pieces can be controlled. Once the part is analyzed, a map (usually a color code) is created allowing you to visually view the results. This type of analysis is also referred to as **finite element analysis** (FEA).

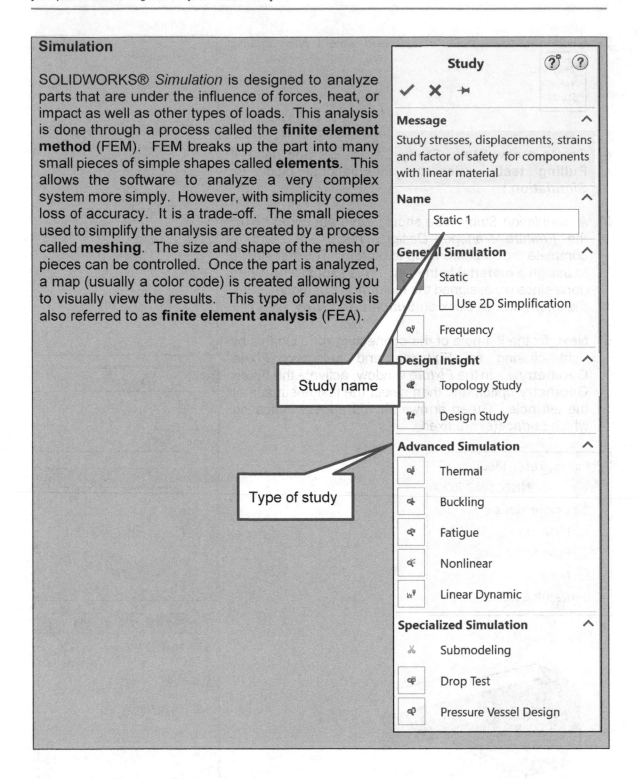

Simulation continued

Part model

Meshed model

Results

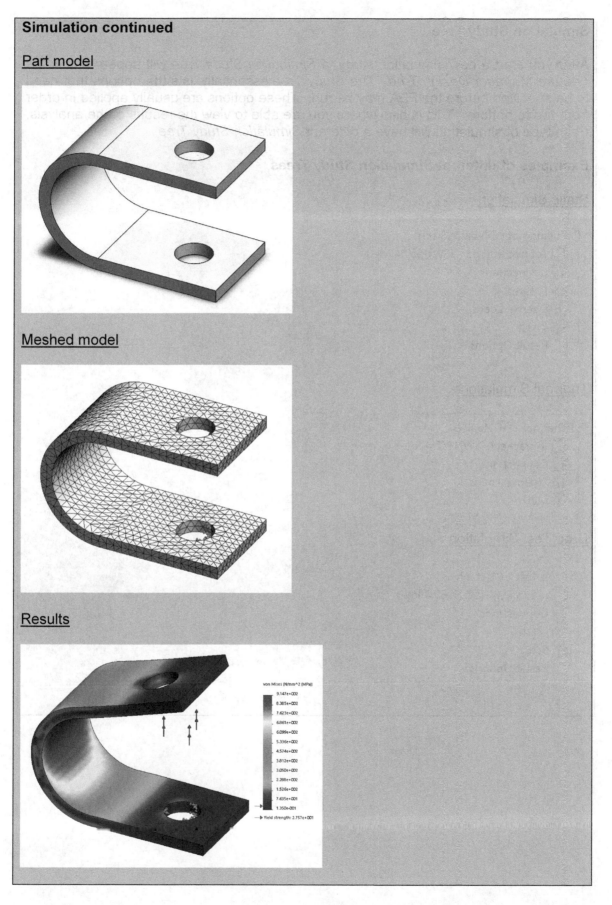

Simulation Study Tree

After you start a new simulation study, a *Simulation Study Tree* will appear below the *Feature Manager Design Tree*. The *Study Tree* essentially lists the options that need to be specified before the FEA may be run. These options are usually applied in order from top to bottom. This is also where you are able to view the results of the analysis. Each type of simulation will have a different *Simulation Study Tree*.

Examples of different *Simulation Study Trees*.

Static Simulation

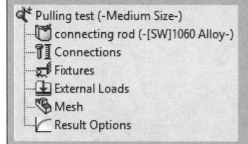

Thermal Simulation

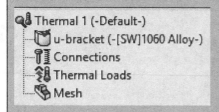

Drop Test Simulation

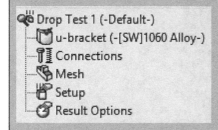

7) Apply a load to the free end of the connecting rod. In the *Simulation Study Tree*, right-click on **External Loads** and select **Force…**. Select the inner surface of the right side hole as the surface that the force will be applied to. Then click on the **Selected direction** and use one of the long edges of the part to define the direction of pull. Enter a force of **1000 N**. You may have to **Reverse direction** so that the part is pulled and not compressed. (See the informational block on *Static Simulation*.)

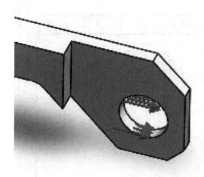

8) Mesh the part. In the *Simulation Study Tree*, right-click on **Mesh** and then select **Create Mesh**. Use the default mesh parameters.

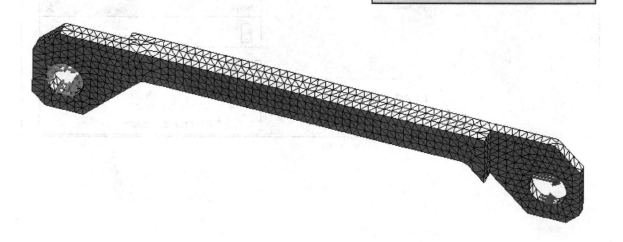

Static Simulation

Static Simulation analyzes a part under load. It can calculate displacements, reaction forces, strains, stresses, and factor of safety distribution.

There are several options in the *Simulation Study Tree* that need to be specified.

- <u>Connections:</u> This is where you would specify any contacts, springs, bolts, bearings, or welds.
- <u>Fixtures:</u> This is where you specify any supports such as fixed geometry or an elastic support.
- <u>External Loads:</u> You may apply a force or a torque to your part.
- <u>Mesh:</u> You can specify your mesh size and shape.

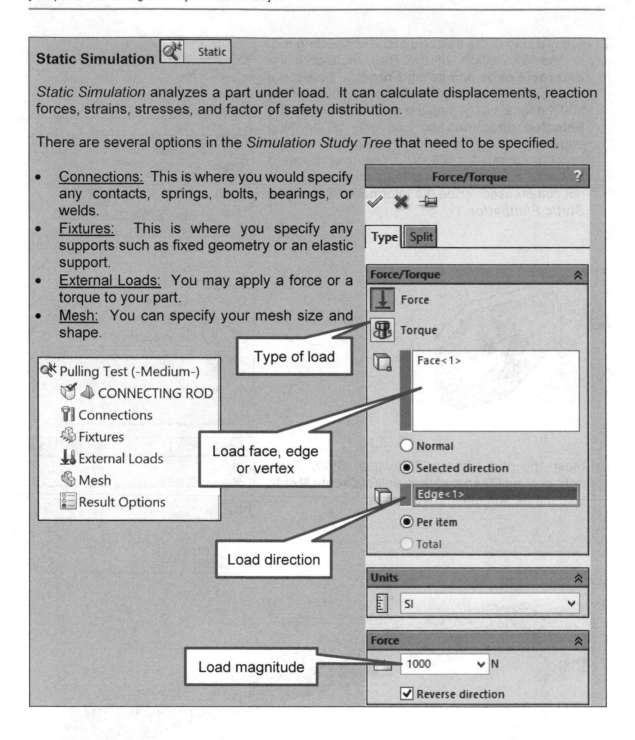

5.4 RUNNING THE ANALYSIS

1) Run this Study [Run This Study]. The analysis may take a while to run. The analysis time will depend on your computer speed. After the analysis is completed, the part will be mapped in colors. A legend indicating what the colors mean will also appear. The default legend will indicate stress (See the informational block on **Stress & Strain**). Note that the highest stress is below the material's yield strength. The maximum stress should be around 4.7e+006 N/m^2 (i.e. 4.7x10^6) and the yield strength is 2.757e+007. This means that the part will not break. You may double click on the other result plots to see the part's **Displacement** and **Strain**.

Pulling Test (-Medium-)
- CONNECTING ROD 2020 (-[SW]1060 Alloy-)
- Connections
- Fixtures
  - Fixed-1
- External Loads
  - Force-1 (:Per item: -1,000 N:)
- Mesh
- Result Options
- **Results**
  - **Stress1 (-vonMises-)**
  - Displacement1 (-Res disp-)
  - Strain1 (-Equivalent-)

von Mises (N/mm^2 (MPa))

4.668e+000
4.279e+000
3.891e+000
3.502e+000
3.113e+000
2.724e+000
2.335e+000
1.946e+000
1.557e+000
1.168e+000
7.796e-001
3.907e-001
1.867e-003

→ Yield strength: 2.757e+001

2) Increase the applied force to **10,000 N**. Do this by right-clicking on **Force – 1** and selecting **Edit Definition**. Re-**Run** the analysis. Note the red arrow that indicates the yield strength of the material. Since the yield strength is within the values of stress experienced by the rod, there is a good chance the part will fail.

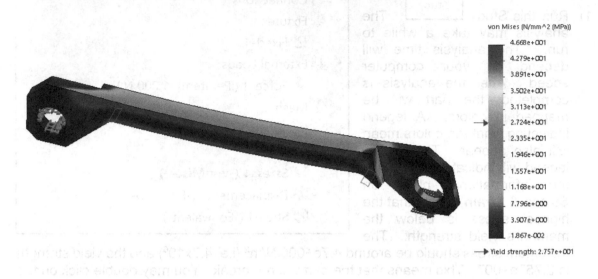

Stress & Strain

Consider a rod being pulled at both ends by a force. As the force pulls on the rod, it stretches (maybe by only an infinitesimal amount.) But, this force is still causing the rod's material to experience what is called *stress* (σ). The bonds between the atoms are being pulled on. If the force becomes large enough, these bonds may break and the material will experience permanent or plastic deformation.

- **Engineering Stress**:
  Engineering stress is equal to the pulling force divided by the original cross-sectional area of the specimen. Stress is measured in Pascal's (Pa) or Newton's per meter squared (N/m^2) or the equivalent in US customary units.
- **Engineering Strain**:
  Engineering strain is equal to the change in length of the material over its original length. Strain is essentially unit less because it is length over length.

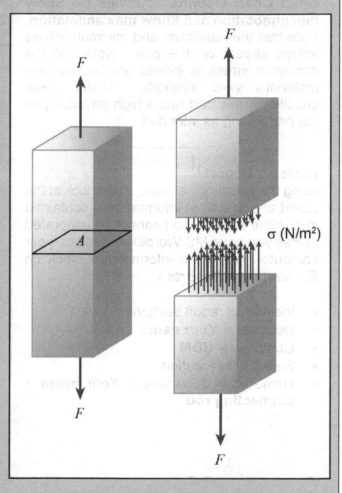

A part will plastically deform at locations where the stress exceeds the yield strength of the material. The **yield strength** is the maximum stress that a material can sustain before plastic or permanent deformation occurs. Think of a paper clip. If you apply a big enough force to the paper clip it will bend and remain bent. This is plastic deformation. In most cases, plastic deformation is bad and should be avoided. The **ultimate** or **tensile strength** is the maximum stress that a material can sustain before fracture.

There are many types of stress and strain. What is described above is called axial stress and strain. However, there is bending and shear stress and strain as well. But, the basic idea behind them all is that you want the actual stress on a part to be low enough so that the part does not permanently deform.

3) Under *Results*, right-click on **Stress** and select **Chart Options**. Activate the **Show min annotation** and **Show max annotation**. Note that the maximum and minimum stress values appear on the part. Note that the maximum stress is indeed greater than the material's yield strength. Under these conditions, this part has a high probability of not performing as intended.

4) Publish a **Report** 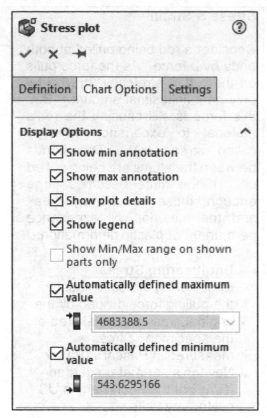 of this analysis using the following settings. Then, look at the report and see what information is contained in it. Note that a report cannot be generated unless you have MS Word® installed on your computer. (See the informational block on *Generating a Reports*.)

- Include all report sections.
- Designer = **Your name**
- Company = **UDM**
- Select a file location
- Name your document = **Your name + connecting rod**

Generating a Report 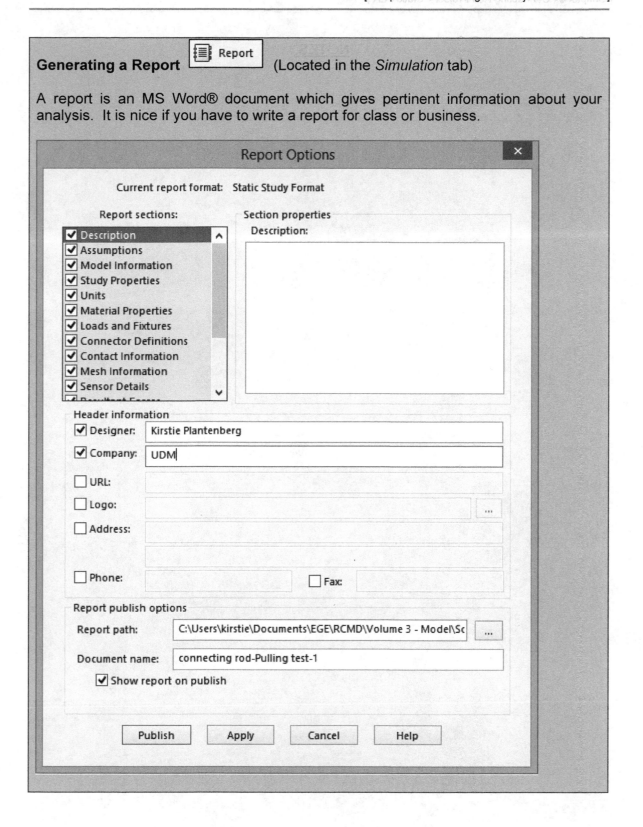 (Located in the *Simulation* tab)

A report is an MS Word® document which gives pertinent information about your analysis. It is nice if you have to write a report for class or business.

Report Options

Current report format: Static Study Format

Report sections:

- ✔ Description
- ✔ Assumptions
- ✔ Model Information
- ✔ Study Properties
- ✔ Units
- ✔ Material Properties
- ✔ Loads and Fixtures
- ✔ Connector Definitions
- ✔ Contact Information
- ✔ Mesh Information
- ✔ Sensor Details

Section properties

Description:

Header information

- ✔ Designer: Kirstie Plantenberg
- ✔ Company: UDM
- ☐ URL:
- ☐ Logo:
- ☐ Address:
- ☐ Phone: ☐ Fax:

Report publish options

Report path: C:\Users\kirstie\Documents\EGE\RCMD\Volume 3 - Model\Sc

Document name: connecting rod-Pulling test-1

✔ Show report on publish

[Publish] [Apply] [Cancel] [Help]

NOTES:

NOTES:

CONNECTING ROD (STATIC) FEA PROBLEMS

P5-1) Use SOLIDWORKS® to create a solid model of the following 1345 Aluminum part. Using SOLIDWORKS® Simulation, determine the maximum force (to the nearest 1/2 lb) that can be applied to the part so that the maximum displacement is less than 0.2 mm. The bottom hole is fixed and the load is applied upward to the inside of the top hole. Generate a report. Include the following information at the end of your report. Dimensions given in inches.

1. Maximum force = _____
2. Maximum displacement = _____
3. Material's Yield strength = _____
4. Maximum stress experienced by the part = _____
5. A picture of where the maximum stress is located.

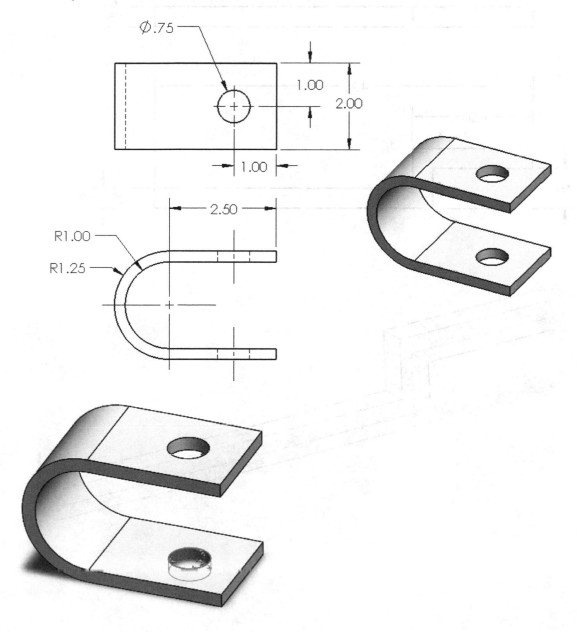

P5-2) Use SOLIDWORKS® to create a solid model of the following Acrylic part. Using SOLIDWORKS® Simulation, apply a downward force of 5 Newtons to the right end of the part. The left end of the part is fixed. Generate a report. Include the following information at the end of your report. Dimensions given in inches. Note that TYP means typical. So, the thickness of the part is 0.25 all over.

1. Material's yield strength = _____
2. Maximum stress experienced by the part = _____
3. Is there a possibility of the part failing due to stress?
4. Include a picture of where the maximum stress is located.
5. If the design parameters state that the part cannot deflect more than 3 mm, does the part perform as intended?

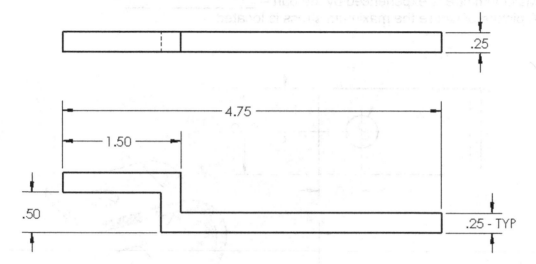

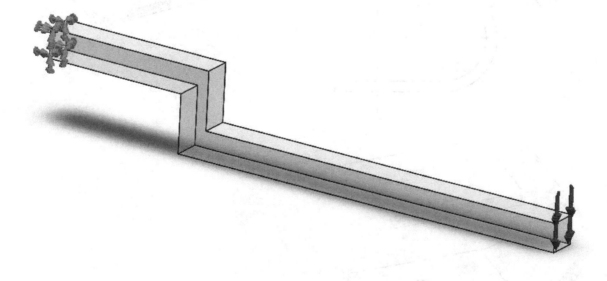

P5-3) Use SOLIDWORKS® to create a solid model of the following AISI 1020 Steel Cold Rolled part. Using SOLIDWORKS® Simulation, determine the maximum torque that can be applied to the part before it yields. The left end of the part is fixed and the torque is applied to the right end. Generate a report. Include the following information at the end of the report. Dimensions given in millimeters.

1. Maximum safe torque = _____ N-m
2. Material's yield strength = _____ Pa
3. Maximum stress experienced by the part = _____ Pa
4. A picture of where the maximum stress is located.

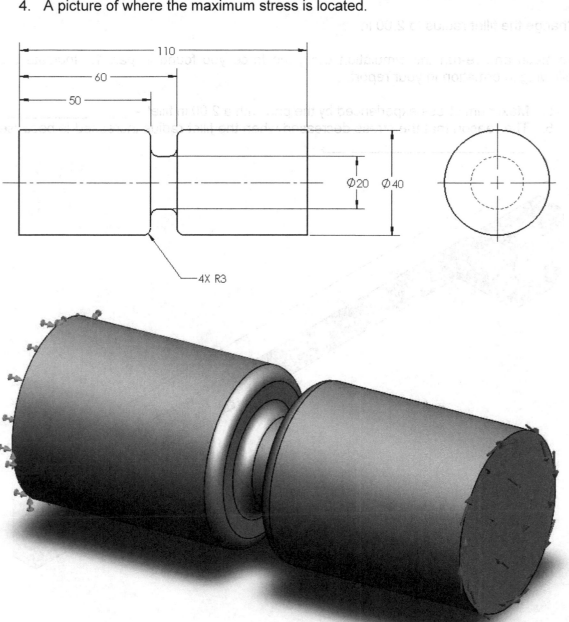

P5-4) Using SOLIDWORKS® Simulation, determine the maximum downward force that can be applied to the connecting rod before it yields. The left hole of the part is fixed and the force is applied to the right hole. Generate a report. Include the following information at the bottom of the report.

    1.   Maximum safe force = _____
    2.   Material's yield strength = _____
    3.   Maximum stress experienced by the part = _____
    4.   A picture of where the maximum stress is located.

Change the fillet radius to 2.00 in.

Re-mesh and re-run the simulation using the force you found in part 1. Indicate the following information in your report.

    5.   Maximum stress experienced by the part with a 2.00 in fillet = _____
    6.   The reason that the stress decreased when the fillet radius increased is because

        _____.

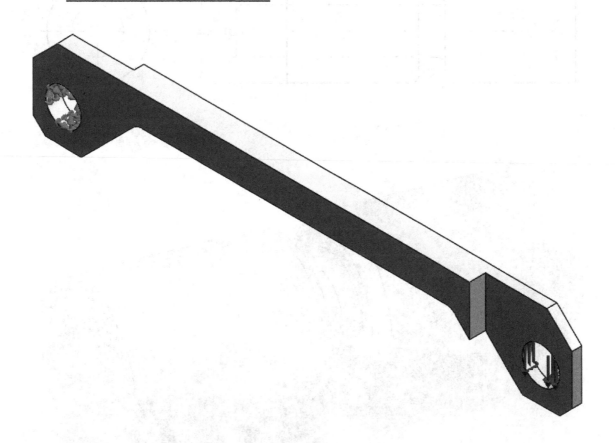

P5-5) Using SOLIDWORKS® Simulation, determine the maximum side force that can be applied to the connecting rod before it yields. The left hole of the part is fixed and the force is applied to the right hole. Generate a report. Include the following information at the bottom of the report.

1. Maximum safe force = _____
2. Material's yield strength = _____
3. Maximum stress experienced by the part = _____
4. A picture of where the maximum stress is located.

Add a 1.00 in fillet to the inside corners of the cut outs (one of which experienced the maximum stress.)

Re-mesh and re-run the simulation using the force you found in part 1. Indicate the following information in your report.

5. Maximum stress experienced by the part with the fillets = _____
6. A picture of where the maximum stress is located after the fillets are added.
7. The reason that the stress decreased when a fillet was added is because _____.

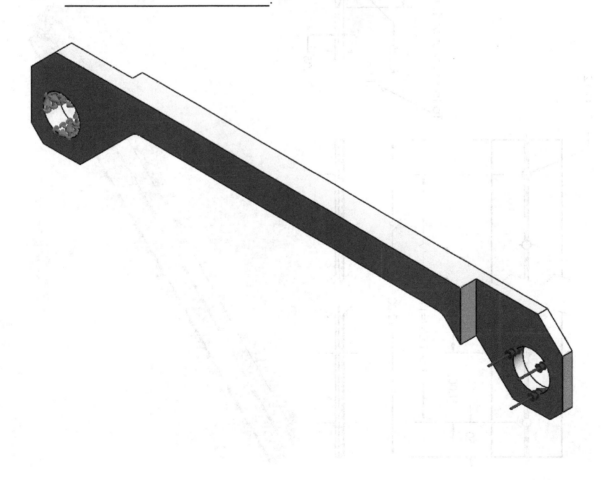

P5-6) Use SOLIDWORKS® to create a solid model of the following Oak ruler. Using SOLIDWORKS® Simulation, determine the maximum downward force that can be applied to the end of the ruler before it yields or breaks. The left end of the ruler is fixed and the force is applied to the right end. Generate a report. Include the following information at the bottom of the report. Dimensions are in inches.

1. Maximum safe force = _____
2. Material's yield strength = _____
3. Maximum stress experienced by the part = _____
4. A picture of where the maximum stress is located.

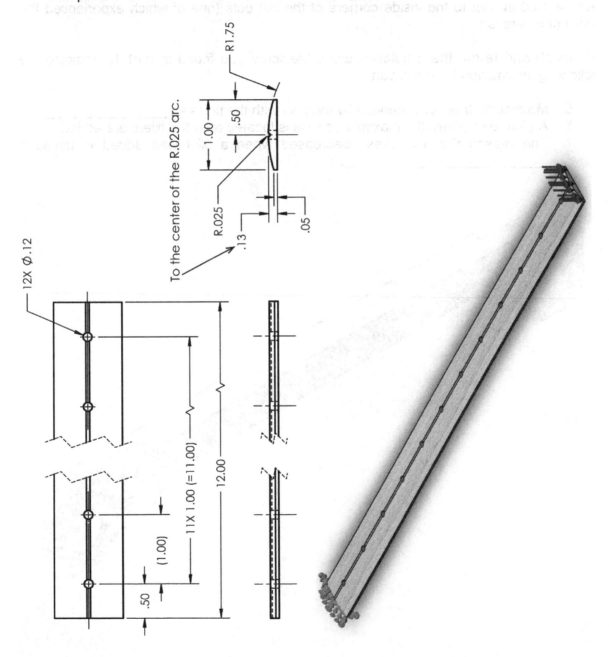

CONNECTING ROD (STATIC FEA) QUIZ PROBLEMS

Q5-1) Model the following part which is made from PE High Density. The dimensions are given in millimeters. Run a Static FEA test on the part. Fix the two holes on the base. Apply a 20 N force to the upright hole pointing in a direction that is away from the two base holes. Note the maximum stress experienced by the part.

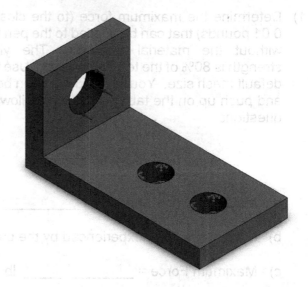

	Group 1	Group 2	Group 3
A	100	110	90
B	50	45	55

Maximum Stress experienced by the part = _____ N/m² (Pa)

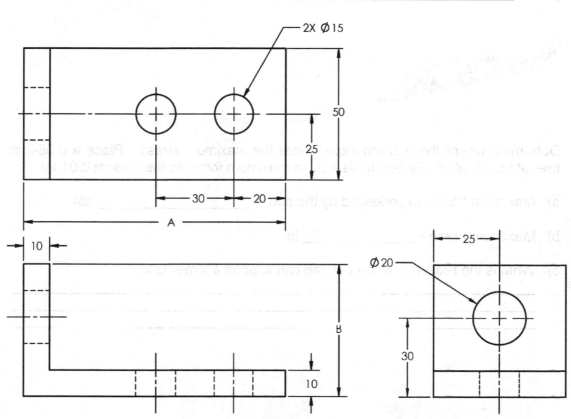

Q5-2) Open "**pen top – Student.SLDPRT**"

1) Determine the maximum force (to the closest 0.01 pounds) that can be applied to the pen tab without the material yielding.   The yield strength is 80% of the tensile strength. Use the default mesh size. You will hold the main body and push up on the tab. Answer the following questions.

   a) Material's Yield Strength = _____ psi

   b) Maximum Stress experienced by the part = _____ psi

   c) Maximum Force = _____ lb

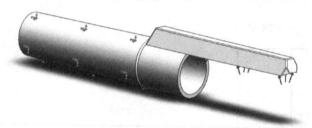

2) Determine where the pen top experiences the maximum stress. Place a 0.05-inch fillet at this location. Re-test to determine maximum force (to the closest 0.01 lb).

   a) Maximum Stress experienced by the part = _____ psi

   b) Maximum Force =_____ lb

   c) What is the reason why the pen tab can support a larger load?
   _____
   _____
   _____.

CHAPTER 6

FLANGED COUPLING PROJECT
Coupling

CHAPTER OUTLINE

6.1) PREREQUISITES

Before starting this tutorial you should complete the following tutorials.

- Connecting Rod Project – Part modeling
- Connecting Rod Project – Part print

It will help if you have the following knowledge.

- A familiarity with section views.
- A familiarity with threads and fasteners.

6.2) WHAT YOU WILL LEARN

The objective of this tutorial is to introduce you to the **revolve** command, simple **patterns**, **holes**, and **section views**. In this tutorial, you will be modeling the *left coupling* for the *Flanged Coupling* assembly shown in Figure 6.2-1. Specifically, you will be learning the following commands and concepts.

Sketching

- Dimensioning using a centerline

Features

- Revolve
- Hole wizard
- Patterns

View

- Rotate

Drawing

- Section view

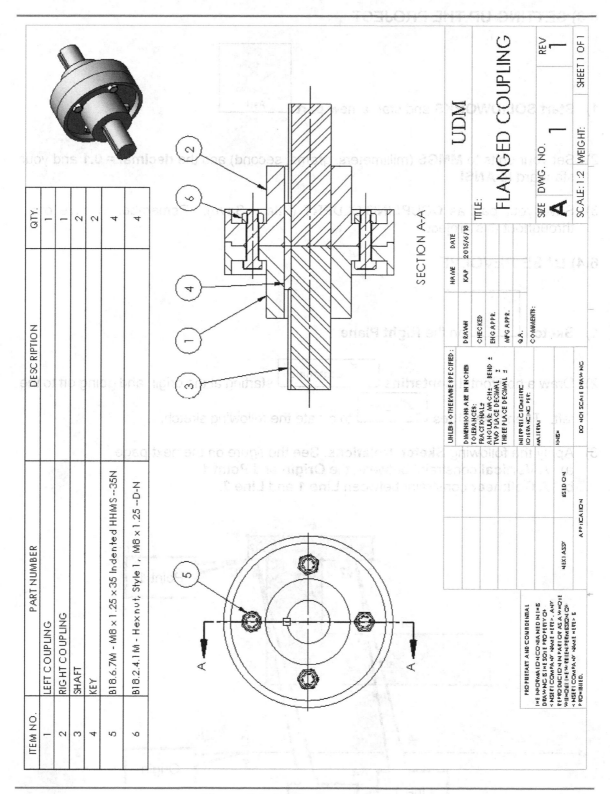

Figure 6.2-1: Flanged Coupling

6.3) SETTING UP THE PROJECT

1) **Start SOLIDWORKS** and start a **new part** .

2) Set your units to **MMGS** (millimeters, grams, second) and the **decimal = 0.1** and your standard to **ANSI**.

3) Save your part as **COUPLING.SLDPRT** (**File – Save**). Remember to save often throughout this project.

6.4) BASE REVOLVE

1) **Sketch** [Sketch] on the **Right Plane**.

2) Draw a horizontal **Centerline** [Centerline] starting at the origin and going off to the left. Then, use **Lines** [Line] to create the following sketch.

3) Apply the following **Sketch Relations**. See the figure on the next page.
   a) A **Vertical** constraint between the **Origin** and **Point 1**.
   b) A **Collinear** constraint between **Line 1** and **Line 2**.

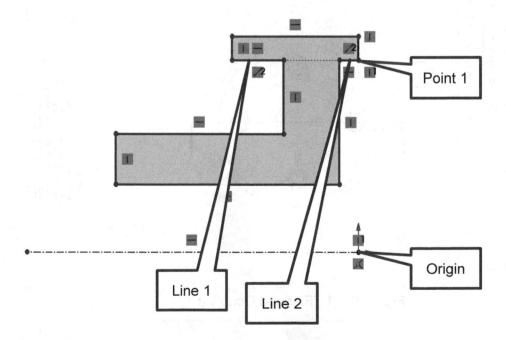

4) **Dimension** 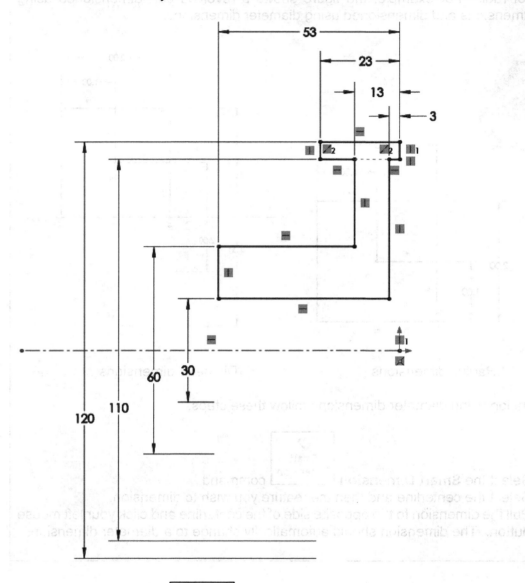 the sketch. See the informational block on **Dimensioning to a centerline**. After you dimension the sketch, all lines should be black.

5) **Revolve Boss/Base** the sketch **360** degrees using the centerline as the axis of revolution and the **Blind** method. See the informational block on **Revolve Boss/Base & Revolve Cut**.

Dimensioning to a centerline

If you are using a centerline as a revolve axis, you may want to dimension diameters instead of radii. For example, the figure shows a revolved part dimensioned using radius dimensions and dimensioned using diameter dimensions.

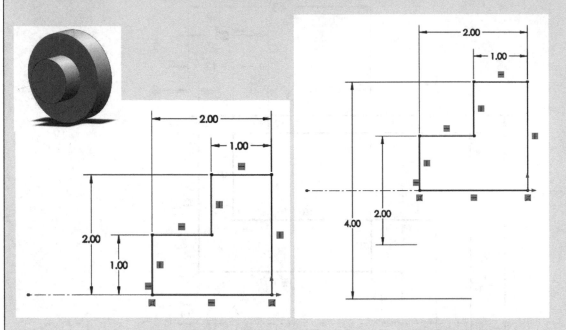

Radius dimensions   Diameter dimensions

To dimension using diameter dimensions follow these steps.

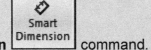

1) Select the **Smart Dimension** command.
2) Select the centerline and then the feature you wish to dimension.
3) Pull the dimension to the opposite side of the centerline and click your left mouse button. The dimension should automatically change to a diameter dimension.

Revolve Boss/Base & Revolve Cut

The **Revolve Boss/Base** and **Revolve Cut** commands are located in the *Features* tab. The revolve commands take a closed profile and revolve it about a specified axis. The *Revolve Boss/Base* and the *Revolve Cut* commands work essentially the same way. The *Revolve Boss/Base* adds material and the *Revolve Cut* removes material. Note that the command **View – Hide/Show - Temporary Axes** may be used to show existing axes that may then be used as the revolve axis.

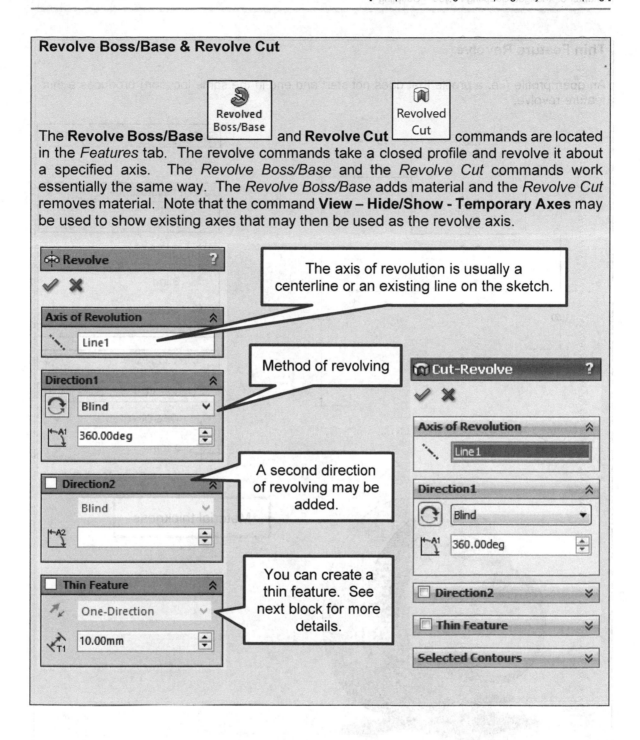

The axis of revolution is usually a centerline or an existing line on the sketch.

Method of revolving

A second direction of revolving may be added.

You can create a thin feature. See next block for more details.

Thin Feature Revolve

An open profile (i.e. a profile that does not start and end in the same location) produces a thin feature revolve.

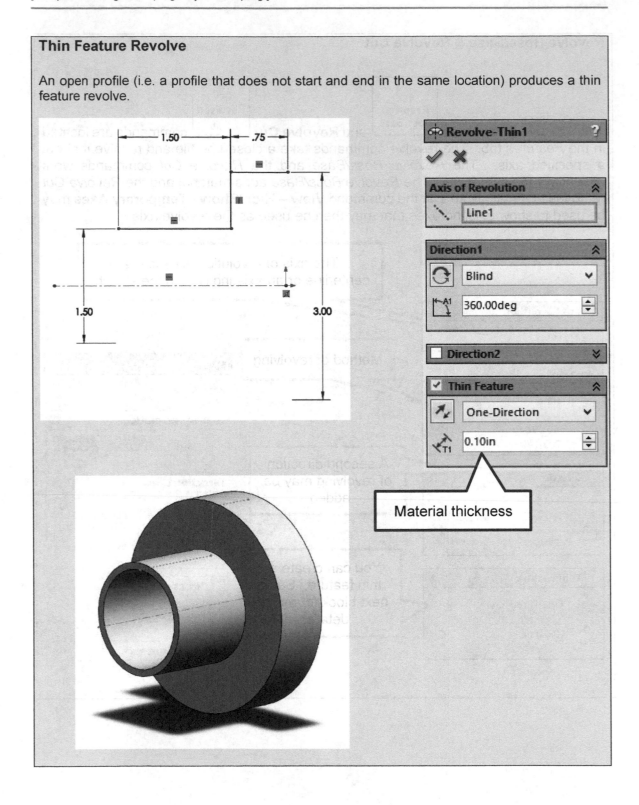

6) Rotate your part to look at the back side. You can use the view cube (**Space bar**) or click and hold the middle button on your mouse and move your mouse.

7) Return to the previous view showing the front side using the view cube (**Space bar**) or **Ctrl + 7**.

6.5) ADDING FEATURES

1) **Sketch** and **Dimension** the square shown, on the front face of the object. Remember, **Ctrl + 8** gives you the normal or straight on view.

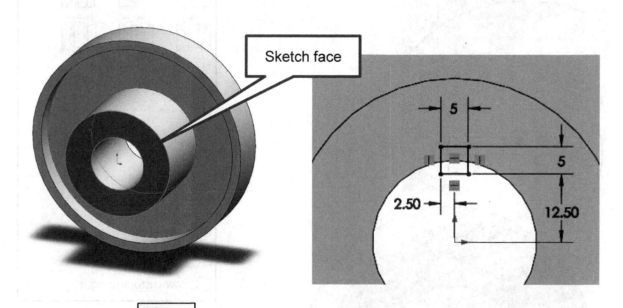

Sketch face

2) **Extrude Cut** the sketch **Through All**.

3) Add a normal **Clearance Hole** 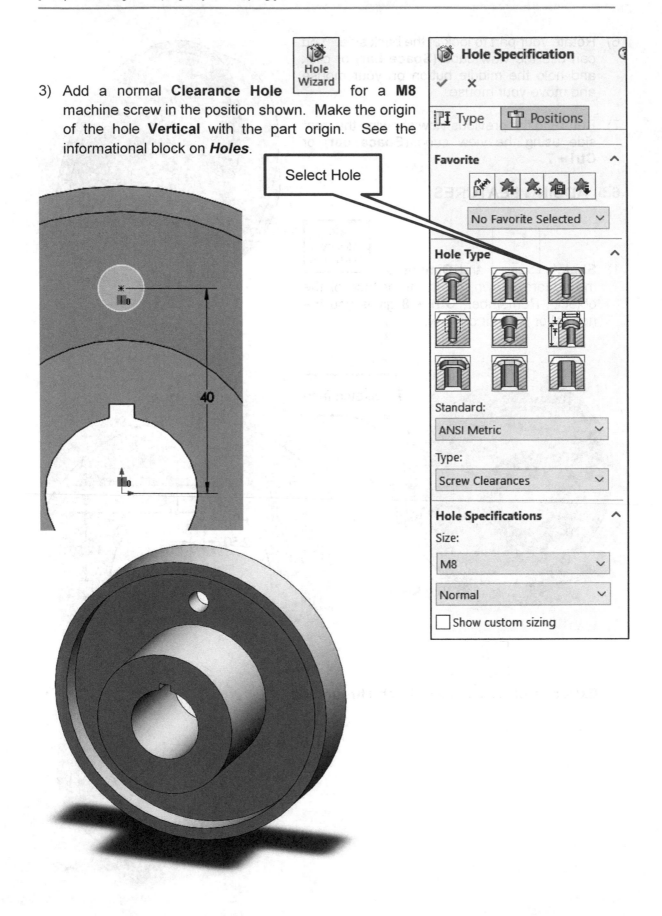 for a **M8** machine screw in the position shown. Make the origin of the hole **Vertical** with the part origin. See the informational block on *Holes*.

Select Hole

Hole Wizard (Located in the *Features* tab)

The **Hole Wizard** command is located in the *Features* tab. The *Holes* command allows you to create various types of holes in your part. The types of holes that can be created are

- Counterbore and Countersink holes
- Clearance hole
- Tapped (threaded) hole
- Legacy hole
- Counterbore and Countersink slots
- Slot

Each type of hole may be associated with a standard fastener or drill size. The figure on the next page shows the *Hole* window. To create a *Hole*, follow these steps.

1. Select the **Holes Wizard** 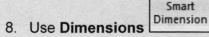 command.
2. Select the hole shape by selecting one of the pictures (e.g. counterbore, countersink, blind).
3. Select the standard (e.g. ANSI Metric, ANSI inch).
4. Select the hole type (e.g. screw clearance, tap drill, letter drill size).
5. Select the hole specification (e.g. drill size, associated fastener).
6. Specify the end condition.
7. Click on the **Positions** tab and then select the surface on which the hole will be placed.
8. Use **Dimensions** and **Sketch Relations** to position the hole.

Hole Wizard continued

Enter the *Position* tab to locate the hole center using **Dimensions** and **Sketch Relations**

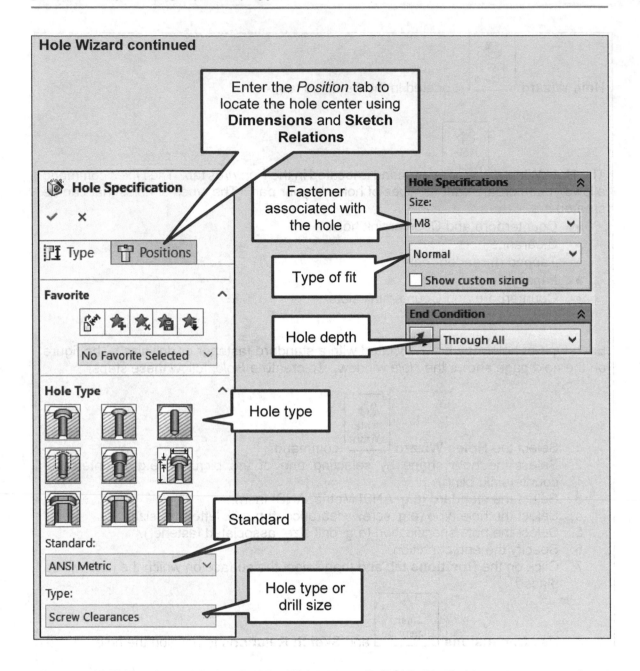

Hole Specification

Type   Positions

Favorite

No Favorite Selected

Hole Type

Hole type

Standard:

ANSI Metric

Type:

Screw Clearances

Fastener associated with the hole

Type of fit

Hole depth

Standard

Hole type or drill size

Hole Specifications

Size:

M8

Normal

☐ Show custom sizing

End Condition

Through All

4) Create a **Circular Pattern**  patterning the **Hole** you just created. Use the center axis of your part and revolve **4** holes using a total angle of **360** degrees. To view your center axis, select **View – Hide/Show - Temporary Axes**. See the informational block on *Patterns* and the information block on *Circular and Linear Patterns*.

5) Make the part out of **1020 Steel**.

6) **Save** your part.

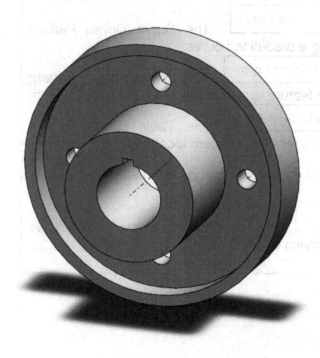

Select the Clearance hole in the Feature Tree

Patterns

The **Pattern** commands are located in the *Features* tab. They allow you to array an existing feature. The most commonly used patterns are *Linear Pattern* and *Circular Pattern*. However, there are other methods of patterning a feature.

1) Linear Pattern: Linear Pattern   The *Linear Pattern* command will repeat a feature along two directions.

2) Circular Pattern: Circular Pattern   The *Circular Pattern* command repeats a feature along a circular path.

3) Mirror: Mirror   The *Mirror* command creates a duplicate feature about a mirror line.

4) Curve Driven Pattern: Curve Driven Pattern   The *Curve Driven Pattern* command allows you to array along a predefined curve.

5) Sketch Driven Pattern: Sketch Driven Pattern   The *Sketch Driven Pattern* command uses sketch points. The feature is copied to each point in the sketch.

6) Table Driven Pattern: Table Driven Pattern   The *Table Driven Pattern* command uses X-Y coordinates, to specify the pattern locations.

7) Fill Pattern: Fill Pattern   The *Fill Pattern* command fills a selected area with the patterned feature.

8) Variable Pattern: Variable Pattern   The *Variable Pattern* command allows you to create patterns that have varying dimensions.

Circular & Linear Patterns

The **Linear Pattern** 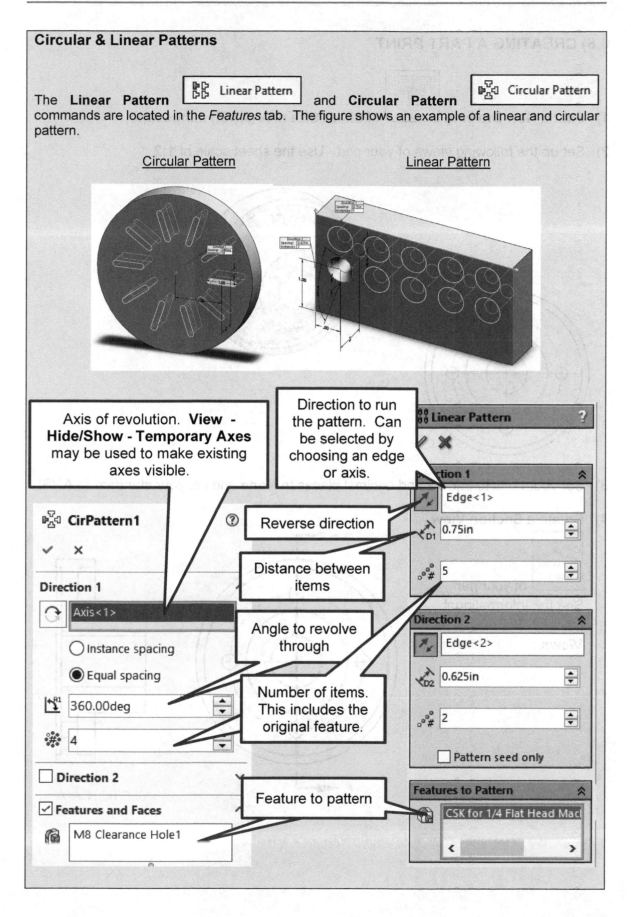 and **Circular Pattern** commands are located in the *Features* tab. The figure shows an example of a linear and circular pattern.

Circular Pattern   Linear Pattern

Axis of revolution. **View - Hide/Show - Temporary Axes** may be used to make existing axes visible.

Direction to run the pattern. Can be selected by choosing an edge or axis.

Reverse direction

Distance between items

Angle to revolve through

Number of items. This includes the original feature.

Feature to pattern

CirPattern1

✓ ✗

Direction 1

Axis<1>

○ Instance spacing
● Equal spacing

360.00deg

4

☐ Direction 2

✓ Features and Faces

M8 Clearance Hole1

Linear Pattern

Direction 1

Edge<1>

0.75in

5

Direction 2

Edge<2>

0.625in

2

☐ Pattern seed only

Features to Pattern

CSK for 1/4 Flat Head Mac

6.6) CREATING A PART PRINT

1) Start a **New Drawing** of **Sheet Size** of **A (ANSI) Landscape**.

2) Set up the following views of your part. Use the sheet scale of **1:2**.

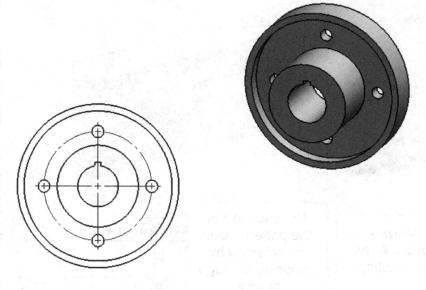

3) Set your units to **MMGS** and decimal places to **None** and set your standard to **ANSI**.

4) Create a **Section View**

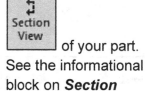 of your part. See the informational block on **Section Views**.

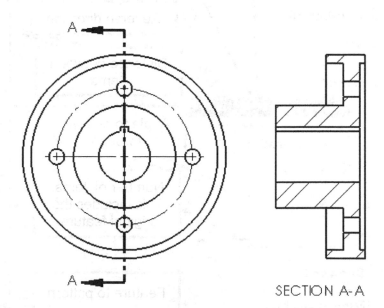

SECTION A-A

Section Views (*View Layout* tab)

The **Section View** command is located in the *View Layout* tab. A section view allows you to look inside of your part. An imaginary cut is made through your part and a portion of the part is mentally removed allowing you a look at the inside of the part. The imaginary cut is indicated on a part print with a **Cutting Plane line**. The material that is actually cut is indicated using **Section lines**. The section line pattern is dependent on the material of the part. This is automatically chosen by the program. To create a section view follow these steps.

1) Select the **Section View** command in the *View Layout* tab of the *Command Manager* ribbon.
2) Select the type of section you wish to make.
3) Place your cutting plane line. Note that more points may be added in order to bend the cutting plane line. Getting an offset section cutting plane line just right may take a little practice.
4) Select OK when your section line is what you want it to be.
5) Place your view.

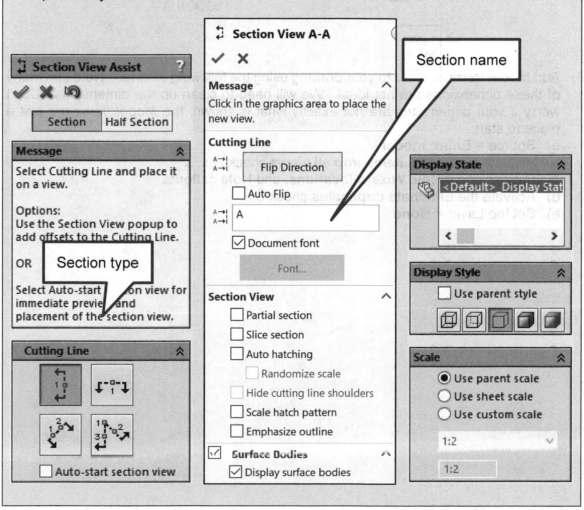

5) Add missing **Centerlines** 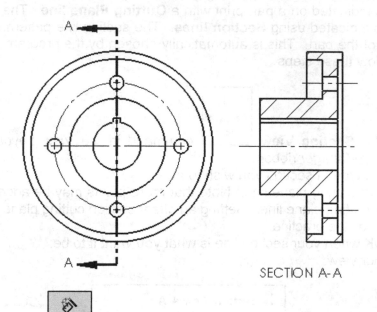 `⊟ Centerline` to your section view. Extend the centerlines as necessary. We do not want the centerlines to end at the boundary of the part.

SECTION A-A

6) Add **Model Items** `Model Items` to your drawing using the following settings. Note that many of these dimensions are not ideal. We will need to clean up the dimensions. Don't worry if your dimensions are not exactly what is shown; the *Model Items* are just a place to start.
   a) Source = **Entire model**
   b) Activate the **Import items into all views** check box.
   c) Dimensions = **Hole Wizard locations,** and **Hole callouts**
   d) Activate the **Eliminate duplicates** check box.
   e) Set the Layer = **None**

7) Move your dimensions away from the part views so that they are not directly on top of the view.

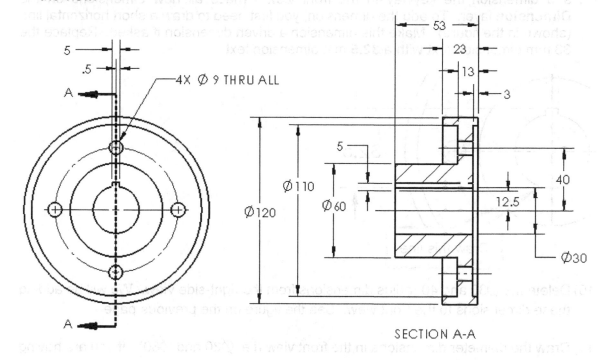

SECTION A-A

8) The 4X Ø9 dimension is gray. Create a **Dimension** layer and move that dimension to this layer. Do this by clicking on the dimension and then selecting the *Dimension* layer.

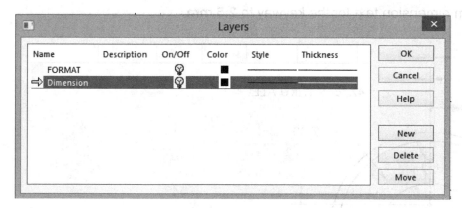

9) **Delete** the 13 mm and 5 mm dimension in the section view that dimension the keyway and dimension the keyway in the front view. Place all new dimensions on the **Dimension** layer. To add the dimension, you first need to draw a short horizontal line (shown in the figure). Make this dimension a driven dimension if asked. Replace the 33 mm dimension text with a **32.5** mm dimension text.

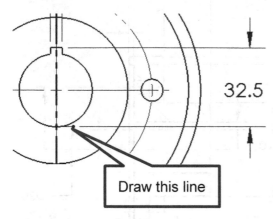

Draw this line

10) Delete the ∅30 and 40 radius dimensions from the right-side view. We will be adding these dimensions to the front view. See the figure on the previous page

11) Draw the diameter dimensions in the front view (i.e. ∅30 and ∅80). If you are having trouble dimensioning the circle of centers, you may need to delete this circle and draw one in manually. Make a new layer called **Centerline** using a centerline line type and place the new circle on this layer. Make the dimensions driven if asked.

12) Change the 3 mm dimension text for the keyway to **2.5 mm**.

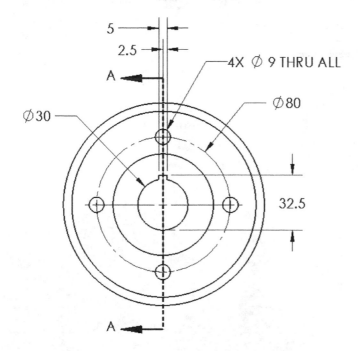

13) The drawing below is how your final views should look. If they do not, make any adjustments necessary.

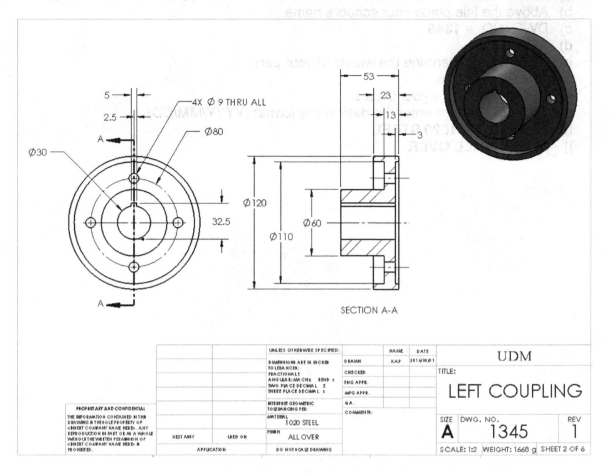

SECTION A-A

		UNLESS OTHERWISE SPECIFIED:		NAME	DATE		UDM	
		DIMENSIONS ARE IN INCHES TOLERANCES:	DRAWN	KAP	2014/28/01	TITLE:		
		FRACTIONAL± ANGULAR: MACH± BEND ± TWO PLACE DECIMAL ± THREE PLACE DECIMAL ±	CHECKED					
			ENG APPR.				LEFT COUPLING	
			MFG APPR.					
PROPRIETARY AND CONFIDENTIAL		INTERPRET GEOMETRIC TOLERANCING PER:	QA.					
THE INFORMATION CONTAINED IN THIS DRAWING IS THE SOLE PROPERTY OF <INSERT COMPANY NAME HERE>. ANY REPRODUCTION IN PART OR AS A WHOLE WITHOUT THE WRITTEN PERMISSION OF <INSERT COMPANY NAME HERE> IS PROHIBITED.		MATERIAL 1020 STEEL	COMMENTS:			SIZE	DWG. NO.	REV
	NEXT ASSY	USED ON	FINISH ALL OVER			A	1345	1
	APPLICATION		DO NOT SCALE DRAWING			SCALE: 1:2	WEIGHT: 1668 g	SHEET 2 OF 6

6 - 21

14) Fill in the title block with the following information.
   a) TITLE = **LEFT COUPLING**
   b) Above the title place your school's name.
   c) DWG. NO. = **1345**
   d) REV = **1**
   e) WEIGHT = Determine the weight of your part.
   f) SHEET = 2 OF 6
   g) DRAWN NAME = your initials
   h) DRAWN DATE = enter the date in this format (YYYY/MM/DD)
   i) MATERIAL = **1020 STEEL**
   j) FINISH = **ALL OVER**

FLANGED COUPLING (COUPLING) PROBLEMS

P6-1) Use SOLIDWORKS® to create a solid model and detailed drawing of the following 1060 Alloy Aluminum **JIG**. Fill in the appropriate information in the drawing's title block.

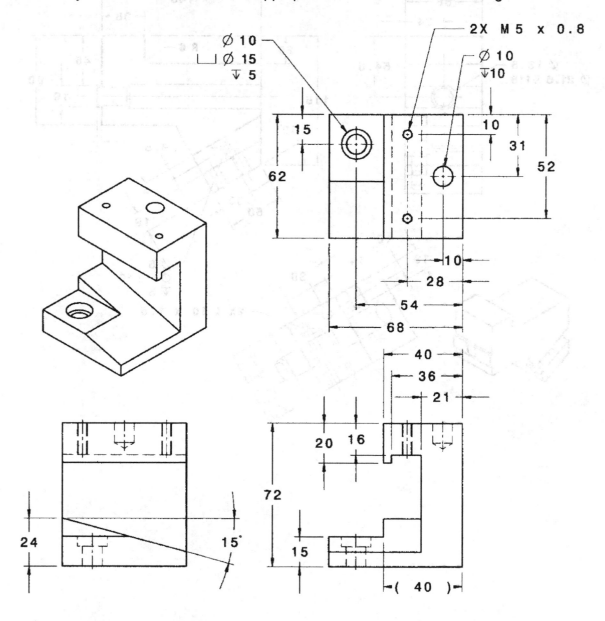

P6-2) Use SOLIDWORKS® to create a solid model and detailed drawing of the following Tool Steel **FIXTURE**. Fill in the appropriate information in the drawing's title block.

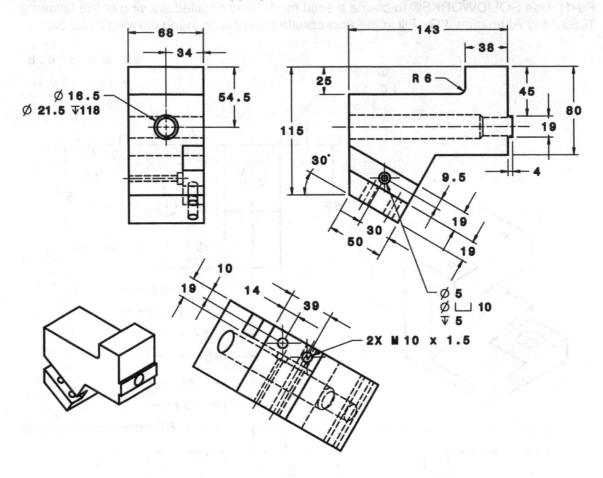

P6-3) Use SOLIDWORKS® to create a solid model and detailed drawing of the following High Density Polyethylene **STEP GEAR MECHANISM**. Fill in the appropriate information in the drawing's title block.

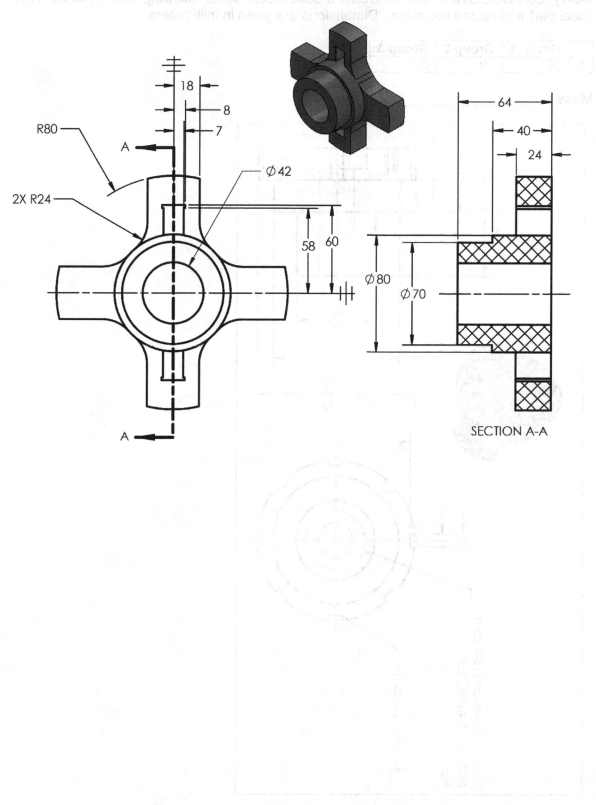

SECTION A-A

FLANGED COUPLING (COUPLING) QUIZ PROBLEMS

Q6-1) Use SOLIDWORKS® to create a solid model of the following AISI Type A2 Tool Steel part and record the mass. Dimensions are given in millimeters.

	Group 1	Group 2	Group 3
A	80	70	60

Mass = _____ grams

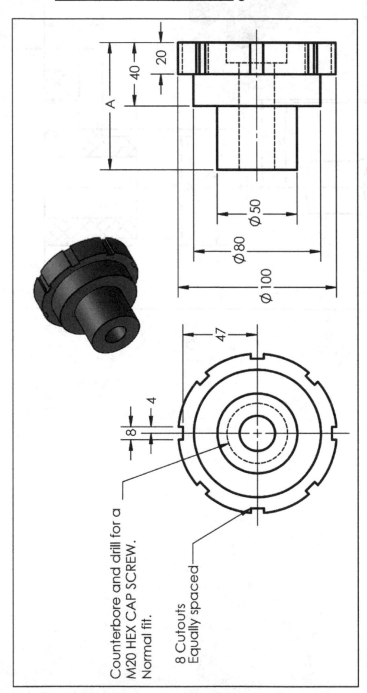

Counterbore and drill for a
M20 HEX CAP SCREW.
Normal fit.

8 Cutouts
Equally spaced

CHAPTER 7

FLANGED COUPLING PROJECT
Assembly

CHAPTER OUTLINE

7.1) PREREQUISITES

Before starting this tutorial, you should complete the following tutorials.

- Connecting rod project - configurations
- Flanged coupling project – coupling

It will help if you have the following knowledge.

- Familiarity with assembly drawings
- Familiarity with threads and fasteners

7.2) WHAT YOU WILL LEARN

The objective of this tutorial is to introduce you to simple assembly models. In this tutorial, you will be creating the remaining parts for the *Flanged Coupling* assembly shown in Figure 7.2-1. You will also assemble the parts using *Mates*. Specifically, you will be learning the following commands and concepts.

Setting up your drawing

- New assembly

Sketch

- Trim

Assembly

- Standard Mates
- Toolbox components
- Exploded view

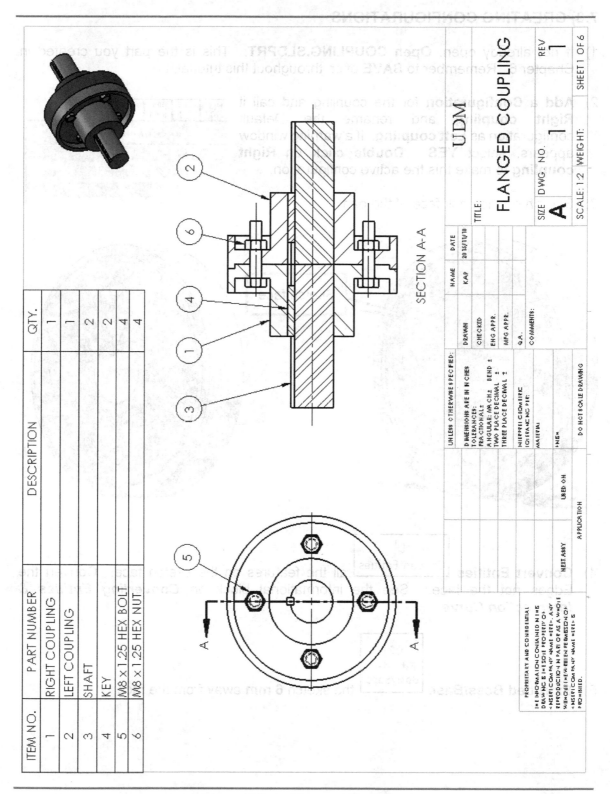

ITEM NO.	PART NUMBER	DESCRIPTION	QTY.
1	RIGHT COUPLING		1
2	LEFT COUPLING		1
3	SHAFT		2
4	KEY		2
5	M8 x 1.25 HEX BOLT		4
6	M8 x 1.25 HEX NUT		4

SECTION A-A

UDM

FLANGED COUPLING

	NAME	DATE
DRAWN	KAP	2015/11/10
CHECKED		
ENG APPR.		
MFG APPR.		
Q.A.		
COMMENTS:		

TITLE:

SIZE	DWG. NO.	REV
A	1	1

SCALE: 1:2   WEIGHT: SHEET 1 OF 6

UNLESS OTHERWISE SPECIFIED:

DIMENSIONS ARE IN INCHES
TOLERANCES:
FRACTIONAL±
ANGULAR: MACH±   BEND ±
TWO PLACE DECIMAL ±
THREE PLACE DECIMAL ±

INTERPRET GEOMETRIC
TOLERANCING PER:

MATERIAL

FINISH

DO NOT SCALE DRAWING

NEXT ASSY   USED ON

APPLICATION

Figure 7.2-1: Flanged Coupling

7.3) CREATING CONFIGURATIONS

1) If not already open, **Open COUPLING.SLDPRT**. This is the part you created in Chapter 6. Remember to **SAVE** often throughout this tutorial.

2) **Add** a **Configuration** for the coupling and call it **Right coupling** and rename the Default configuration as **Left coupling**. If a warning window appears, select **YES**. **Double click** on **Right coupling** to make this the active configuration.

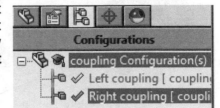

3) **Sketch** on the back face of the part.

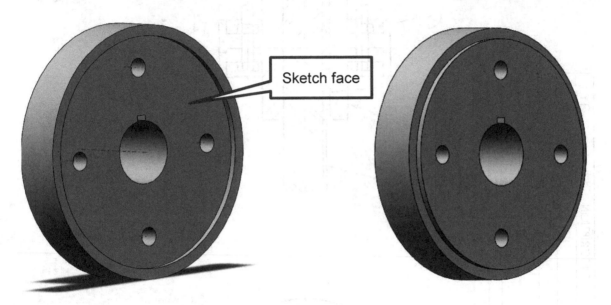

Sketch face

4) **Convert Entities**  all the features on the sketch face. Convert the Edges not the face. See the informational block on **Converting Entities & Intersection Curve**.

5) **Extruded Boss/Base** the sketch **6 mm** away from the face.

Convert Entities  & **Intersection Curve**
(Located in the *Sketch* tab)

The *Convert Entities* and *Intersection Curve* commands allow you to create sketches based on existing geometry. The *Convert Entities* command converts solid geometry edges or sketch entities to a sketch on a selected plane. The *Intersection Curve* command creates a sketch of the intersection between planes, solid bodies, and surface bodies.

Example of a *Convert Entities*   Example of an *Intersection Curve*

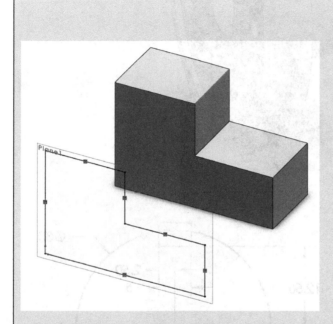 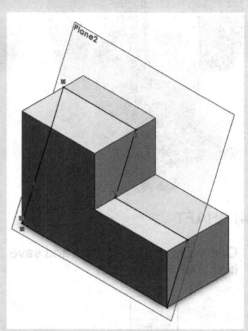

Convert Entities

1) Select a plane or face to sketch on.

2) Select the **Convert Entities** [Convert Entities] command.
3) Select the faces and/or edges you wish to convert.

Intersection Curve

1) Select at least two entities such as planes, faces, or surfaces. If you are sketching on a plane, the plane is automatically selected as one of the items.

2) Select the **Intersection Curve** [Intersection Curve] command.

6) Go to your *Configuration* tab and click between the **Left** and **Right coupling** to make sure that the configurations work. **Save** your part.

7.4) SHAFT

1) Open a **new MMGS part** and save it as **SHAFT.SLDPRT**.

2) **Sketch** 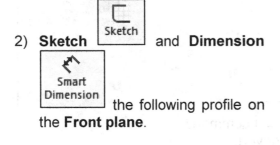 and **Dimension**

Smart Dimension the following profile on the **Front plane**.

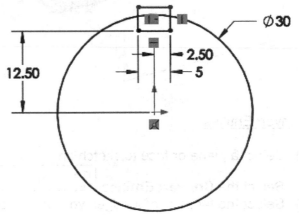

3) **Trim (To closest)** 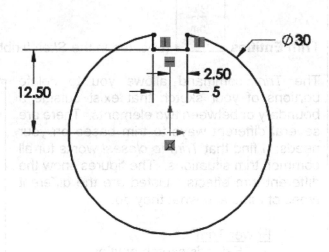 the excess lines to create the key seat. See the informational block for information on **Trimming Entities**.

4) **Extrude** the sketch **50 mm** and make the part out of **1020 Steel**.

5) **Save** your part.

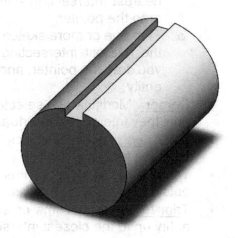

Trim Entities (Located in the *Sketch* ribbon)

The *Trim* command allows you to delete portions of your sketch that exist outside a boundary or between two elements. There are several different ways to trim based on your needs. I find that *Trim to closest* works for all common trim situations. The figures show the different trim effects. Listed are the different types of trims and what they do.

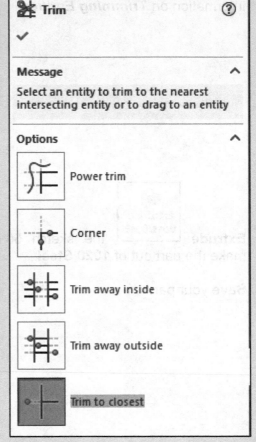

- Power Trim
  - ○ Extends sketch entities.
  - ○ Trim single sketch entities to the nearest intersecting entity as you drag the pointer.
  - ○ Trim one or more sketch entities to the nearest intersecting entity as you drag the pointer, and cross the entity.
- Corner: Modifies two selected entities until they intersect at a virtual corner.
- Trim away inside: Trims an entity between two intersections.
- Trim away outside: Trims an entity outside of two intersections.
- Trim to closest: Trims or extends an entity up to the closest intersection.

Corner trim example

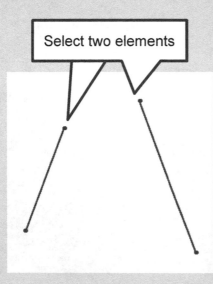

Select two elements

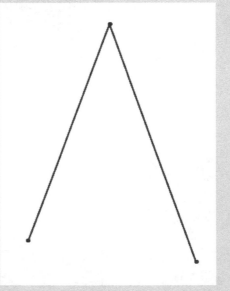

Trim continued

Trim away inside example

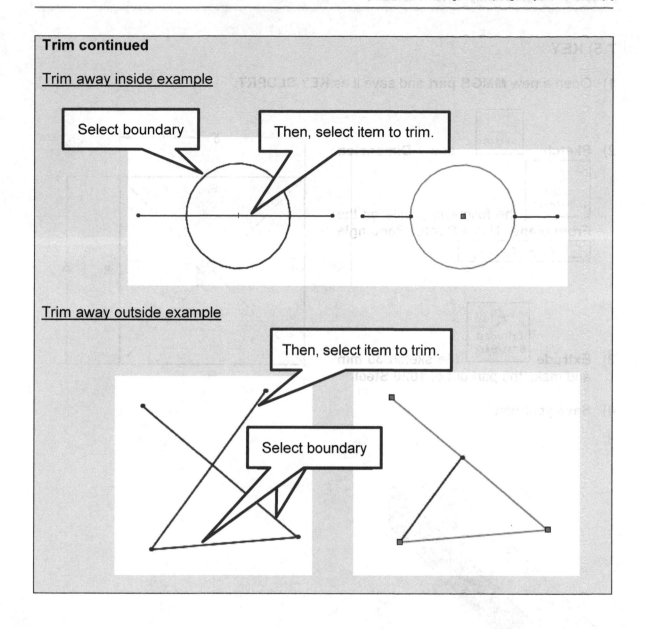

Trim away outside example

7.5) KEY

1) Open a **new MMGS part** and save it as **KEY.SLDPRT**.

2) **Sketch** | Sketch | and **Dimension** | Smart Dimension | the following profile on the **Front plane**. Use a **Center Rectangle** | □ Center Rectangle |.

3) **Extrude** | Extruded Boss/Base | the sketch **30 mm** and make the part out of **1020 Steel**.

4) **Save** your part.

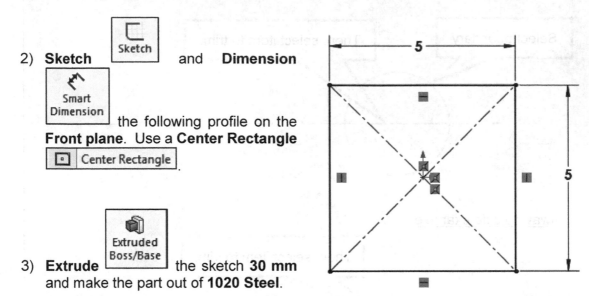

7.6) SETTING UP THE ASSEMBLY

1) Open **COUPLING.SLDPRT**, **SHAFT.SLDPRT**, and **KEY.SLDPRT**

2) Create a **new Assembly** .

3) In the *Begin Assembly* window you should see all three of your parts in the *Open documents* field. Multiple select all the parts (Hold the **Ctrl** key to multiple select).

4) Move your mouse onto the drawing area. One of your parts will appear. Place the part by clicking the left mouse button. Note, if the part is the *COUPLING*, it will ask you which configuration of the *COUPLING* you want to insert. Choose the *Left Coupling*. If it doesn't ask you to select a coupling, the configuration chosen will be shown in the design tree. Another one of your parts will appear. Place this one and the next.

> ▸ 🐚 🚩 (f) KEY<1> (Default<<Default>_Display State 1>)
> ▸ 🐚 🚩 (-) SHAFT<1> (Default<<Default>_Display State 1>)
> ▸ 🐚 🚩 (-) COUPLING<1> (Left Coupling<<Default>_Display State 1>)

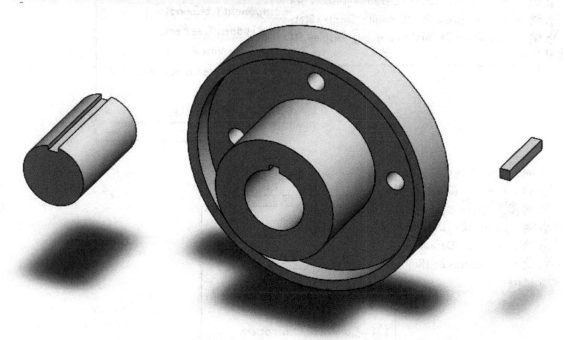

5) Make sure your units are **MMGS,** your standard is set to **ANSI**, and then save your assembly as **FLANGED COUPLING.SLDASM**

6) Make a copy of each of your parts. Do this by holding the **Ctrl** key, clicking on your part and then drag it to a new location.

7) Notice, in your *Feature Manager Design Tree*, it lists 6 parts (two couplings, two shafts and two keys). One of the parts has an (f) next to it. This is the fixed part (i.e. non-movable part). *Float* that part and *Fix* shaft<1>. Do this by right-clicking on the part and choosing either **Float** or **Fix**.

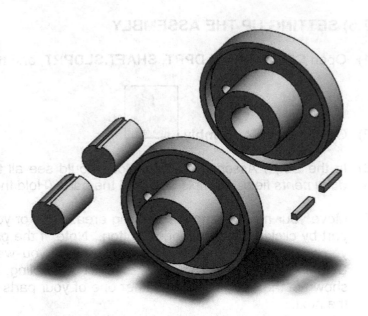

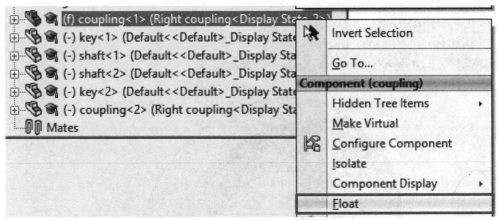

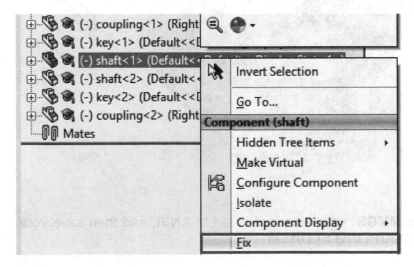

8) Notice that you either have two of the *left couplings* or two of the *right couplings*. We need one of each. To change the part's configuration, click on the part in the *Feature Manager Design Tree* and select the configuration. V isually confirm that you have one of each coupling configuration in the assembly. SOLIDWORKS® may have automatically chosen the non-represented configurations when you copied the coupling.

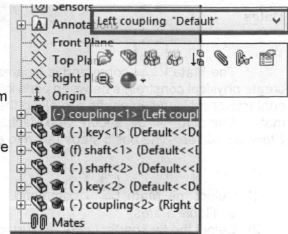

9) **Save**. If a warning window appears, choose **Rebuild and save the document**.

7.7) CREATING MATES

1) **Hide** *shaft< 2>* , *k ey<2>* and the *right coupling*. Do this by right-clicking on the part in the *Feature Manager Design Tree* and selecting **Hide Components**.

2) Apply the following **Mates**. Your assembly should look like what is shown. See the informational block on *Mates*.
   a) **Concentric** mate between the **Left Coupling's** center hole and **SHAFT< 1>'s** circumference.
   b) **Coincident** mate between the back edge of the **Left Coupling** and the back surface of **SHAFT< 1>** .
   c) **Coincident** mate between the **Right Plane** of the **Left Coupling**, and the **Right Plane** of the **SHAFT< 1>**. You will have to open up the design tree to do this.
   d) Create three **Coincident** mates that will place the **K EY** in its correct position.

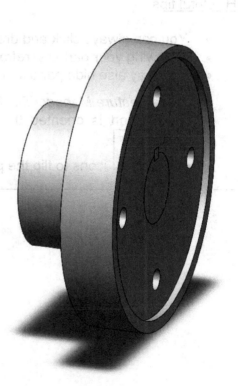

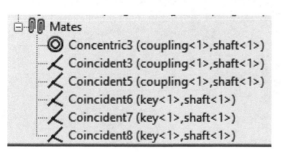

Mates

The **Mate** [Mate] command is located in the *A ssem bly.* *Mates* allow you to create physical constraints between parts in an assembly. For example, making surface contacts or making two shafts run along the same axis. There are three categories of mates: *Standard, A dv anced, and Mechanical.* This tutorial will introduce you to applying *Standard Mates*. The basic steps taken to apply a *Mate* are

1) Select the **Mate** [Mate] command. A *Mate* window will appear showing the available *Mates*.
2) Select the two parts, features, surfaces or planes to which you want the mate to be applied.
3) SOLIDWORKS will automatically select the mate that it thinks is most appropriate. If the default mate is good select **OK**, if not select the mate that you wish to apply.
4) The *Mate* window will stay active so that you can apply your next mate.
5) Select **OK** in the *Mate* window to end the *Mate* command.

H elpful tips

- You can always click and drag to move your parts out of the way.
- V iewing your part in wireframe may help you get to features that are hidden.
- You may also hide parts that are in the way. Do this by right-clicking on the part in the *Feature Manager Design* tree and selecting **Hide** [icon].
- If your part is oriented the wrong way, select one of the **Mate alignment**

Mate alignment:
[icons] icons to flip the part.

Standard Mates

The following are a description of the available *Standard mates*.

- <u>Coincident</u>: Makes points, edges and surfaces occupy the same point, line or plane.
- <u>Perpendicular</u>: Makes edges and surfaces perpendicular.
- <u>Tangent</u>: Makes edges and surfaces tangent.
- <u>Concentric</u>: Makes cylindrical surfaces and circular edges share the same center point.
- <u>Distance</u> 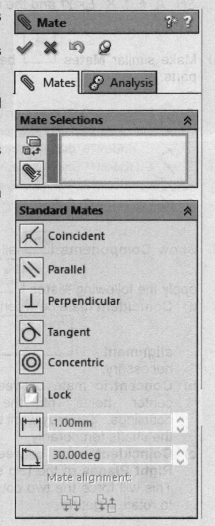: Make points, edges and surfaces a specified distance from each other.
- <u>Angle</u>: Make edges and surfaces a specified angle apart.

3) **Show Components** 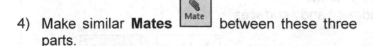 *SH A ⟨T2⟩ K, E⟨Y2⟩*

and the *right coupling*. **Hide Components** 🚫
SH A ⟨T⟩ K, E⟨Y1⟩ and the *left coupling*.

4) Make similar **Mates** between these three
parts.

> ◎ Concentric4 (shaft<2>,coupling<2>)
> ⟋ Coincident9 (shaft<2>,coupling<2>)
> ⟋ Coincident10 (shaft<2>,coupling<2>)
> ⟋ Coincident11 (shaft<2>,key<2>)
> ⟋ Coincident12 (shaft<2>,key<2>)
> ⟋ Coincident13 (shaft<2>,key<2>)

5) **Show Components** 👁 all of your parts and

apply the following **Mates** [Mate].

a) **Coincident** mate between the contacting surfaces of the couplings. Flip the **Mate**

    alignment [Mate alignment:] if
necessary.

b) **Concentric** mate between the
center holes of the two
couplings. You may want to hide
the shafts temporarily.

c) **Coincident** mate between the
Right Planes of the two shafts.
This will force the two couplings
to rotate together.

> ⟋ Coincident15 (coupling<1>,coupling<2>)
> ◎ Concentric5 (coupling<1>,coupling<2>)
> ⟋ Coincident16 (shaft<1>,shaft<2>)

6) Open, if not already open, **SHAFT.SLDPRT** and change the shaft length to **100 mm**. Do this by right-clicking on the **Extrude** feature and selecting **Edit Feature**.

7) **Save** the file and return to your assembly.

8) If the assembly file doesn't automatically update, select **rebuild** 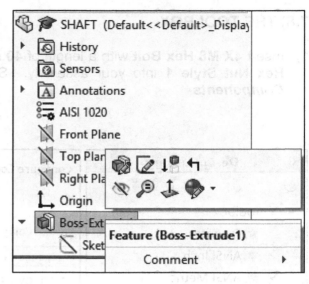.

9) **Save all** your assembly.

7.8) THE TOOLBOX

1) Insert **4X M8 Hex Bolt** with a length of **40 mm** into the assembly. Then add **4X M8 Hex Nut Style 1** into your assembly. See the informational block on *Toolbox Components*.

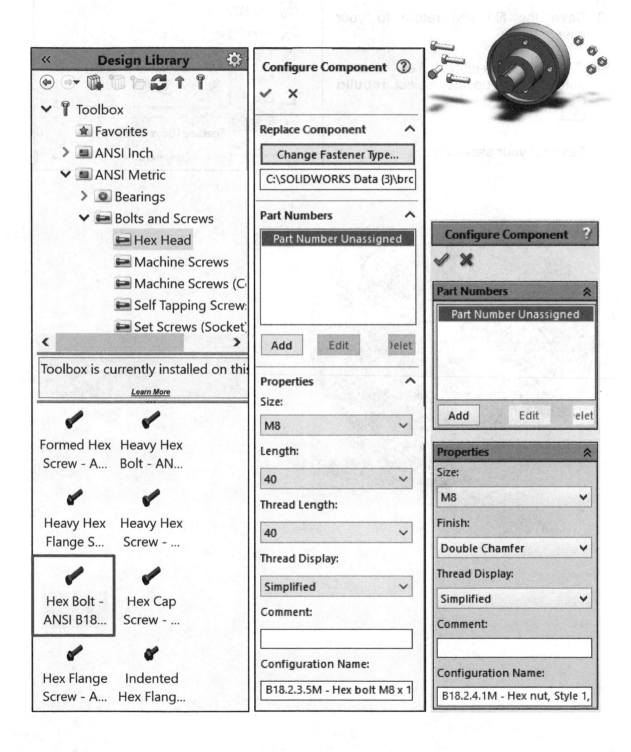

Toolbox components

The **Toolbox** [Toolbox] is located in the *Design Library* . The *Design library* is located in the *Task Pane* on the right side of your drawing area. The **Toolbox** gives you access to standard parts such as bolts, nuts and gears. This saves you the effort of having to model them.

To access the *Toolbox*, follow these steps.

1) In the *Task Pane* on the right side of the screen, select the **Design Library** icon.

2) Expand the **Toolbox** [Toolbox]. If the Toolbox is not loaded, **Add in now**.
3) Select the standard that controls your model (e.g ANSI inch, ANSI Metric).
4) Select the type of standard part that you want to insert into your assembly.
5) Drag the part into the drawing area.
6) A window will appear allowing you to adjust the parameters of the part.

Toolbox is not added in
Add in now

If you need to change the size of a toolbox component that you have already inserted, right-click on the component in the *Feature Manager Design Tree* and select **Edit Toolbox component**.

Toolbox components continued

To preload the *Toolbox* perform the following steps.

1) **Select Tools – Add-ins....**
2) In the *Add-Ins* window, activate the **SOLIDWORKS Toolbox Library** and **SOLIDWORKS Toolbox Utilities** checkbox in the **Active Add-ins** column. If you want the *Toolbox* to activate each time you open the program, activate them in the *Start Up* column as well.

Add-Ins			✕
Active Add-ins	**Start Up**	**Last Load Time**	
⊟ **SOLIDWORKS Premium Add-ins**			
☐ CircuitWorks	☐	--	
☐ FeatureWorks	☐	--	
☐ PhotoView 360	☐	1s	
☐ ScanTo3D	☐	--	
☐ SOLIDWORKS Design Checker	☐	< 1s	
☐ SOLIDWORKS Motion	☐	--	
☐ SOLIDWORKS Routing	☐	--	
☑ SOLIDWORKS Simulation	☑	1s	
☑ SOLIDWORKS Toolbox Library	☑	< 1s	
☑ SOLIDWORKS Toolbox Utilities	☑	1s	
☐ SOLIDWORKS Utilities	☐	--	
☐ TolAnalyst	☐	--	
⊟ **SOLIDWORKS Add-ins**			
☐ Autotrace	☐	--	
☑ SOLIDWORKS Composer	☑	< 1s	
☐ SOLIDWORKS Electrical	☐	--	
☐ SOLIDWORKS Flow Simulation 2016	☐	--	
☑ SOLIDWORKS Forum 2016	☑	< 1s	

OK	Cancel

2) Apply the following **Mates** to put the bolt and nut into position. Do this for every bolt-nut pair.

◎ Concentric6 (coupling<1>,hex screw_am<2>)
╳ Coincident17 (coupling<1>,hex screw_am<2>)
◎ Concentric7 (hex screw_am<2>,hex nut style 1_am<1>)
╳ Coincident18 (coupling<2>,hex nut style 1_am<1>)

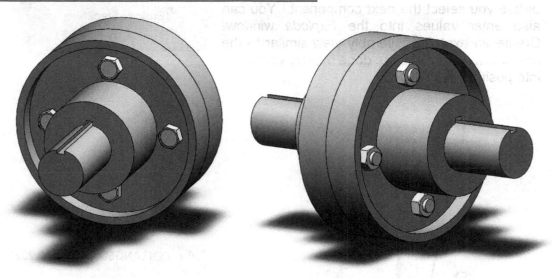

3) **Save all** your assembly.

7.9) EXPLODED ASSEMBLY

1) Select the **Exploded View**  command in the *Assembly* tab of the *Command Manager* ribbon. Select a component and then click and drag on one of the axes to move it. Select **Done** before you select the next component. You can also enter values into the *Explode* window. Create an explode assembly view similar to the one shown. After you are done moving your parts into position, select **OK**.

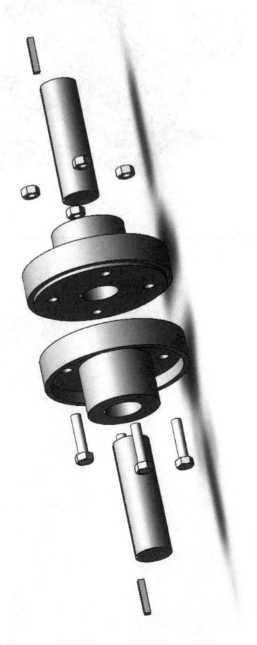

2) Enter the **Configurations** tab and expand your *Default* configuration. Notice that there is a new *Exploded View1* configuration. Double-click on **Exploded View1** to see the change.

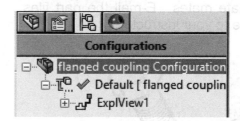

3) Make your unexploded view current. Right-click on *ExplView1* and select **Animate explode**. Note that an *Animation Controller* will appear allowing you to manipulate the explode as well as to record it.

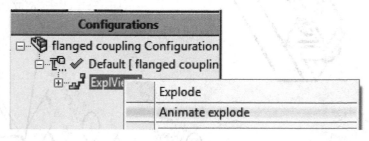

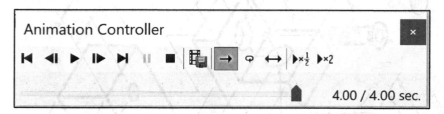

FLANGED COUPLING (ASSEMBLY) PROBLEMS

P7-1) Use SOLIDWORKS® to create a solid model of the following parts. Create an assembly model of the *Drill Jig* applying the appropriate mates. E-mail the part files, including the toolbox components, and the assembly file to your instructor.

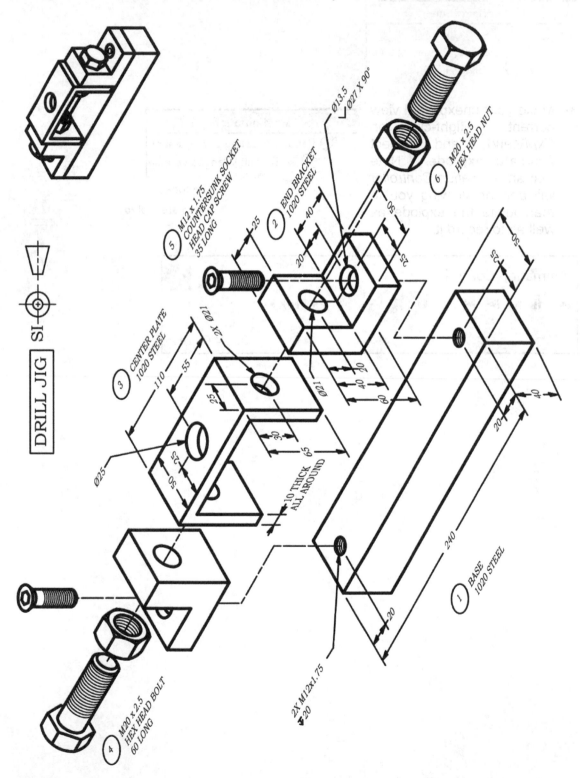

P7-2) Use SOLIDWORKS® to create a solid model of the following parts. Create an assembly model of the *Linear Bearing* applying the appropriate mates. E-mail the part files, including the toolbox components, and the assembly file to your instructor.

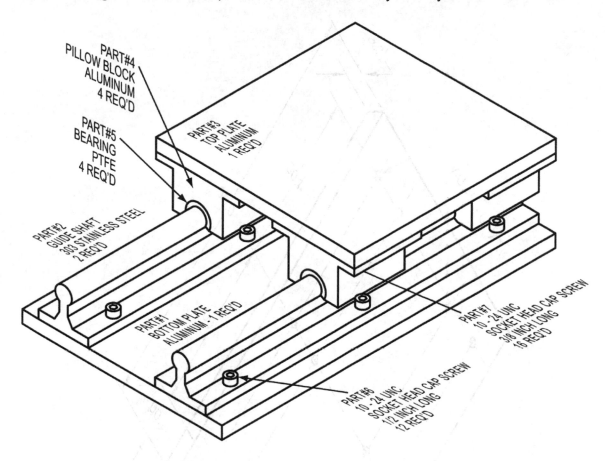

Part#1: Bottom Plate If you are just studying the basics and have not covered threads and fasteners, replace the 12X 10 – 24 UNC dimension with a 12x ∅.19 dimension.

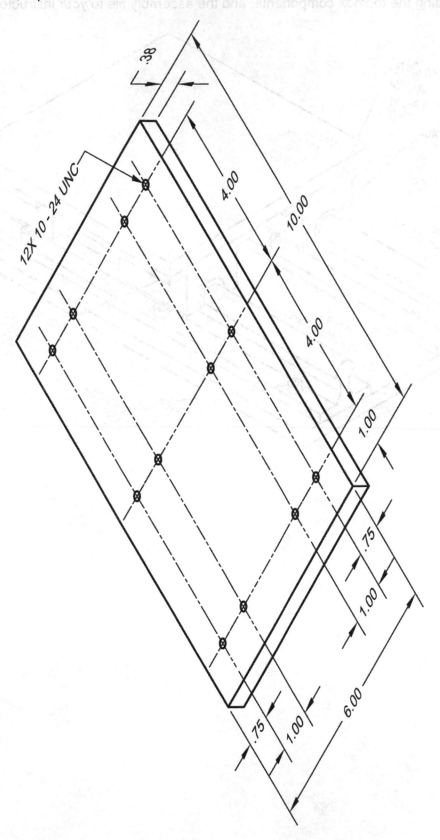

Part#2: Guide Shaft If you are just studying the basics and have not covered tolerancing, ignore the RC4 tolerance. NOTE TO DRAFTER: This part is symmetric, and all fillets are R.12.

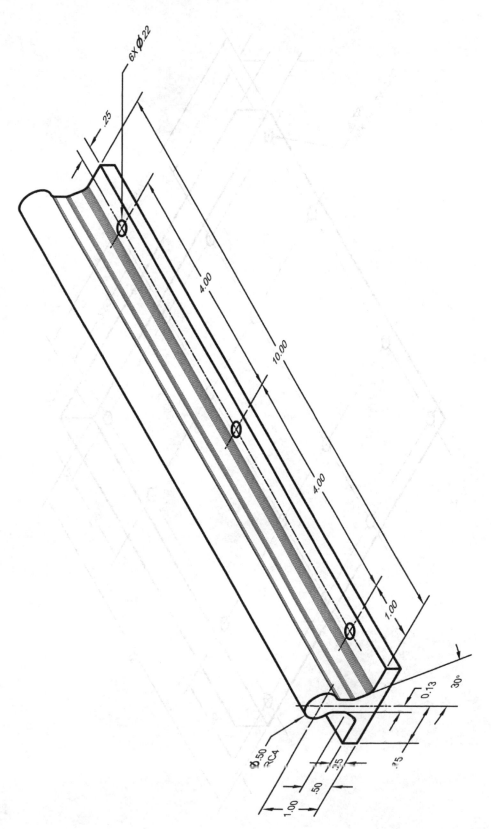

Part#3: Top Plate If you are just studying the basics and have not covered threads and fasteners, replace the 16X 10 – 24 UNC dimension with a 16x ⌀.19 dimension.

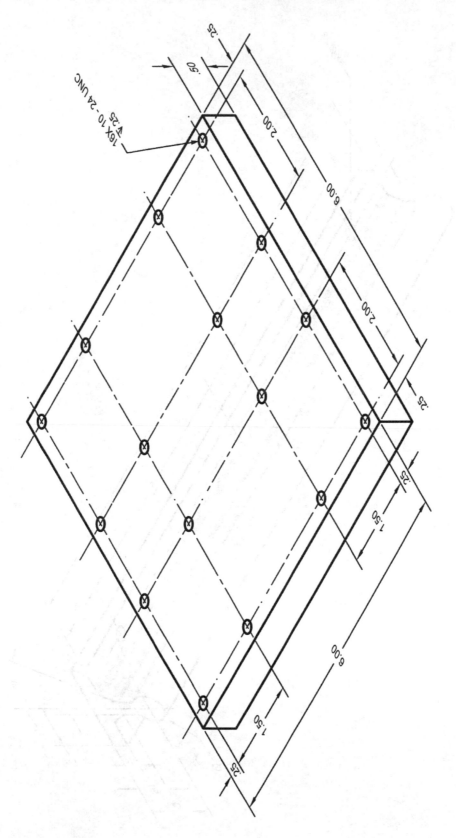

Part#4: Pillow Block If you are just studying the basics and have not covered tolerancing, ignore the FN1 tolerance.

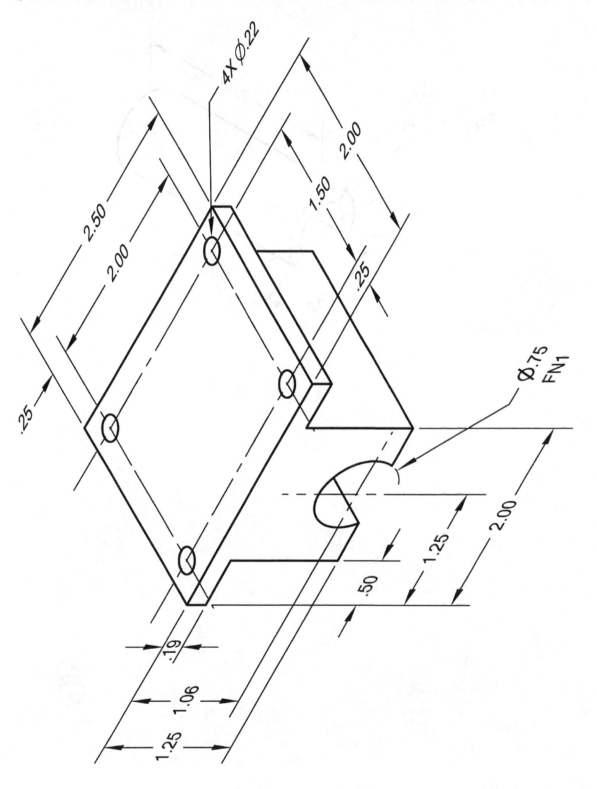

Part#5: Bearing If you are just studying the basics and have not covered tolerancing, ignore the RC4 and FN1 tolerances.

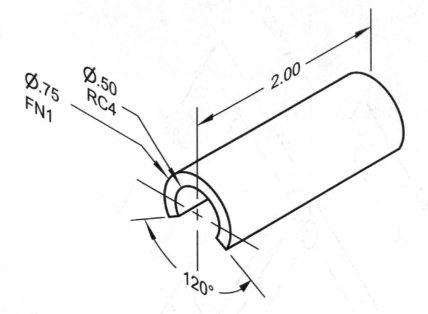

FLANGED COUPLING (ASSEMBLY) QUIZ PROBLEMS

Q7-1) Build a realistic assembly of the fidget spinner shown.

    1) Download the following files.

        • Fidget Spinner Body
        • Fidget Spinner Cap
        • Bearing

    2) Open a new assembly and insert the above parts.
    3) Make a copy of the Fidget Spinner Cap and three copies of the Bearing.
    4) Fix one of the Fidget Spinner Caps and Float the rest of the parts.
    5) Assemble the Fidget Spinner using the appropriate mates.

NOTES:

CHAPTER 8

FLANGED COUPLING PROJECT
Assembly Drawing

CHAPTER OUTLINE

8.1) PREREQUISITES

Before starting this tutorial you should complete the following tutorials.

- Flanged coupling project – Coupling
- Flanged coupling project – Assembly

It will help if you have the following knowledge.

- Familiarity with assembly drawings

8.2) WHAT YOU WILL LEARN

The objective of this tutorial is to introduce you to simple assembly drawings. In this tutorial, you will be creating the *Flanged Coupling* assembly drawing shown in Figure 8.2-1. Specifically, you will be learning the following commands and concepts.

Drawing

- Assembly drawing
- Ballooning
- Bill of Materials

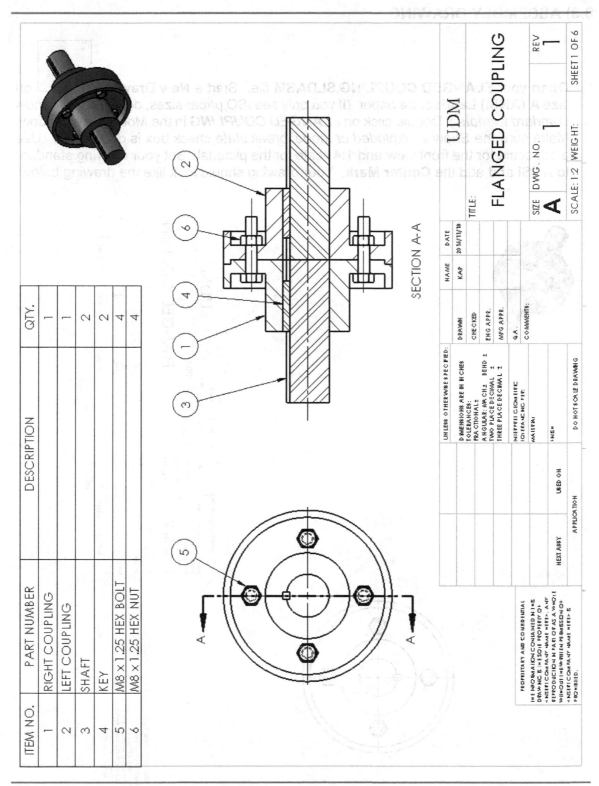

ITEM NO.	PART NUMBER	DESCRIPTION	QTY.
1	RIGHT COUPLING		1
2	LEFT COUPLING		1
3	SHAFT		2
4	KEY		2
5	M8 x 1.25 HEX BOLT		4
6	M8 x 1.25 HEX NUT		4

SECTION A-A

	NAME	DATE
DRAWN	KAP	2016/11/10
CHECKED		
ENG APPR.		
MFG APPR.		
Q.A.		
COMMENTS:		

UNLESS OTHERWISE SPECIFIED:

DIMENSIONS ARE IN INCHES
TOLERANCES:
FRACTIONAL±
ANGULAR: MACH± BEND ±
TWO PLACE DECIMAL ±
THREE PLACE DECIMAL ±

INTERPRET GEOMETRIC
TOLERANCING PER:

MATERIAL

FINISH

DO NOT SCALE DRAWING

UDM

TITLE:

FLANGED COUPLING

SIZE **A** DWG. NO. 1 REV 1

SCALE: 1:2 WEIGHT: SHEET 1 OF 6

NEXT ASSY USED ON

APPLICATION

PROPRIETARY AND CONFIDENTIAL

THE INFORMATION CONTAINED IN THIS
DRAWING IS THE SOLE PROPERTY OF
<INSERT COMPANY NAME HERE>. ANY
REPRODUCTION IN PART OR AS A WHOLE
WITHOUT THE WRITTEN PERMISSION OF
<INSERT COMPANY NAME HERE> IS
PROHIBITED.

Figure 8.2-1: Flanged Coupling

8.3) ASSEMBLY DRAWING

1) **Open** your **FLANGED COUPLING.SLDASM** file. Start a **New Drawing** [Drawing] on size **A (ANSI) Landscape** paper. (If you only see ISO paper sizes, deselect *Only show standard formats.*) Double click on ***FLANGED COUPLING*** in the *Model View* window. Make sure the *Show in exploded or model break state* check box is deselected. Use a **1:2** scale for the front view and **1:4** scale for the pictorial. Set your drawing standard to **ANSI** and add the **Center Mark**. Your drawing should look like the drawing below.

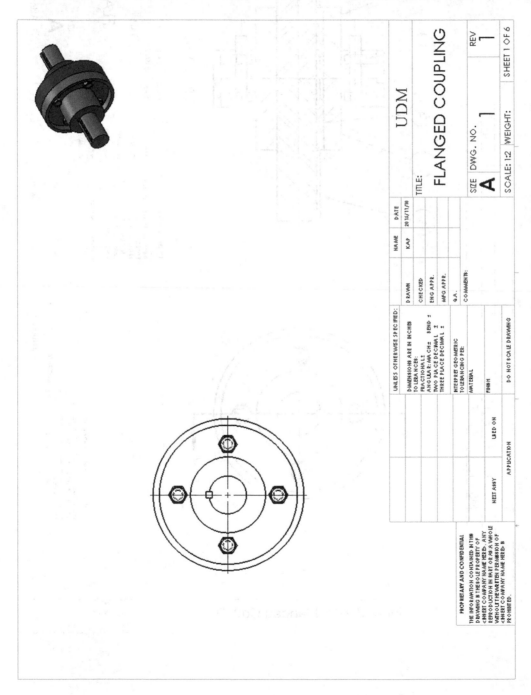

2) **Save** your drawing as **FLANGED COUPLING**.

3) Create a **Section View** 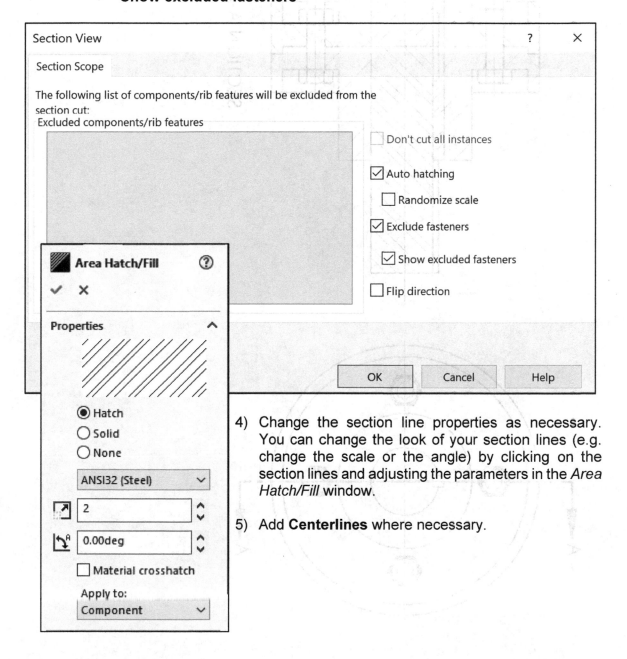 that looks like the section view shown on the next page. Note that the section lines, in the section view, run in different directions and have different scales. This is to show physically different parts. When you create the section view, activate the following options.
- **Auto hatching**
- **Exclude fasteners** (We don't want to section the fasteners.)
- **Show excluded fasteners**

4) Change the section line properties as necessary. You can change the look of your section lines (e.g. change the scale or the angle) by clicking on the section lines and adjusting the parameters in the *Area Hatch/Fill* window.

5) Add **Centerlines** where necessary.

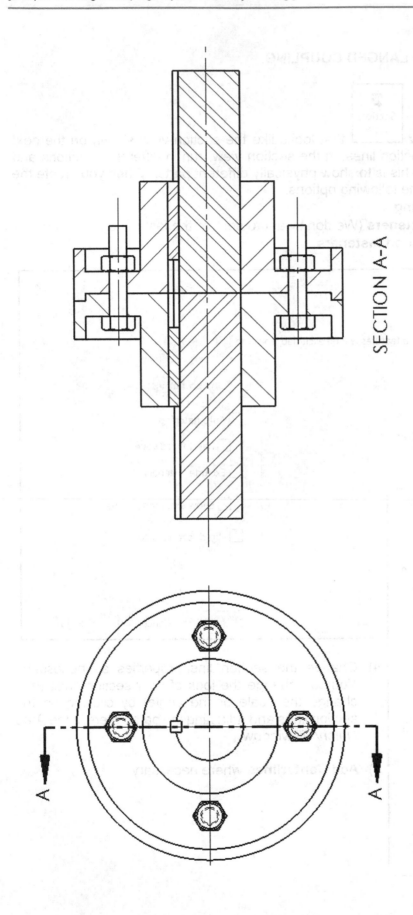

SECTION A-A

6) Add a **Bill of Materials** that contains the parts shown. (See the informational block on *Bill of Materials*.)

ITEM NO.	PART NUMBER	DESCRIPTION	QTY.
1	LEFT COUPLING		1
2	RIGHT COUPLING		1
3	SHAFT		2
4	KEY		2
5	B18.6.7M - M8 x 1.25 x 35 Indented HHMS --35N		4
6	B18.2.4.1M - Hex nut, Style 1, M8 x 1.25 --D-N		4

Bill of Materials [Bill of Materials] (Located in the *Annotation* tab)

1) Expand the **Table** icon in the *Annotation* tab and select **Bill of Materials**.
2) Select a view that has all the parts in it.
3) Set your bill of material properties in the *Bill of Materials* window and then select **OK**.
4) Place your table. Usually in the upper left corner.
5) The text may be edited by double clicking on it. Also, if a window shows up that asks you about the link between the text and part, select **Keep Link**.

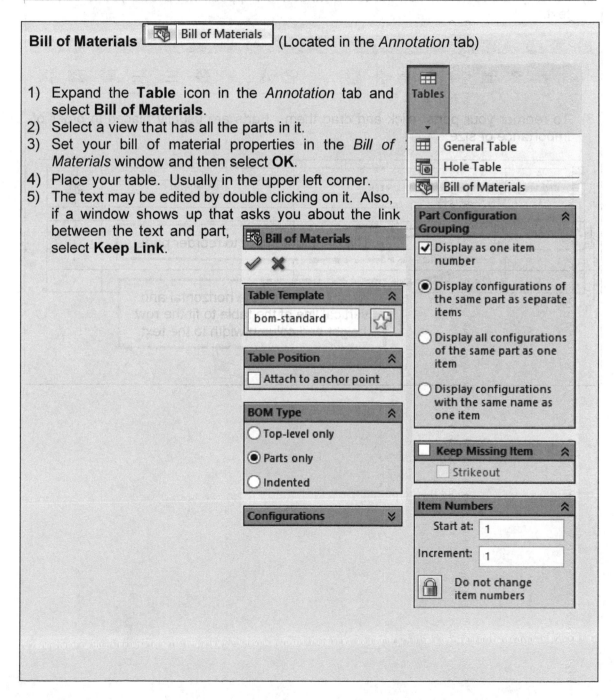

Bill of Materials cont. 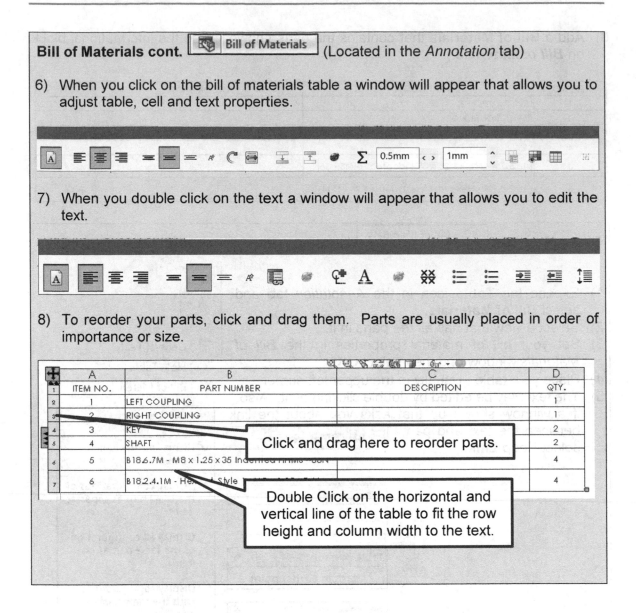 Bill of Materials (Located in the *Annotation* tab)

6) When you click on the bill of materials table a window will appear that allows you to adjust table, cell and text properties.

7) When you double click on the text a window will appear that allows you to edit the text.

8) To reorder your parts, click and drag them. Parts are usually placed in order of importance or size.

Click and drag here to reorder parts.

Double Click on the horizontal and vertical line of the table to fit the row height and column width to the text.

7) Use the **Balloon** 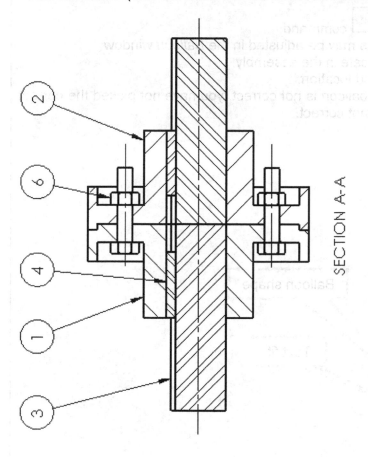 <!-- Balloon button icon --> command, located in the *Annotation* tab, to add the part identification. (See the informational block on ***Ballooning***.)

SECTION A-A

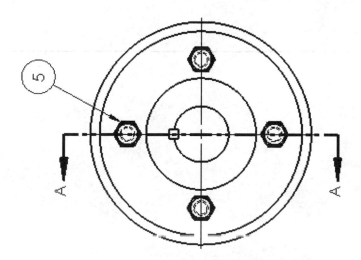

Ballooning 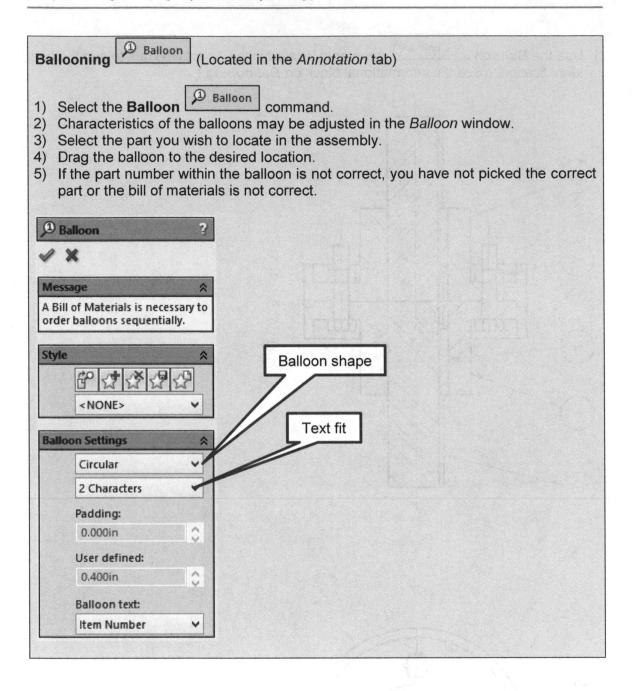 Balloon (Located in the *Annotation* tab)

1) Select the **Balloon** ⊕ Balloon command.
2) Characteristics of the balloons may be adjusted in the *Balloon* window.
3) Select the part you wish to locate in the assembly.
4) Drag the balloon to the desired location.
5) If the part number within the balloon is not correct, you have not picked the correct part or the bill of materials is not correct.

FLANGED COUPLING (ASSEMBLY DRAWING) PROBLEMS

P8-1) Use SOLIDWORKS® to reproduce the assembly drawing of the *Drill Jig* shown. The part dimensions are given in Chapter 7.

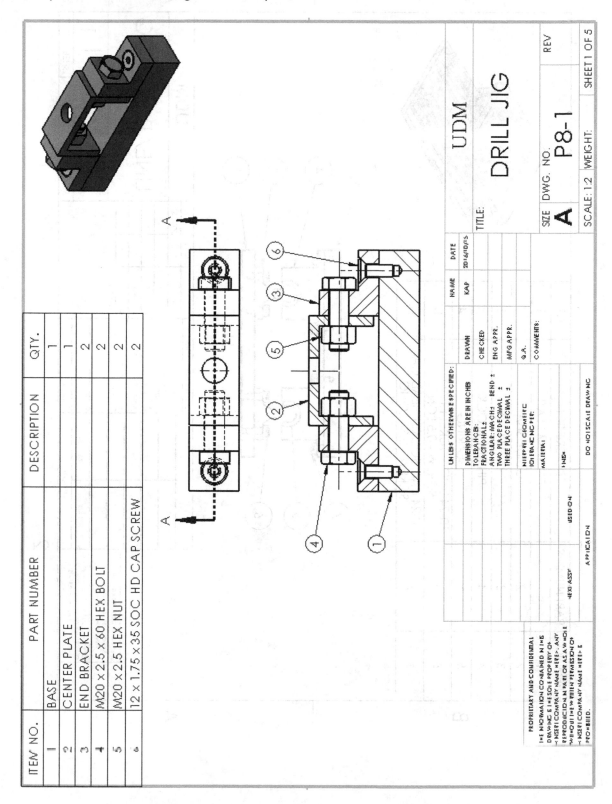

P8-2) Use SOLIDWORKS® to reproduce the assembly drawing of the *Linear Bearing* shown. The part dimensions are given in the Chapter 7.

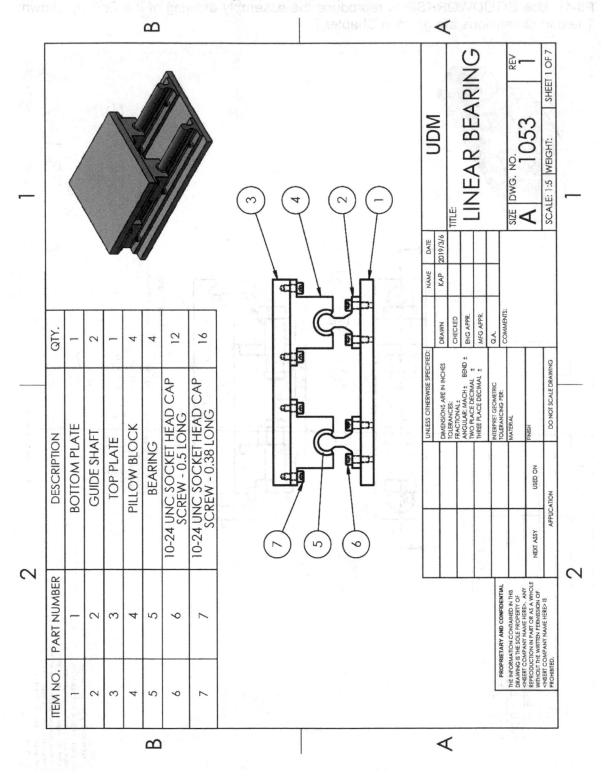

ITEM NO.	PART NUMBER	DESCRIPTION	QTY.
1	1	BOTTOM PLATE	1
2	2	GUIDE SHAFT	2
3	3	TOP PLATE	1
4	4	PILLOW BLOCK	4
5	5	BEARING	4
6	6	10-24 UNC SOCKET HEAD CAP SCREW - 0.5 LONG	12
7	7	10-24 UNC SOCKET HEAD CAP SCREW - 0.38 LONG	16

UDM

TITLE:

LINEAR BEARING

		NAME	DATE
DRAWN		KAP	2019/3/6
CHECKED			
ENG APPR.			
MFG APPR.			
Q.A.			
COMMENTS:			

UNLESS OTHERWISE SPECIFIED:

DIMENSIONS ARE IN INCHES
TOLERANCES:
FRACTIONAL±
ANGULAR: MACH± BEND ±
TWO PLACE DECIMAL ±
THREE PLACE DECIMAL ±

INTERPRET GEOMETRIC
TOLERANCING PER:

MATERIAL

FINISH

DO NOT SCALE DRAWING

SIZE	DWG. NO.	REV
A	1053	1

SCALE: 1:5 WEIGHT: SHEET 1 OF 7

NEXT ASSY | USED ON

APPLICATION

FLANGED COUPLING (ASSEMBLY DRAWING) QUIZ PROBLEM

Q8-1) Create a technically correct assembly drawing of *Cork Screw* shown.

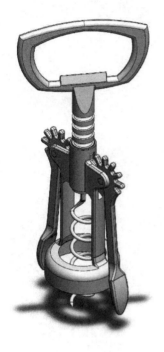

1. **Download** the following files.
   - Cork Screw Assembly.SLDASM
   - Cork Screw.SLDPRT
   - Body.SLDPRT
   - Arm.SLDPRT
   - Pin.SLDPRT
2. Open the **Cork Screw Assembly.SLDASM** file.
3. Create an **assembly drawing** of the *Cork Screw* that contains the following items.
   - At least one view of the *Cork Screw* plus a pictorial.
   - A Bill of Materials.
   - Ballooning that identifies and locates all of the parts in the assembly.

CHAPTER 9

LINEAR BEARING PROJECT
Assembly

CHAPTER OUTLINE

9.1) PREREQUISITES

Before starting this tutorial you should complete the following tutorial.

- Flanged coupling project – Assembly

9.2) WHAT YOU WILL LEARN

The objective of this tutorial is to introduce you to *Advanced Mates*. You will assemble the parts that comprise the *Linear Bearing* assembly shown in Figure 9.2-1. Specifically, you will be learning the following commands and concepts.

Assembly

- Advanced mates
- Distance mate
- Width mate

Evaluate

- Interference Detection
- Sensors
- Assembly Visualization

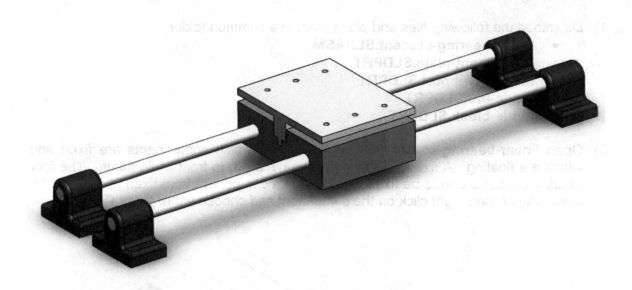

Figure 9.2-1: Linear bearing assembly

9.3) STANDARD MATES

1) Download the following files and place them in a common folder.
   - **linear-bearing-student.SLDASM**
   - **attachment-plate.SLDPRT**
   - **bearing-support.SLDPRT**
   - **guide-bar.SLDPRT**
   - **guide-block.SLDPRT**

2) Open **linear-bearing-student.SLDASM**. Notice which components are fixed and which are floating. A fixed component will have an **(f)** in front of its name. The four bearing supports should be fixed. To change a component from fixed to float, or the other way around, right click on the component and choose either **fix** or **float**.

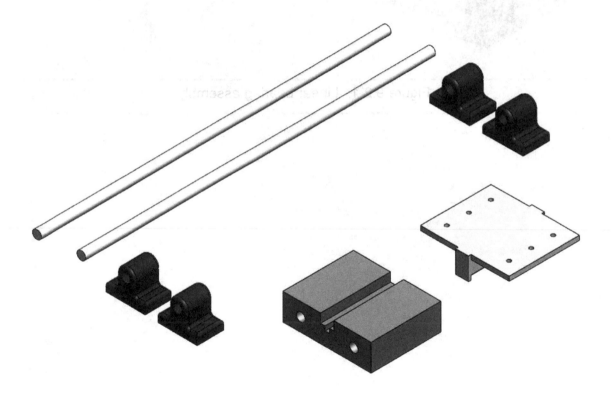

    (-) guide-block<1> (Defaı

    (-) guide-bar<1> (Default

    (-) guide-bar<2> (Default

    (f) bearing-support<1> ([

    (f) bearing-support<2> ([

    (f) bearing-support<3> ([

    (f) bearing-support<4> ([

    (-) attachment-plate<1> ı

3) Apply the following **Standard mates**.
- **Concentric** between the **Guide Bars** and the appropriate **Bearing Support**.
- Make one end of each **Guide Bar Coincident** with the face of the **Bearing Support**.
- **Concentric** between the **Guide Bars** and the **Guide Block**.

Once completed, your linear bearing assembly should look like the figure.

⊚ Concentric1 (guide-bar<2>,bearing-support<4>)
⊚ Concentric2 (guide-bar<1>,bearing-support<3>)
⅄ Coincident17 (guide-bar<1>,bearing-support<2>)
⅄ Coincident18 (guide-bar<2>,bearing-support<1>)
⊚ Concentric3 (guide-block<1>,guide-bar<1>)
⊚ Concentric4 (guide-block<1>,guide-bar<2>)

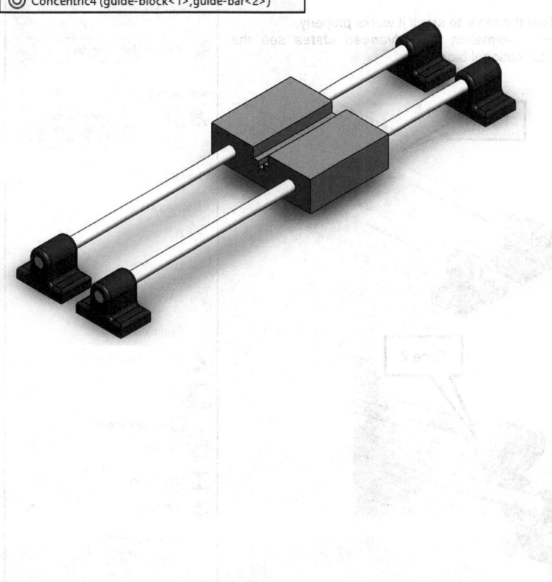

9.4) ADVANCED MATES

1) Move the *Guide Block* to the left and notice that it will pass through the *Bearing Supports*. This is not realistic. Move the *Guide Block* back to the center.

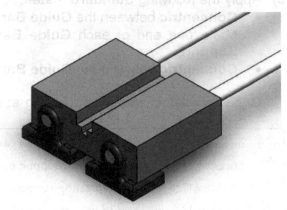

2) Apply a **Limit Distance** mate (under *Advanced Mates*) between the face of the **Guide Block** (Face 1) and the face of the **Bearing Support** (Face 2). Use the following settings.
   - Default distance = **200 mm**
   - Minimum distance = **0**
   - Maximum distance = **260 mm**.

   Test the mate to see if it works properly.
   For information on **Advanced Mates** see the informational block.

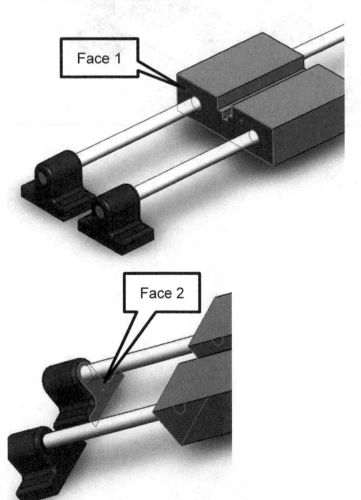

Advanced Mates

Along with the *Standard Mates*, there is a set of *Advanced Mates*. The available *Advanced Mates* are

- **Profile Center:** This mate aligns two geometric profiles with their centers.
- **Symmetric:** This mate forces two similar entities to be symmetric about a plane or face of an assembly.
- **Width:** This mate centers a tab with the width of a groove.
- **Path Mate:** This mate constrains a selected point on a component to a path. You can define pitch, yaw, and roll of the component as it travels along the path.
- **Linear/Linear Coupler:** This mate establishes a relationship between the translation of one component and the translation of another component.
- **Distance Limit:** This mate allows a component to move within a range of distance values. You may specify a starting distance as well as a maximum and minimum value.
- **Angle Limit:** This mate allows a component to move within a range of angle values. You may specify a starting angle as well as a maximum and minimum value.

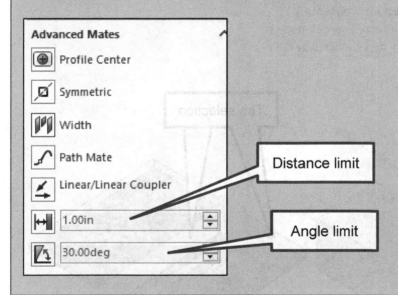

3) Apply the following mates. (See the informational block on **A d vanced Mates**.)

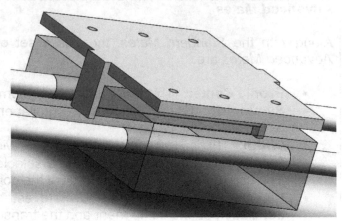

- **Width** mate between the groove of the **Guide Block** and the tab of the **Attachment Plate** (see figure),
- **Coincident** mate between the bottom surface of the **Guide Block** groove and bottom surface of the **Attachment Plate** tab.
- **Coincident** mate between the ends of the **Guide Block** and inner surface of the **Attachment Plate** groove (see figure).

If you get confused about what surfaces to use in the mates, just think about how the bearing should function in real life.

> Width1 (Guide block<1> ,Attachment plate<1>)
> Coincident21 (Guide block<1>,Attachment plate<1>)
> Coincident22 (Guide block<1>,Attachment plate<1>)

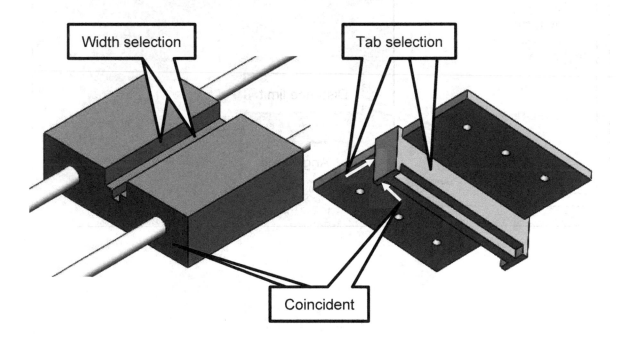

Width selection

Tab selection

Coincident

9.5) INTERFERENCE

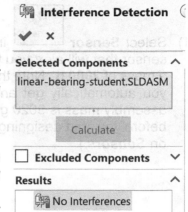

1) Select **Interference Detection** in the *Evaluate* tab. Select **linear-bearing assembly** in your *Feature Design Tree*. Click on **Calculate** to detect any interferences in the assembly. No interferences should be detected.

2) Create an interference by changing the diameter of the *Guide bar* to **10.1 mm**. Note that the holes in the *Bearing Supports* and *Guide Block* are 10 mm. **Rebuild** your assembly. Run the **Interference Detection** again. Several interferences should be detected. When you click on each interference, it should be highlighted in red. (Hint: To edit the *Guide bar*, right-click on it in the *Feature Design Tree* and select **Edit Part**. When you are done, right-click and select **Edit Assembly**.)

3) Change the diameter of the *Guide bar* back to **9.8 mm**.

9.6) SENSORS AND VISUALIZATION

1) Select **Sensor** in the *Evaluate* tab. Create a sensor that will alert you when your assembly exceeds a mass of **2000 g**. Note that when you apply the sensor, you automatically get an alert. This is because your assembly mass is 3020 g. Sensors are usually applied before you start designing. (See the informational block on *Sensors*.)

2) Select **Assembly Visualization** in the *Evaluate* tab. Click the arrow that points to the right and select **Mass**. This is the property that we want to visualize. Notice that the *Guide Block* is the heaviest and that the assembly is now color coded. If your assembly is not colored, click on the key that indicates color. Colors in the legend may be added or taken away and the sliders may be moved. Play around with the colors. (See the informational block on *Assembly Visualization*.)

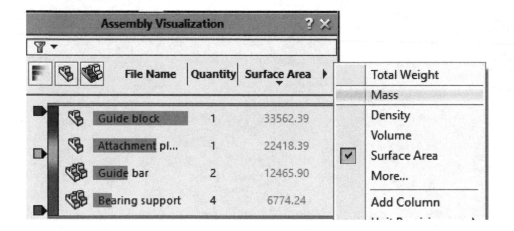

3) Click on the **Group/Ungroup View** 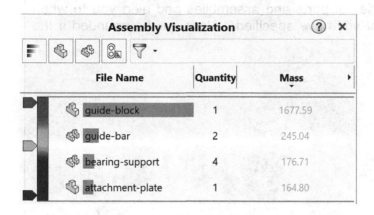 icon. This will show every individual part and not group like parts.

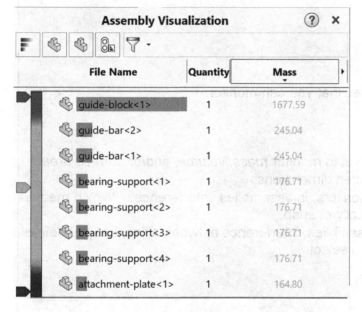

Sensor 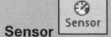 (Located in the *Evaluate* tab)

Sensors monitor selected properties of parts and assemblies and alert you to when values deviate from the limits that you have specified. Alerts will be sounded if the monitored value is

- Greater than
- Less than
- Exactly
- Not greater than
- Not less than
- Not exactly
- Between
- Not between

In some cases,

- True or False

The following is a list of all the values that you can monitor.

Properties

- **Mass properties:** May be set to monitor *mass*, *volume*, and/or *surface area*.
- **Dimension:** Monitors selected dimensions.
- **Interference detection:** Monitors, in assemblies, interferences. Which means that two components physically overlap.
- **Proximity:** Monitors, in assemblies, interference between a line that you define and a component(s) that you select.

Motion Data

Monitors a result(s) that is being calculated by the motion study.

Simulation Data

Defines locations for measuring result quantities in simulations.

Assembly Visualization   (Located in the *Evaluate* tab)

Assembly Visualization provides different ways to display and sort assembly components. It sorts the components in a list and also graphically by coloring the components in the assembly. You can sort using the following properties. However, there are many other properties that may be used to sort that are not listed.

- Mass
- Density
- Volume
- Surface area
- Face count
- Fully mated
- Quantity

Example of Assembly Visualization

The following *Trolley* assembly is sorted for mass. The colors of the assembly correspond to the color key shown on the left.

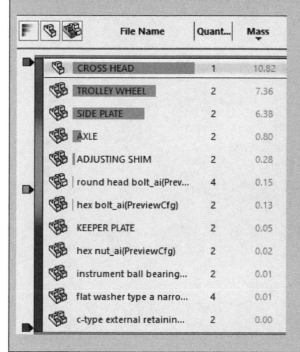

File Name	Quant...	Mass
CROSS HEAD	1	10.82
TROLLEY WHEEL	2	7.36
SIDE PLATE	2	6.38
AXLE	2	0.80
ADJUSTING SHIM	2	0.28
round head bolt_ai(Prev...	4	0.15
hex bolt_ai(PreviewCfg)	2	0.13
KEEPER PLATE	2	0.05
hex nut_ai(PreviewCfg)	2	0.02
instrument ball bearing...	2	0.01
flat washer type a narro...	4	0.01
c-type external retainin...	2	0.00

NOTES:

LINEAR BEARING (ASSEMBLY) QUIZ PROBLEMS

Q9-1) Create a realistic assembly of the following *Hinge*.

1. Download the following files.
   - **Hinge Plate.SLDPRT**
   - **Pin.SLDPRT**
2. Open a **new assembly** file and insert the above parts.
3. Make a **copy** of the **Hinge**.
4. Represent each **configuration** of the **Hinge Plate** (i.e. Three Guides, Two Guides).
5. Assemble the hinge in a realistic way (e.g. the two hinge plates should not pass through each other).

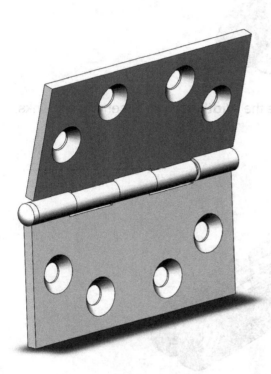

Q9-2) Create a realistic assembly of the following *Chain*.

1) Download the following files:
   - **Link.SLDPRT**
   - **Connecting Link.SLDPRT**
   - **Outer Pin.SLDPRT**
   - **Inner Pin.SLDPRT**
2) Open a **new assembly** file and insert the above parts.

3) Construct the following assembly. Use the **Width** mate to assemble the Links. **Fix** the first component in the chain.

CHAPTER 10

MICROPHONE PROJECT
Base

CHAPTER OUTLINE

10.1) PREREQUISITES

Before starting this tutorial you should complete the following tutorials.

- Connecting Rod Project – Part modeling

10.2) WHAT YOU WILL LEARN

The objective of this tutorial is to introduce you to creating more complex solid geometries. You will be modeling the *Base* of the *Microphone* assembly shown in Figure 10.2-1. Specifically, you will be learning the following commands and concepts.

<u>Sketch</u>

- Arc
- Convert Entities
- Mirror entities
- Construction Geometry

<u>Feature</u>

- Loft
- Mirror
- Shell
- Rib
- Reference Geometry (e.g. Plane, Axis, Coordinates)

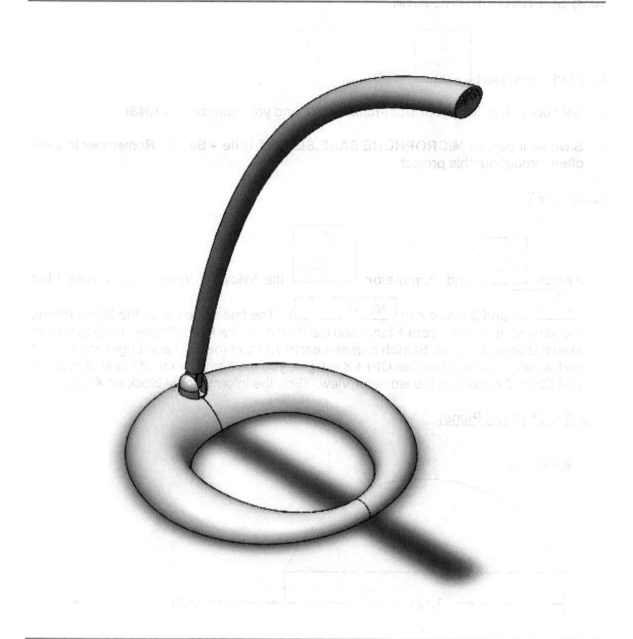

Figure 10.2-1: Microphone Assembly

10.3) SETTING UP THE ARM

1) Start a **new part** .

2) Set your unit to **IPS,** your **Decimals = .123,** and your standard to **ANSI**.

3) Save your part as **MICROPHONE BASE.SLDPRT** (**File – Save**). Remember to save often throughout this project.

10.4) LOFT

1) **Sketch** and **Dimension** the following three profiles (use **Line** and **3 Point Arc**). The first sketch is on the **Right Plane**, the second is on the **Front Plane**, and the third is on the **Right Plane**. Note that each sketch is separate (**Exit Sketch** between each) and that the line and origin are aligned horizontally. Remember that **Ctrl + 8** will give you the normal view of the sketch plane and **Ctrl + 7** gives you the isometric view. (See the informational block on **Arcs**.)

First Sketch (Right Plane)

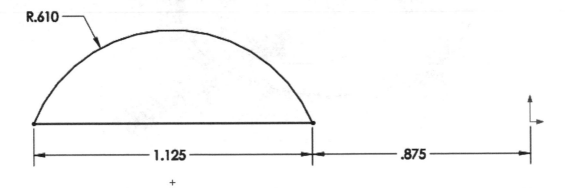

Second Sketch (Front Plane)

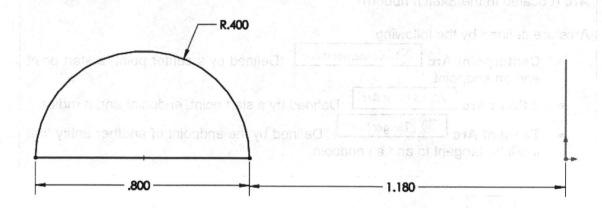

R.400

.800   1.180

Third Sketch (Right Plane)

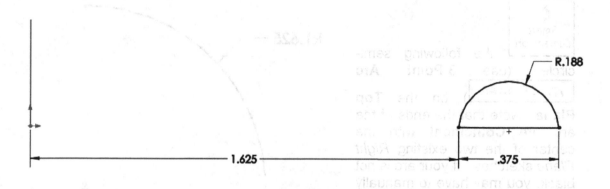

R.188

1.625   .375

Final result (Hit Ctrl+7 to view the isometric)

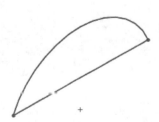

Arc (Located in the *Sketch* ribbon)

Arcs are defined by the following.

- **Centerpoint Arc** [Centerpoint Arc]: Defined by a center point, a start point and an endpoint.
- **3 Point Arc** [3 Point Arc]: Defined by a start point, endpoint and a radius.
- **Tangent Arc** [Tangent Arc]: Defined by the endpoint of another entity that it will be tangent to and an endpoint.

2) **Sketch** [Sketch] and **Dimension** [Smart Dimension] the following semi-circle (use **3 Point Arc** [3 Point Arc]) on the **Top Plane**. Note that the ends of the arc are **Coincident** with the center of the two existing *Right Plane* sketches. If your arc is not black, you may have to manually add the *Sketch Relations*.

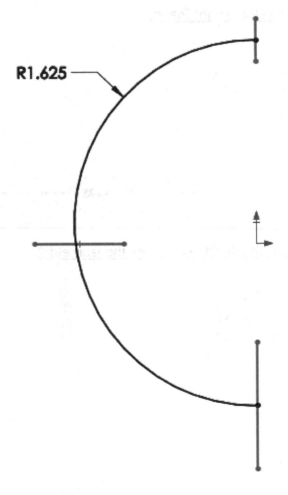

R1.625

3) **Loft** 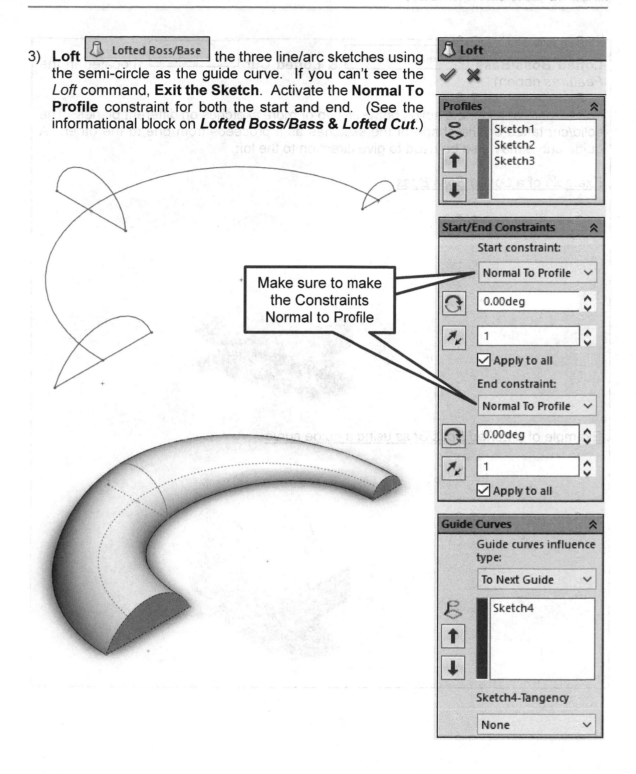 the three line/arc sketches using the semi-circle as the guide curve. If you can't see the *Loft* command, **Exit the Sketch**. Activate the **Normal To Profile** constraint for both the start and end. (See the informational block on *Lofted Boss/Bass & Lofted Cut*.)

Make sure to make the Constraints Normal to Profile

Loft

Profiles

Sketch1
Sketch2
Sketch3

Start/End Constraints

Start constraint:

Normal To Profile

0.00deg

1

☑ Apply to all

End constraint:

Normal To Profile

0.00deg

1

☑ Apply to all

Guide Curves

Guide curves influence type:

To Next Guide

Sketch4

Sketch4-Tangency

None

Lofted Boss/Bass 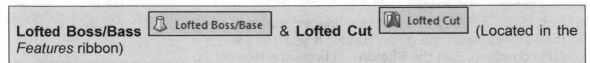 & **Lofted Cut** (Located in the *Features* ribbon)

Lofts create or eliminate solids between two or more sketches on different planes. The solid/cut takes on the shape of the sketches as it proceeds from one to the other. A guide curve may also be used to give direction to the loft.

Example of a *Lofted Boss/Bass*

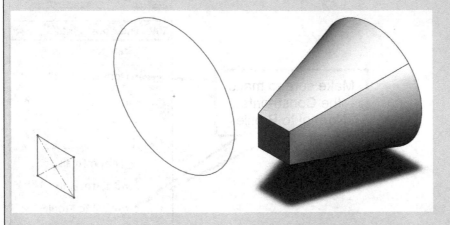

Example of a *Lofted Boss/Bass* using a guide curve

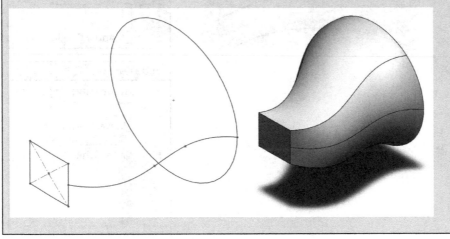

Lofted Boss/Bass 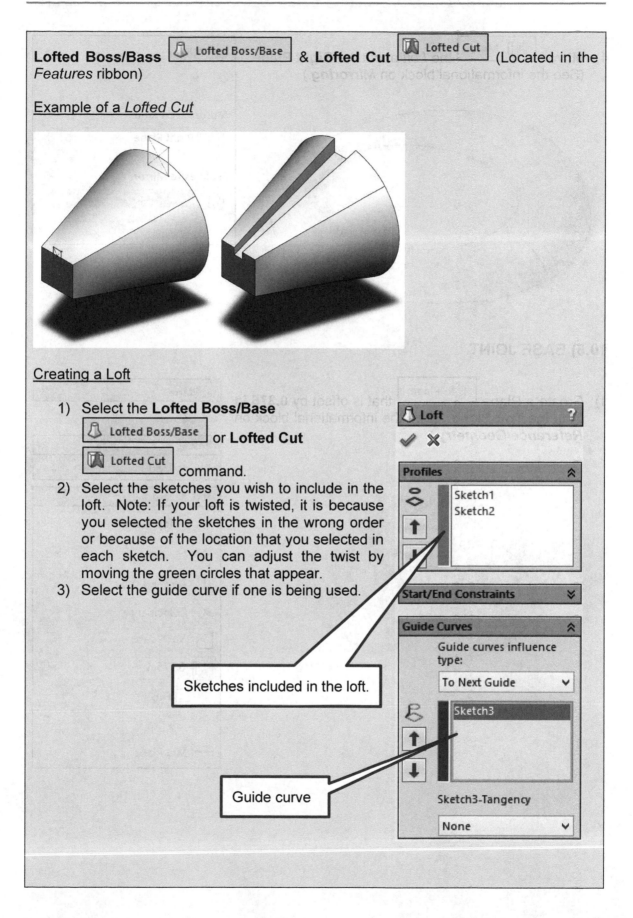 Lofted Boss/Base & **Lofted Cut** Lofted Cut (Located in the *Features* ribbon)

Example of a *Lofted Cut*

Creating a Loft

1) Select the **Lofted Boss/Base** Lofted Boss/Base or **Lofted Cut** Lofted Cut command.

2) Select the sketches you wish to include in the loft. Note: If your loft is twisted, it is because you selected the sketches in the wrong order or because of the location that you selected in each sketch. You can adjust the twist by moving the green circles that appear.

3) Select the guide curve if one is being used.

Sketches included in the loft.

Guide curve

Loft

Profiles
Sketch1
Sketch2

Start/End Constraints

Guide Curves
Guide curves influence type:
To Next Guide
Sketch3
Sketch3-Tangency
None

4) **Mirror**  the *Loft* about the **Right Plane**.
(See the informational block on ***Mirroring***.)

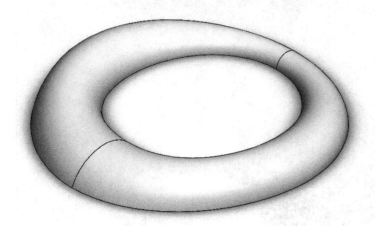

10.5) BASE JOINT

1) Create a **Plane** 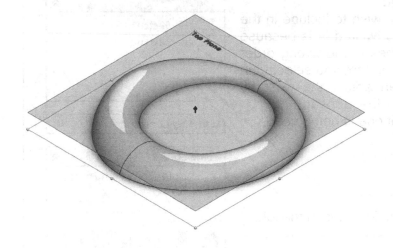 that is offset by **0.375 in** from the **Top Plane**. (See the informational block on ***Reference Geometry***.)

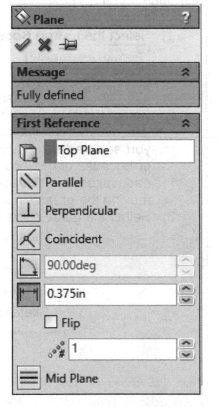

Mirror [⊩⊣ Mirror] (Located in the *Features* ribbon)

The *Mirror* command allows you to duplicate a solid with its mirror image about a selected plane or face.

Example of a mirrored object

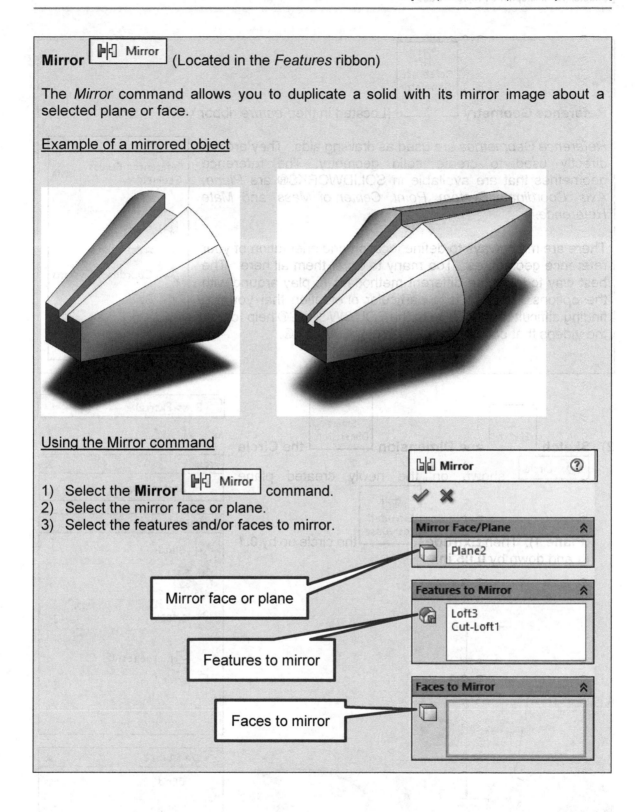

Using the Mirror command

1) Select the **Mirror** [⊩⊣ Mirror] command.
2) Select the mirror face or plane.
3) Select the features and/or faces to mirror.

Mirror face or plane

Features to mirror

Faces to mirror

Mirror ⑦

Mirror Face/Plane
Plane2

Features to Mirror
Loft3
Cut-Loft1

Faces to Mirror

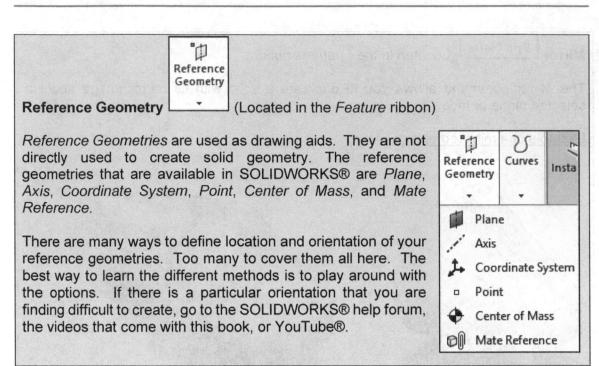

Reference Geometry (Located in the *Feature* ribbon)

Reference Geometries are used as drawing aids. They are not directly used to create solid geometry. The reference geometries that are available in SOLIDWORKS® are *Plane*, *Axis*, *Coordinate System*, *Point*, *Center of Mass*, and *Mate Reference*.

There are many ways to define location and orientation of your reference geometries. Too many to cover them all here. The best way to learn the different methods is to play around with the options. If there is a particular orientation that you are finding difficult to create, go to the SOLIDWORKS® help forum, the videos that come with this book, or YouTube®.

2) **Sketch** and **Dimension** the **Circle** shown on the newly created plane (**Plane 1**). Then **Extrude** the circle up by **0.1 in** and down by **0.05 in**.

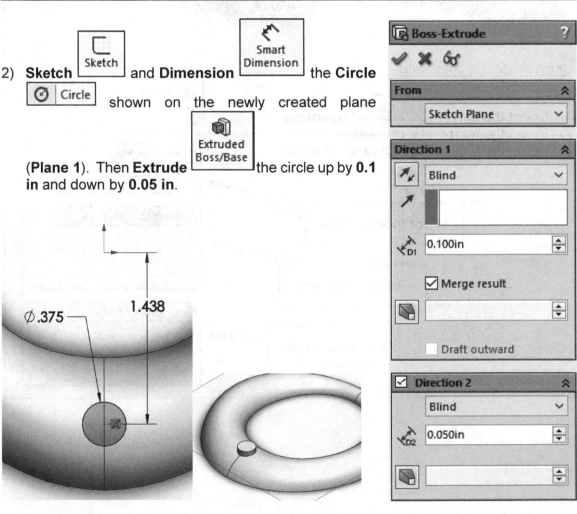

3) Add a **Dome** 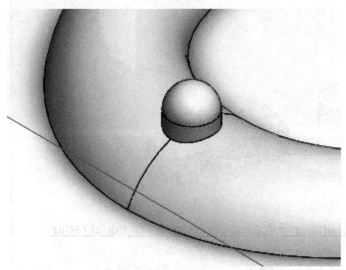 (**Insert – Feature – Dome**) to the top of the *Extrude* with a radius of **0.1875 in**. (See the informational block on **Domes**.)

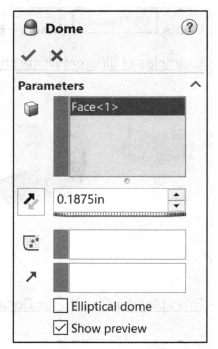

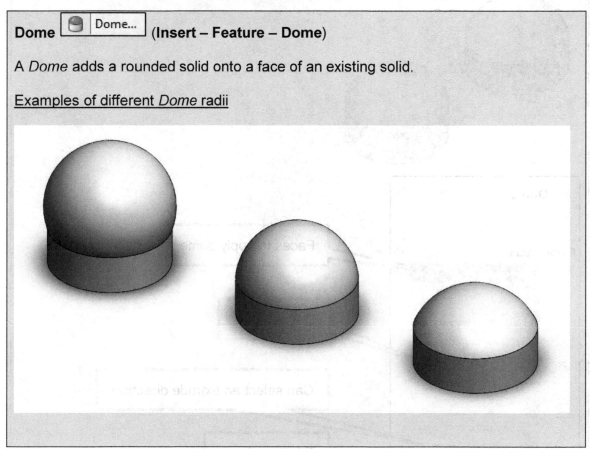

Dome 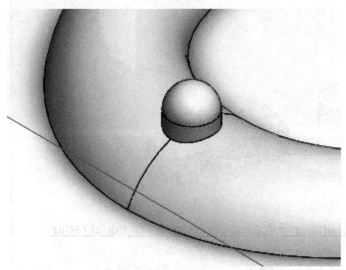 (**Insert – Feature – Dome**)

A *Dome* adds a rounded solid onto a face of an existing solid.

Examples of different *Dome* radii

Dome 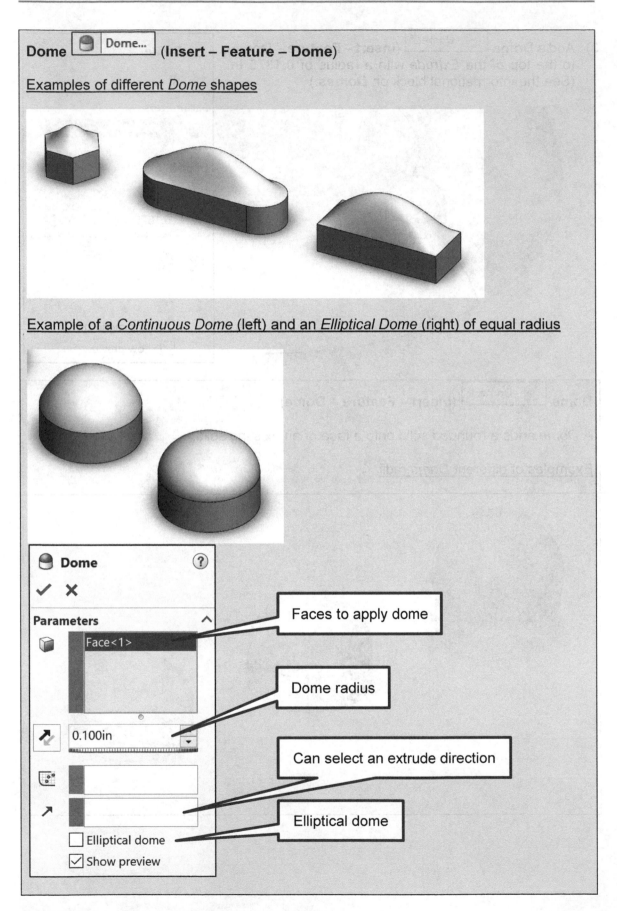 Dome... **(Insert – Feature – Dome)**

Examples of different *Dome* shapes

Example of a *Continuous Dome* (left) and an *Elliptical Dome* (right) of equal radius

Dome

Parameters

Face<1>

0.100in

□ Elliptical dome

☑ Show preview

Faces to apply dome

Dome radius

Can select an extrude direction

Elliptical dome

4) **Sketch** [Sketch] and **Dimension** [Smart Dimension] the following **Rectangle** [Corner Rectangle] on the newly created plane (**Plane 1**). Then, **Extrude Cut** [Extruded Cut] the sketch **Through All** reversing the direction if necessary.

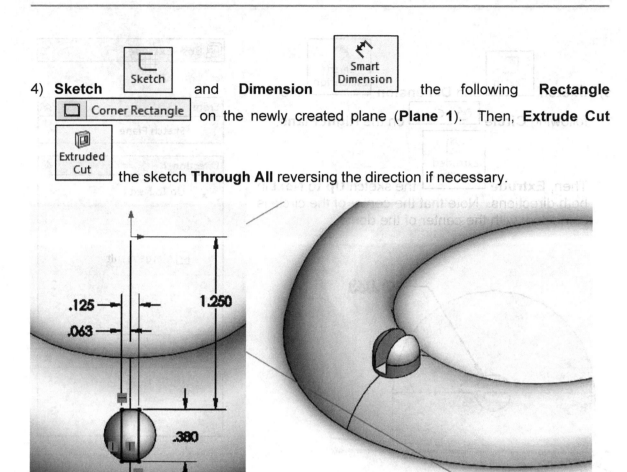

5) **Sketch** 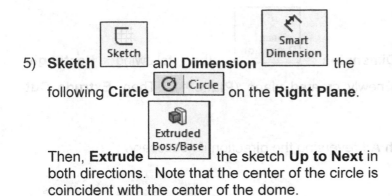 and **Dimension** the following **Circle** on the **Right Plane**.

Then, **Extrude** the sketch **Up to Next** in both directions. Note that the center of the circle is coincident with the center of the dome.

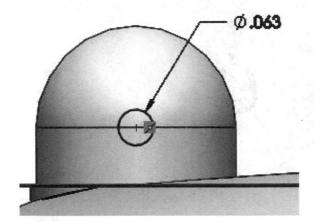

Ø.063

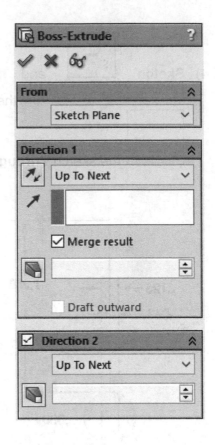

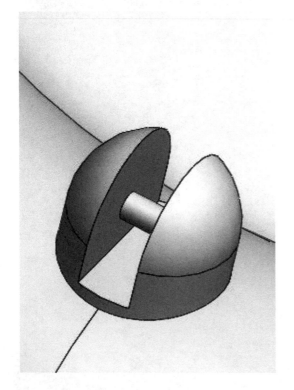

10.6) SHELL

1) We would like to *Shell* the base, but not the base joint. In order to accomplish this, we will **Roll Back** the *Feature Manager Design Tree* to a place before we started to model the joint. Notice the line at the bottom of the *Design Tree*. Hover your mouse over this line. When a hand appears, click and drag the line until it is under **Mirror1**.

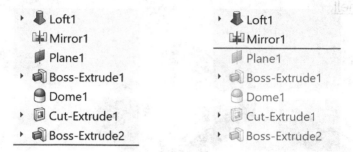

2) **Shell** 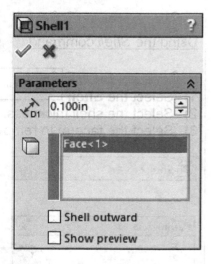 the base to a thickness of **0.1 in** removing the bottom surface. (See the informational block on **Shells**.)

3) **Roll Forward** the *Design Tree* until after the last step.

4) We will not be needing **Plane1** anymore so **Hide** it.

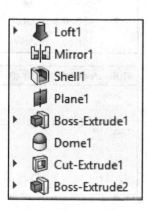

Shell 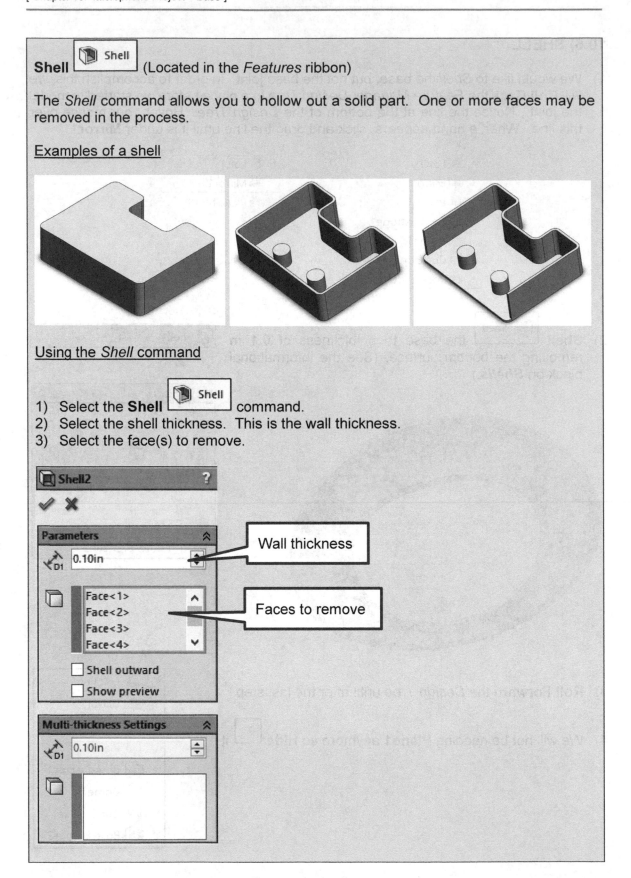 (Located in the *Features* ribbon)

The *Shell* command allows you to hollow out a solid part. One or more faces may be removed in the process.

Examples of a shell

Using the *Shell* command

1) Select the **Shell** command.
2) Select the shell thickness. This is the wall thickness.
3) Select the face(s) to remove.

10.7) RIBS

1) **Sketch** 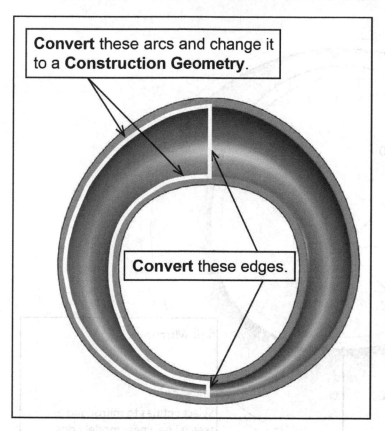 **Sketch** on the **Top Plane**. View the part from the bottom. **Convert Entities** **Convert Entities** the edge shown in the figure and change the element into a **Construction Geometry** if indicated in the figure. (See the information block on *Converting Entities* and *Construction Geometry*.)

Convert these arcs and change it to a **Construction Geometry**.

Convert these edges.

2) Draw and **Dimension** Smart Dimension the three **Centerlines** Centerline and **Arcs** 3 Point Arc shown in the figure. Note that the endpoints of each arc are **Coincident** with the construction geometry arcs. Make sure all the arcs are black, which means that they are completely constrained. **Mirror** Mirror Entities the three arcs using one of the converted lines to mirror about. (See the informational block on *Mirroring*.)

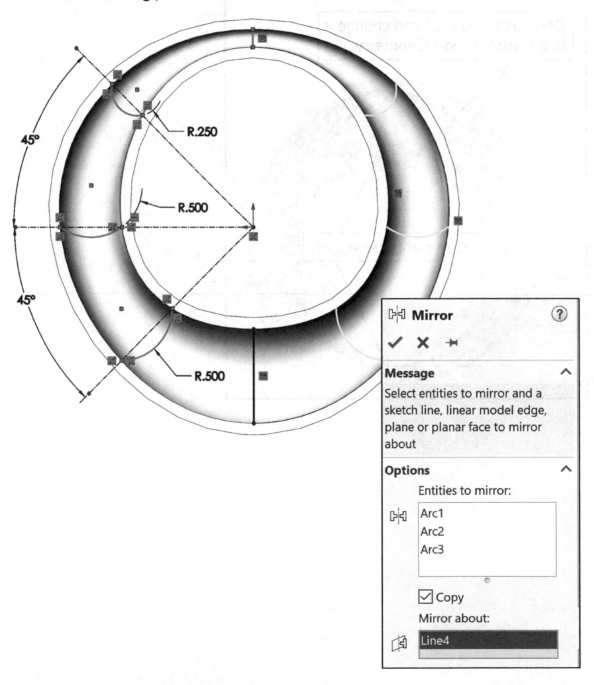

Mirror ⌾

✓ ✕ ✦

Message ⌃

Select entities to mirror and a sketch line, linear model edge, plane or planar face to mirror about

Options ⌃

Entities to mirror:

Arc1
Arc2
Arc3

☑ Copy

Mirror about:

Line4

Converting Entities ⬚ Convert Entities (Located in the *Sketch* ribbon)

The *Convert Entities* command allows you to create one or more curves in a sketch by projecting an edge, face, or curve of an existing solid or sketch.

Examples of the *Convert Entities* command

In the figure the solid part is used to create a sketch on a distant plane.

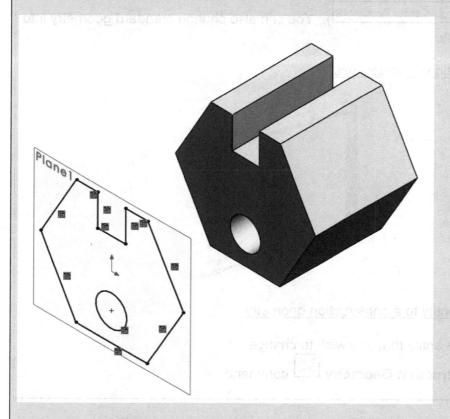

Using the *Convert Entities* command

1) Select the **Convert Entities** ⬚ Convert Entities command.
2) Select the face, edge or curve that you wish to convert.
3) Select OK.

Construction Geometry ⇄

Construction geometry are sketch entities that will not be used to create solid features. They are used as construction aids. Construction geometries are shown as center lines.

Centerlines [┊ | Centerline] are automatically created as construction geometry. Construction geometries are also created when drawing certain sketch entities (i.e. *Center Rectangle* [▫ | Center Rectangle]). You can also change standard geometry into construction geometry.

Example of construction geometry use

Changing a sketch entity to a construction geometry

1) Right click on the entity that you wish to change.

2) Select the **Construction Geometry** ⇄ command.

Mirror Entities 　⊢╫⊣ Mirror Entities 　(Located in the *Sketch* ribbon)

The *Mirror Entities* command mirrors 2D sketches about a chosen line.

Using the *Mirror Entities* command

1) Select the **Mirror Entities** ⊢╫⊣ Mirror Entities command.
2) Select the entities that you want to mirror.
3) Select the mirror line.
4) Choose whether or not you want to copy the entities or replace them.

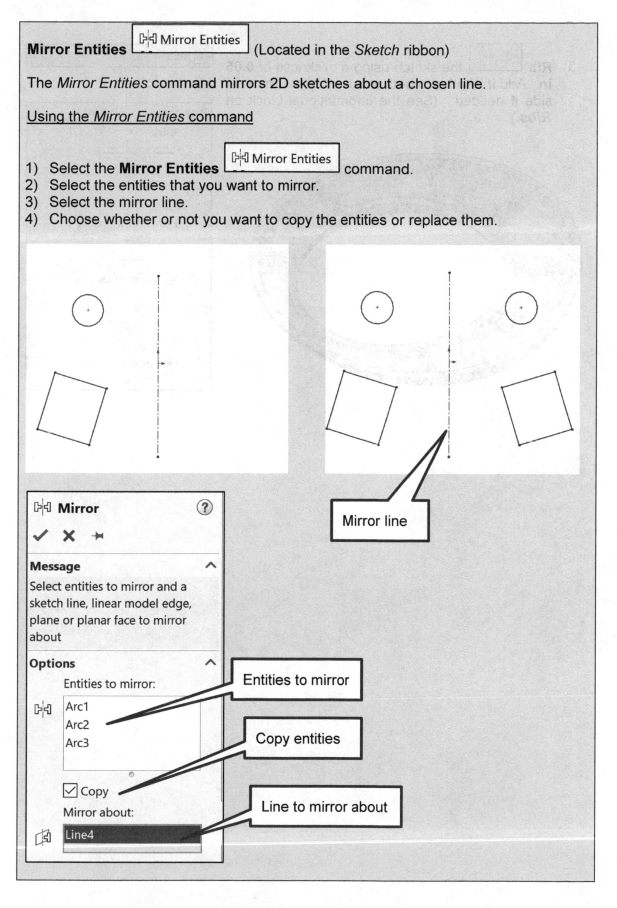

Mirror line

⊢╫⊣ **Mirror** ⟨?⟩

✓ ✗ ✚

Message ⌄

Select entities to mirror and a sketch line, linear model edge, plane or planar face to mirror about

Options ⌄

Entities to mirror:

⊢╫⊣   Arc1
  Arc2
  Arc3

Entities to mirror

☑ Copy

Copy entities

Mirror about:

🪞 Line4

Line to mirror about

3) **Rib** 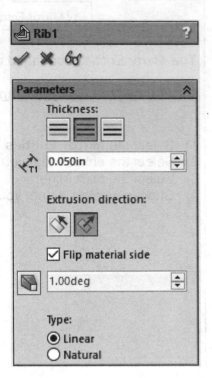 the sketch using a thickness of **0.05 in**. Add thickness to both sides. Flip the material side if needed. (See the informational block on *Ribs*.)

Rib1 ?

Parameters ⌃

Thickness:

0.050in

Extrusion direction:

☑ Flip material side

1.00deg

Type:
  ⦿ Linear
  ○ Natural

Rib 🖱️ Rib (Located in the *Features* ribbon)

A *Rib* is a support structure. It is used to strengthen a part that is otherwise brittle or flimsy. They are usually thin relative to their length. A rib is created using a single sketch entity.

<u>Example of a rib</u>

<u>Creating *Ribs*</u>

1) Select the sketch that will be used to create the rib(s).
2) Select the rib thickness method. The options are to add material on one side only or both sides.
3) Enter the rib thickness.
4) Select the direction of rib travel.
5) You may apply a draft to the rib.

Add thickness method

Rib thickness

Normal or parallel to sketch

Flip material side

Apply draft

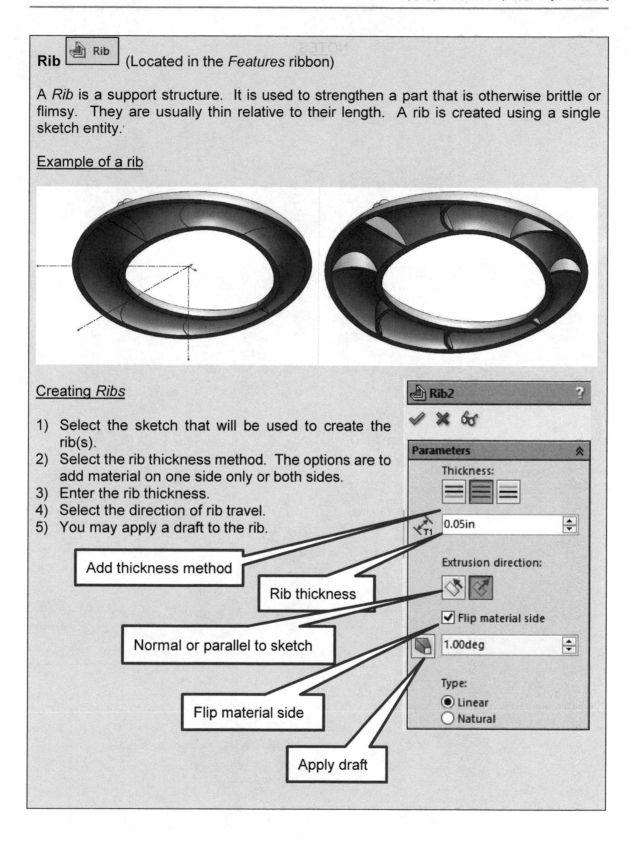

NOTES:

MICROPHONE PROJECT – BASE PROBLEMS

P10-1) Use SOLIDWORKS® to create a solid model of the following Cast Iron object. Use at least one LOFT command.

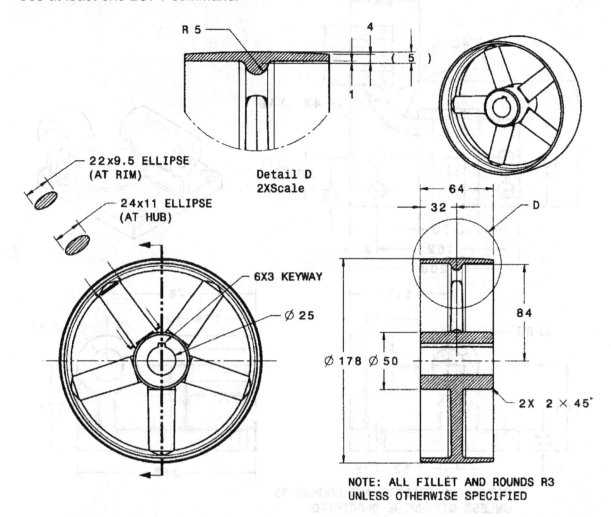

R 5

4

(5)

1

22x9.5 ELLIPSE
(AT RIM)

Detail D
2XScale

24x11 ELLIPSE
(AT HUB)

6X3 KEYWAY

Ø 25

64

32

D

84

Ø 178 Ø 50

2X 2 × 45°

NOTE: ALL FILLET AND ROUNDS R3
UNLESS OTHERWISE SPECIFIED

P10-2) Use SOLIDWORKS® to create a solid model of the following Cast Iron object. Use at least one RIB command.

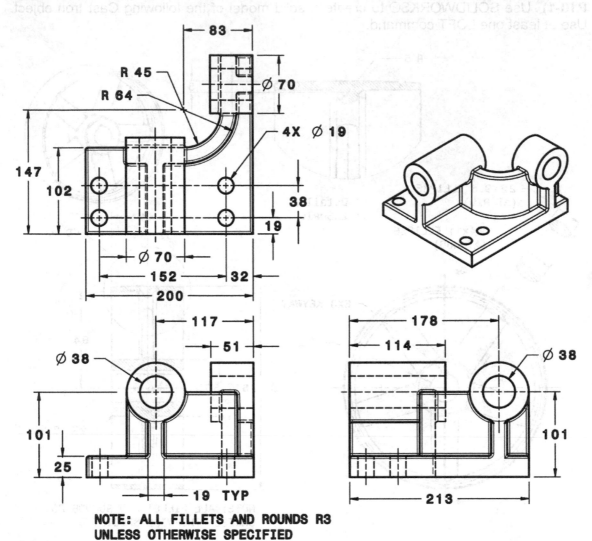

NOTE: ALL FILLETS AND ROUNDS R3
UNLESS OTHERWISE SPECIFIED

P10-3) Model one of the following. Use at least one LOFT command. Apply the appropriate materials.

    a) Tire iron

    b) A wine glass

    c) A screw driver

    d) Bicycle tire wrench

    e) A soft drink bottle

NOTES:

CHAPTER 11

MICROPHONE PROJECT
Arm

CHAPTER OUTLINE

11.1) PREREQUISITES

Before starting this tutorial you should complete the following tutorial.

- Microphone Project – Base
- Flanged Coupling Project - Assembly

11.2) WHAT YOU WILL LEARN

The objective of this tutorial is to introduce you to creating more complex solid geometries. You will be modeling the *Arm* of the *Microphone* assembly shown in Figure 11.2-1 and then assembling the base and arm.

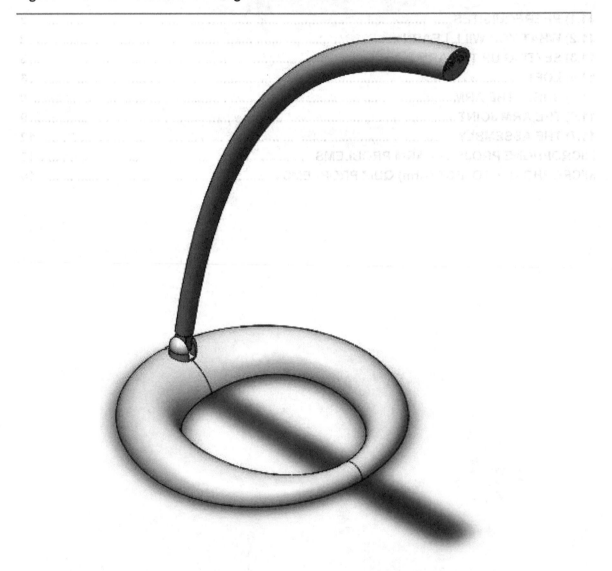

Figure 11.2-1: Microphone Assembly

11.3) SETTING UP THE ARM

1) Start a **new part** .

2) Set your unit to **IPS**, set your **Decimals = .123,** and your standard to **ANSI**.

3) Save your part as **MICROPHONE ARM.SLDPRT** (**File – Save**). Remember to save often throughout this project.

11.4) LOFT

1) **Sketch** and **Dimension** the following **Circle** on **Top Plane**. **Exit Sketch**.

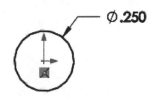

2) Create a **Plane** [Plane] that is **4.5 in** from the **Right Plane**.

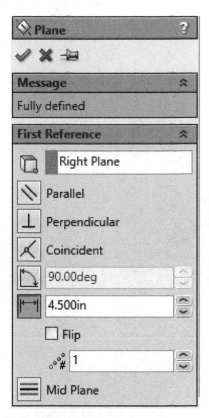

3) **Sketch** and **Dimension** the following **Circle** on **Plane1** (the newly created plane). Make the circle center and origin aligned **Vertically**. **Exit Sketch**.

4) **Sketch** and **Dimension** the following **Centerline**

   [✎ Centerline] on the **Front Plane**. Note that the end of the *Centerline* is aligned **Horizontally** with the origin and **Coincident** with Plane1. **Exit Sketch**.

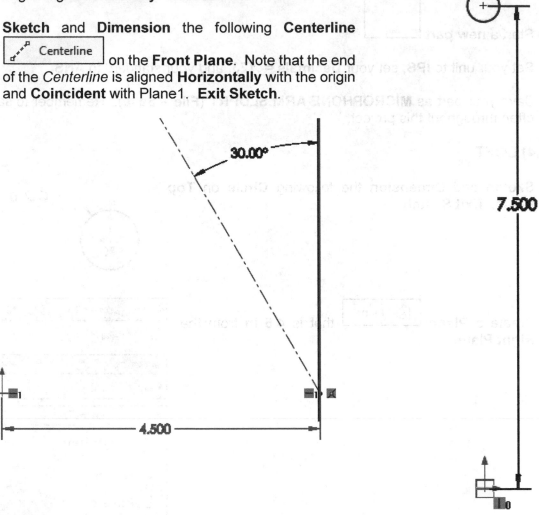

5) Create two **Planes** 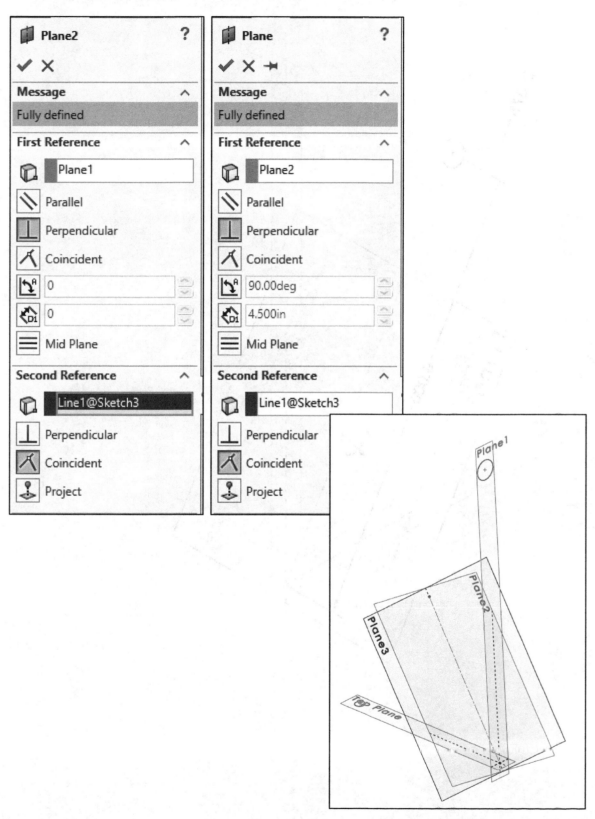 . For the first plane, make it **Perpendicular** to **Plane1** and **Coincident** to the **Centerline**. For the second plane, make it **Perpendicular** to **Plane2** and **Coincident** to the **Centerline**.

Plane2	?
✔ ✕	

Message ∧
Fully defined

First Reference ∧
Plane1
◻ Parallel
⊥ Perpendicular
⊿ Coincident
↱ 0
◈ 0
≡ Mid Plane

Second Reference ∧
Line1@Sketch3
⊥ Perpendicular
⊿ Coincident
⬇ Project

Plane	?
✔ ✕ ➤	

Message ∧
Fully defined

First Reference ∧
Plane2
◻ Parallel
⊥ Perpendicular
⊿ Coincident
↱ 90.00deg
◈ 4.500in
≡ Mid Plane

Second Reference ∧
Line1@Sketch3
⊥ Perpendicular
⊿ Coincident
⬇ Project

6) **Sketch** and **Dimension** the following **Circle** on **Plane3** (the last plane created). **Exit Sketch**. Note that the center of the circle is **Coincident** with the centerline.

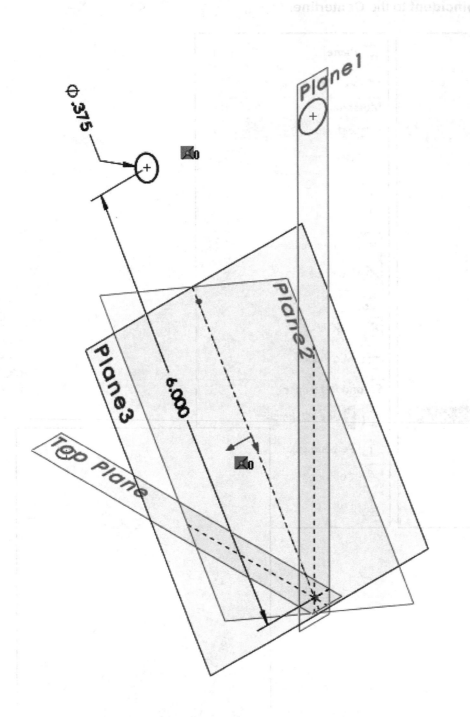

7) **Loft**  the three circles. Make sure that when you choose the circles you choose them in approximately the same location (e.g. all at the bottom quadrant or all at the top quadrant). The green circles indicate the twist. If they are all in the same location, there is no twist. You can click and drag on the green circles to adjust the twist.

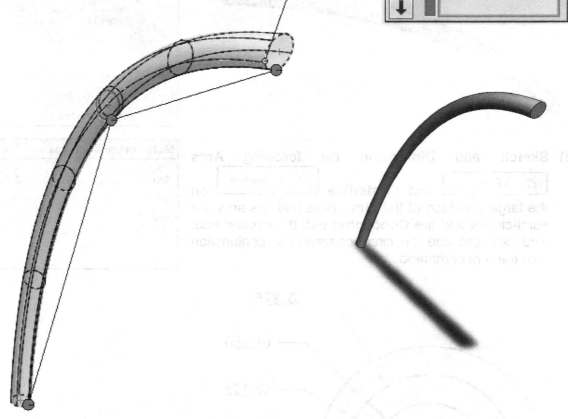

8) **Hide** 👁 all the planes and the centerline.

11.5) SHELL THE ARM

1) **Shell** 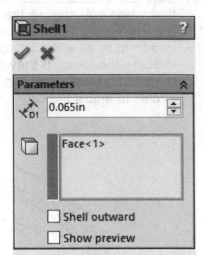 the arm to a thickness of **0.065 in** removing the small end.

2) **Sketch** and **Dimension** the following **Arcs** 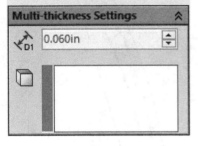 and **Centerline** on the large end face of the arm. Note that the arcs are semi-circles and are **Concentric** with the circular end. You can also use the *circle* command in conjunction with the *trim* command.

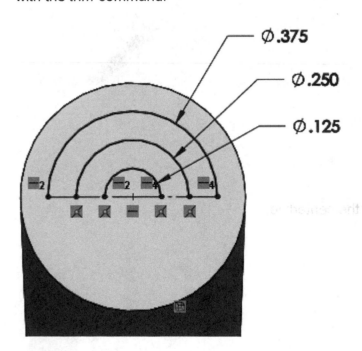

Ø.375

Ø.250

Ø.125

3) **Extrude Cut**  the sketch using the **Thin Feature** option with a thickness of **0.02 in** and a depth of **0.065 in.**

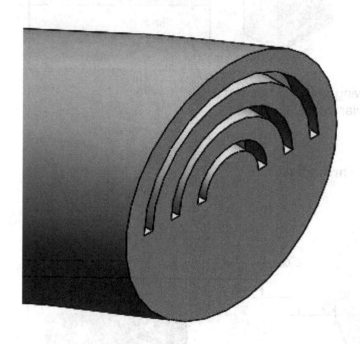

11.6) THE ARM JOINT

1) **Sketch** and **Dimension** the following **Rectangle** on **Right Plane**.

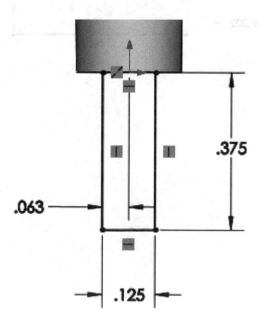

2) **Extrude** 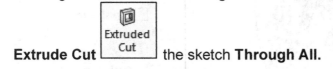 the sketch to a distance of **0.1 in** in **both directions**.

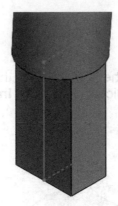

3) **Sketch** and **Dimension** the following profile on one of the large faces of the rectangular extrude. Then,

Extrude Cut 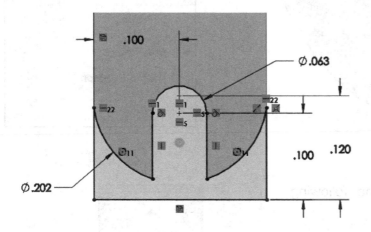 the sketch **Through All.**

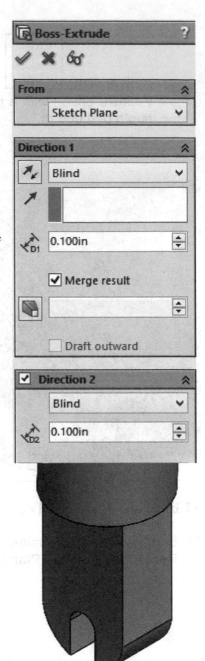

4) **Sketch** and **Dimension** the following **Circle** on the **Right Plane**. The circle center is vertical with the origin. Then, **Extrude Cut**

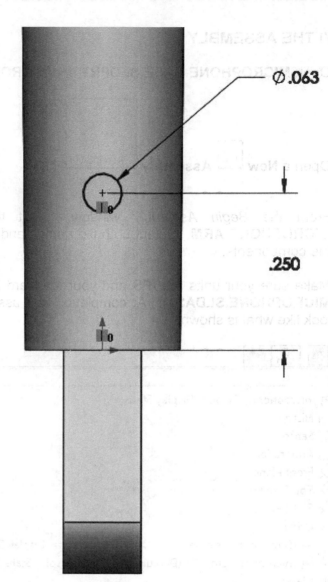

the sketch **Through All** towards the outside curve of the arm.

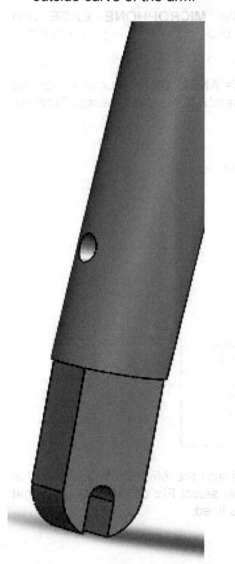

11.7) THE ASSEMBLY

1) Open **MICROPHONE BASE.SLDPRT** and **MICROPHONE ARM.SLDPRT**

2) Open a **New**  **Assembly** .

3) From the *Begin Assembly* window, insert the **MICROPHONE BASE** and **MICROPHONE ARM**. Select both file names and click in the drawing area to place the components.

4) Make sure your units are **IPS** and your standard is **ANSI**. Save your assembly as **MICROPHONE.SLDASM**. At completion, the assembly's *Feature Design Tree* will look like what is shown.

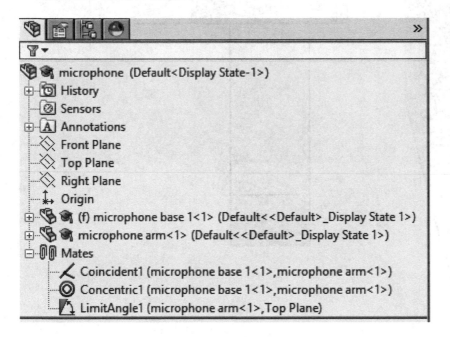

5) Make sure that the *MICROPHONE BASE* is fixed and the *MICROPHONE ARM* is floating. To do this, right click on the part and either select **Fix** or **Float**. Notice that the *base* will have an (f) next to it indicating that it is fixed.

6) Apply the following **Mates** 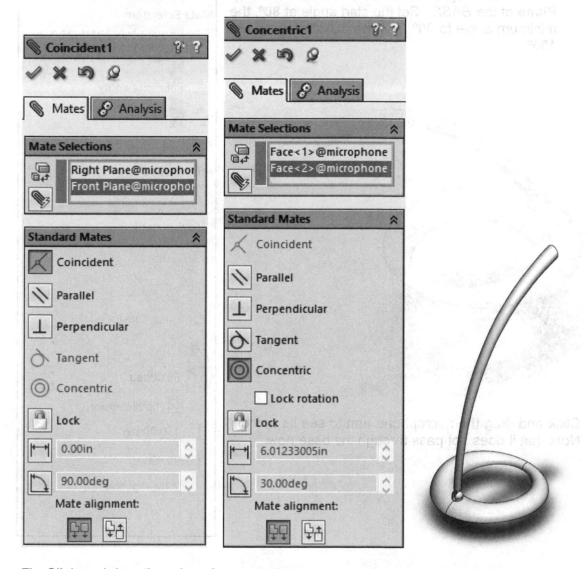.
   a) A **Coincident** mate between the **Right Plane** of the *BASE* and the **Front Plane** of the *ARM*. Reverse the **Mate alignment** if necessary.
   b) A **Concentric** mate between the round shaft of the *base joint* and the round slot of the *arm joint*.

Coincident1

Mates | Analysis

Mate Selections
Right Plane@microphor
Front Plane@microphor

Standard Mates
Coincident
Parallel
Perpendicular
Tangent
Concentric
Lock
0.00in
90.00deg
Mate alignment:

Concentric1

Mates | Analysis

Mate Selections
Face<1>@microphone
Face<2>@microphone

Standard Mates
Coincident
Parallel
Perpendicular
Tangent
Concentric
☐ Lock rotation
Lock
6.01233005in
30.00deg
Mate alignment:

7) Click and drag the microphone arm to see its motion. Note that it will pass through the base, which is not very realistic.

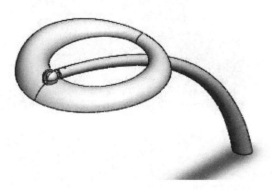

8) Apply the following **Mate** 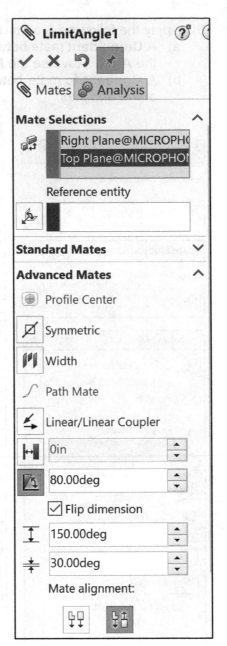. Before applying the mate, make sure that the *ARM* makes an acute angle with the *BASE*.

   a) A **Limit Angle** mate (under **Advanced Mates**) between the **Right Plane** of the *ARM* and the **Top Plane** of the *BASE*. Set the start angle at **80°**, the minimum angle to **30°**, and the maximum angle to **150°**.

LimitAngle1

Mates | Analysis

Mate Selections

Right Plane@MICROPH(
Top Plane@MICROPHON

Reference entity

Standard Mates

Advanced Mates

⊕ Profile Center

⊘ Symmetric

Width

Path Mate

Linear/Linear Coupler

0in

80.00deg

☑ Flip dimension

150.00deg

30.00deg

Mate alignment:

9) Click and drag the microphone arm to see its motion. Note that it does not pass through the base now.

MICROPHONE PROJECT - ARM PROBLEMS

P11-1) Model one of the following. Use the appropriate materials and mates.

a) Scissors

b) Pliers

c) Bicycle

MICROPHONE PROJECT (ARM) QUIZ PROBLEMS

Q11-1) Model the following **Oak** part and calculate its mass. Dimensions are in **inches**.

Mass = _____ grams

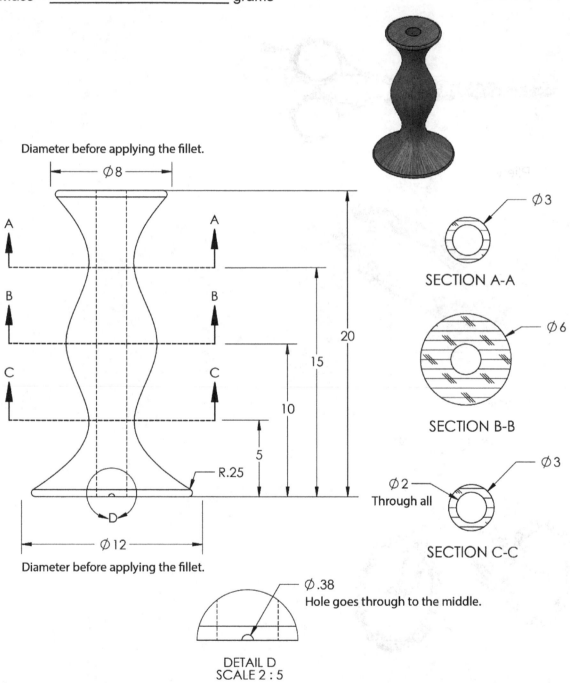

Diameter before applying the fillet.

$\phi 8$

A   A

B   B

C   C

20

15

10

5

R.25

D

$\phi 12$

Diameter before applying the fillet.

$\phi 3$

SECTION A-A

$\phi 6$

SECTION B-B

$\phi 3$

$\phi 2$
Through all

SECTION C-C

$\phi .38$
Hole goes through to the middle.

DETAIL D
SCALE 2 : 5

CHAPTER 12

BOAT PROJECT

CHAPTER OUTLINE

12.1) PREREQUISITES

Before starting this tutorial, you should complete the following tutorial.

- Microphone – Base

12.2) WHAT YOU WILL LEARN

The objective of this tutorial is to introduce you to creating complex solid geometries. You will be modeling the boat shown in Figure 12.2-1. Specifically, you will be learning the following commands and concepts.

Sketching

- Conic
- Scale
- Construction geometry

Features

- Sweep

Figure 12.2-1: Boat model

12.3) SETTING UP THE PROJECT

1) Start a **new part** .

2) Set your unit to **MMGS,** your **Decimals = none** and your standard to **ANSI**.

3) Save your part as **BOAT.SLDPRT** (**File – Save**). Remember to save often throughout this project.

12.4) LOFT

1) **Sketch** and **Dimension** an **Ellipse** [⊘ Ellipse] on the **Right Plane**. Then draw a **Line** that cuts the ellipse in half. (See the informational block on *Drawing a Conic*.)

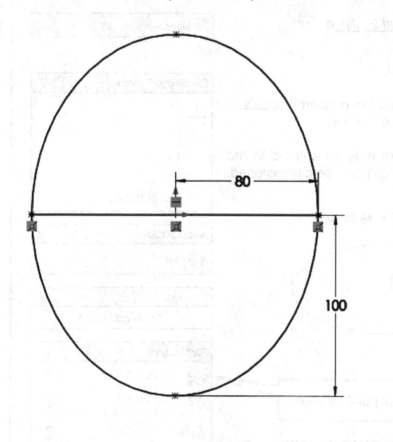

Draw ing a conic (Located in the *Sk etch* ribbon)

A conic is a curve obtained by intersecting a cone with a plane. Conics available in SOLIDWORKS® include the shapes: *E llipse, Partial E llipse, Parab ola, and Conic*.

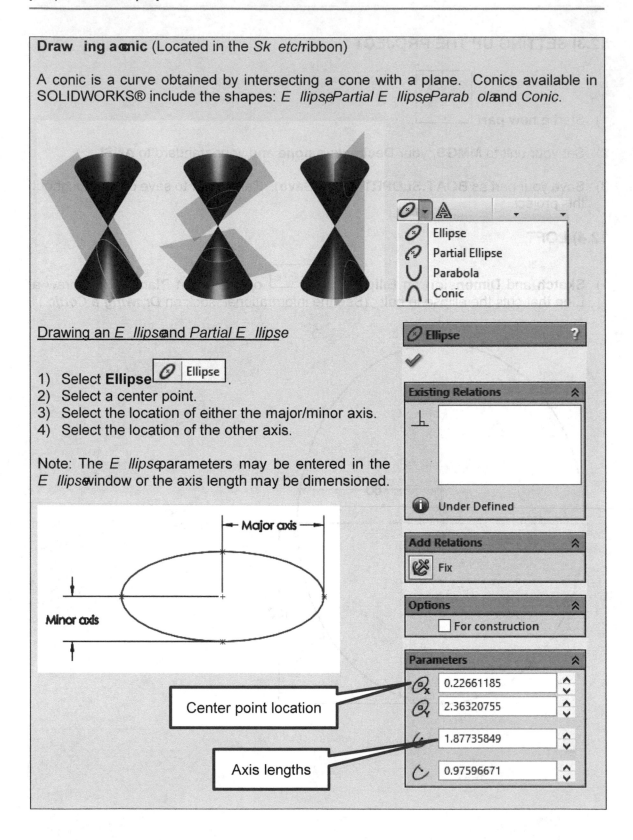

Drawing an *E llipse* and *Partial E llipse*

1) Select **Ellipse** .
2) Select a center point.
3) Select the location of either the major/minor axis.
4) Select the location of the other axis.

Note: The *E llipse* parameters may be entered in the *E llipse* window or the axis length may be dimensioned.

Center point location

Axis lengths

Drawing a conic (Located in the *Sketch* ribbon)

Drawing a *Partial Ellipse*

1) Select **Partial Ellipse** 🔲 Partial Ellipse .
2) Select a center point.
3) Select the location of either the major/minor axis.
4) Select the location of the other axis.
5) Select the extents of the *Partial Ellipse*.

Note: The *Ellipse* parameters may be entered in the *Ellipse* window or the axis length may be dimensioned.

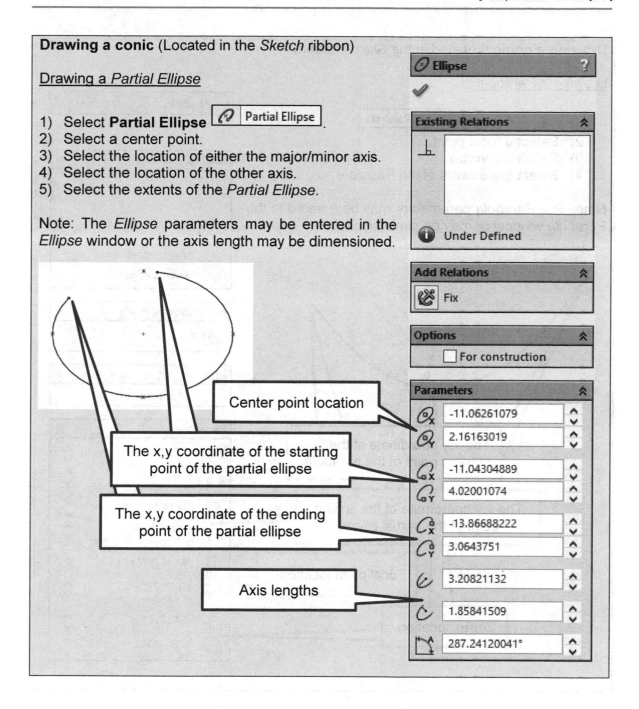

Center point location

The x,y coordinate of the starting point of the partial ellipse

The x,y coordinate of the ending point of the partial ellipse

Axis lengths

Ellipse

Existing Relations

Under Defined

Add Relations

Fix

Options

☐ For construction

Parameters

$\emptyset_X$	-11.06261079
$\emptyset_Y$	2.16163019
G_X	-11.04304889
G_Y	4.02001074
C_X	-13.86688222
C_Y	3.0643751
	3.20821132
	1.85841509
	287.24120041°

Drawing a conic (Located in the *Sketch* ribbon)

Drawing a *Parabola*

1) Select **Parabola** ⎿∪⏌ Parabola .
2) Select a focal point.
3) Select the vertex.
4) Select the extents of the *Parabola*.

Note: The *Parabola* parameters may be entered in the *Parabola* window or may be dimensioned.

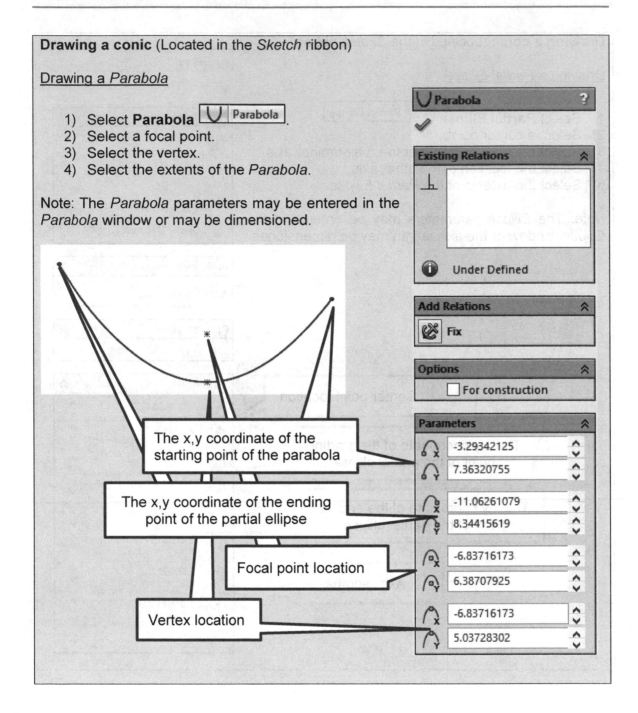

∪ Parabola ?

Existing Relations ≫
⊥
ⓘ Under Defined

Add Relations ≫
⚓ Fix

Options ≫
☐ For construction

Parameters ≫

The x,y coordinate of the starting point of the parabola
x -3.29342125
y 7.36320755

The x,y coordinate of the ending point of the partial ellipse
x -11.06261079
y 8.34415619

Focal point location
x -6.83716173
y 6.38707925

Vertex location
x -6.83716173
y 5.03728302

Drawing a conic (Located in the *Sketch* ribbon)

Drawing a *Conic*

1) Select **Conic** 〔∩ Conic〕.
2) Select the start point.
3) Select the end point.
4) Select the top vertex.
5) Select the shoulder point.

Note: The *Conic* parameters may be entered in the *Conic* window or may be dimensioned.

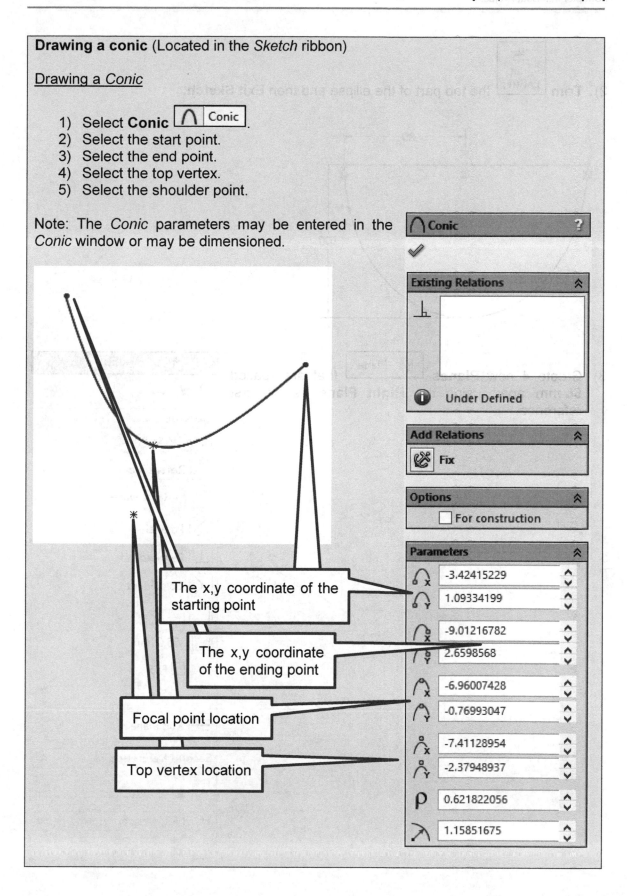

The x,y coordinate of the starting point

The x,y coordinate of the ending point

Focal point location

Top vertex location

2) **Trim** 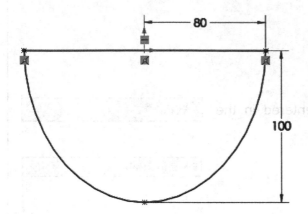 the top part of the ellipse and then **Exit Sketch.**

3) Create **4** new **Planes** 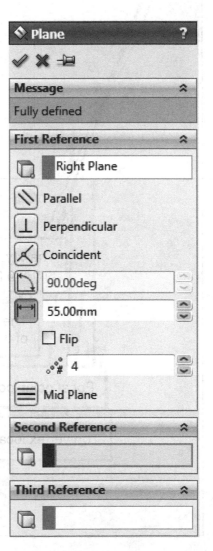 that are spaced **55 mm** apart using the **Right Plane** as the first reference.

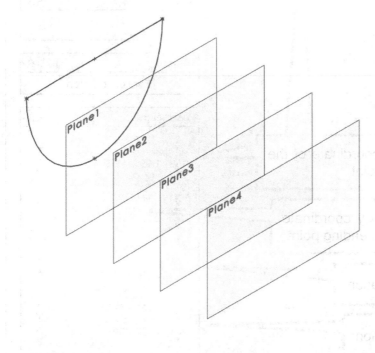

4) **Sketch** on the plane that is closest to the *Right Plane*. Use **Convert Entities** 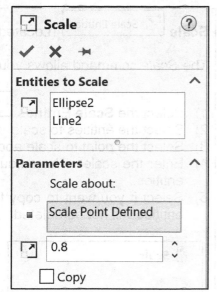 to create a new sketch on the plane that contains the half ellipse and line that you drew on the right plane.

Scale the sketch by a factor of **80%** using the **ellipse center point** as the point to scale about. Repeat for all the planes on the right side to achieve the following sketches. Each successive sketch is 80% the size of the previous sketch. (See the informational block on *Scaling*.)

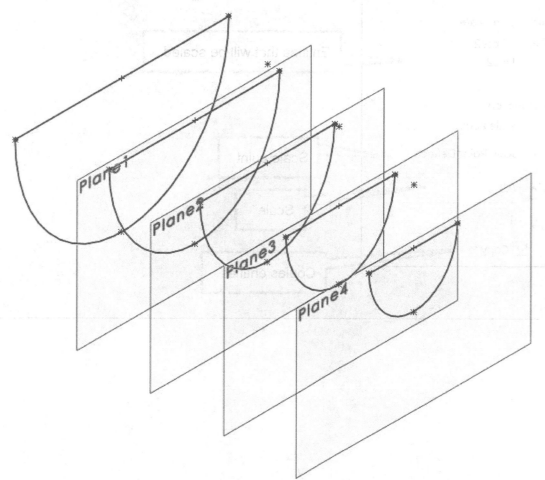

Scale 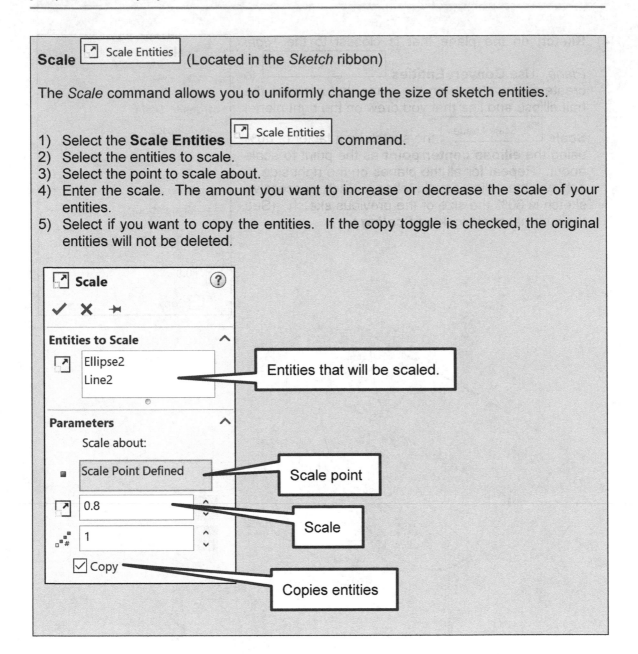 (Located in the *Sketch* ribbon)

The *Scale* command allows you to uniformly change the size of sketch entities.

1) Select the **Scale Entities** command.
2) Select the entities to scale.
3) Select the point to scale about.
4) Enter the scale. The amount you want to increase or decrease the scale of your entities.
5) Select if you want to copy the entities. If the copy toggle is checked, the original entities will not be deleted.

5) Use **Loft Boss/Base** [⌂ Lofted Boss/Base] to create the right side of the boat. Select the sketches in order from largest to smallest. It is easiest if you select the sketches in the *Design Tree*. In this way, you avoid twist.

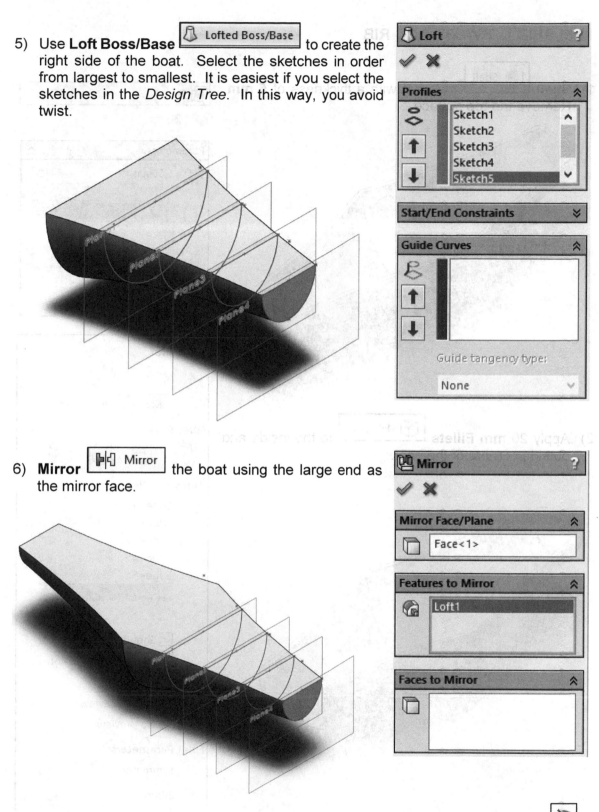

6) **Mirror** [⊢⊣ Mirror] the boat using the large end as the mirror face.

7) Hide the 4 created planes. Do this by clicking on the plane and selecting **Hide** ⊘.

12.5) SHELL, SWEEP AND RIB

1) **Shell** 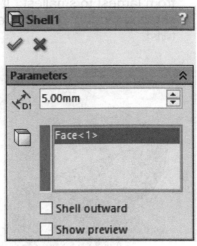 the boat with a thickness of **5 mm**. Remove the top surface.

2) Apply **20 mm Fillets** to the inside and outside corners of the boat.

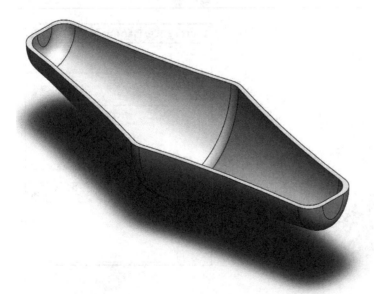

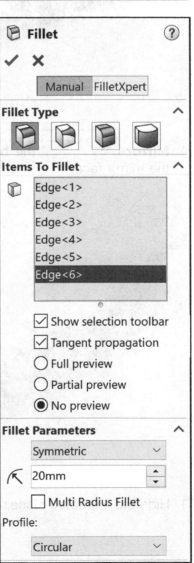

3) **Sketch** and **Dimension** the following profile on the **Right Plane** and then **Exit Sketch**.

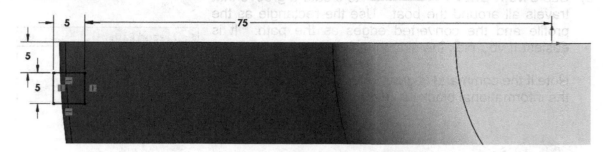

4) **Sketch** on the **Top Plane** and use **Convert Entities** 📦 Convert Entities to create a sketch of the outer profile of the boat. The 2 sketches will look like the second figure with the boat hidden.

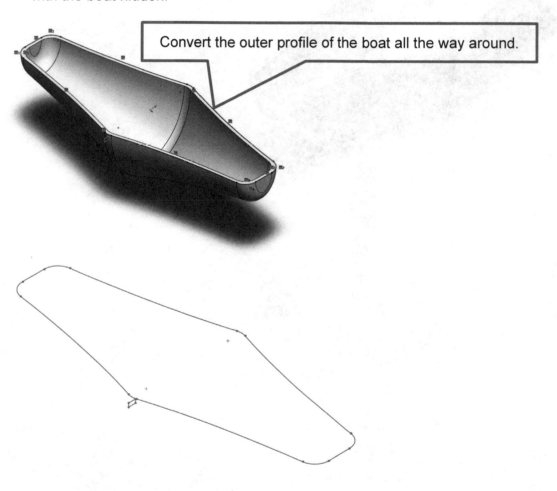

Convert the outer profile of the boat all the way around.

5) Use **Swept Cut** 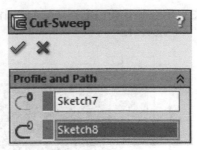 to create a groove that travels all around the boat. Use the rectangle as the profile and the converted edges as the path. It is easiest if you pick the sketches from the Design Tree.

Note if the command is gray, select **Rebuild** 🔘. (See the informational block on *Sweeps*.)

Swept Boss/Bass 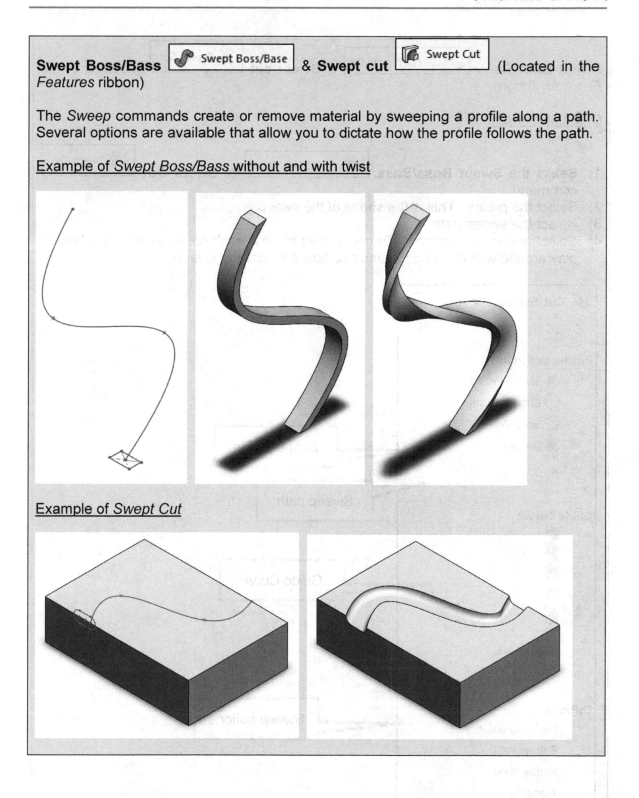 Swept Boss/Base   & **Swept cut** Swept Cut   (Located in the *Features* ribbon)

The *Sweep* commands create or remove material by sweeping a profile along a path. Several options are available that allow you to dictate how the profile follows the path.

Example of *Swept Boss/Bass* without and with twist

Example of *Swept Cut*

Swept Boss/Bass 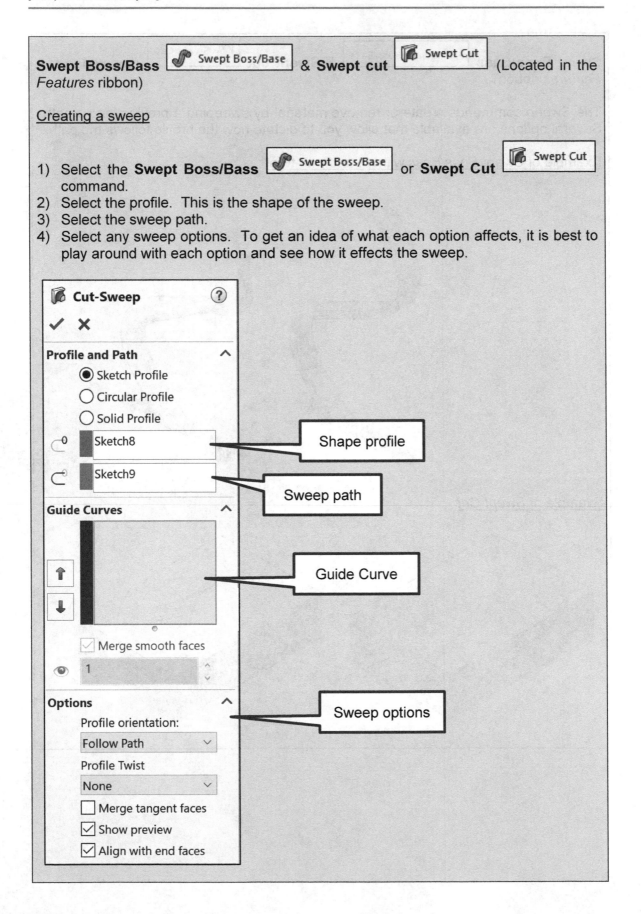 Swept Boss/Base & **Swept cut** Swept Cut (Located in the *Features* ribbon)

Creating a sweep

1) Select the **Swept Boss/Bass** Swept Boss/Base or **Swept Cut** Swept Cut command.
2) Select the profile. This is the shape of the sweep.
3) Select the sweep path.
4) Select any sweep options. To get an idea of what each option affects, it is best to play around with each option and see how it effects the sweep.

6) **Sketch** on **Plane 2** (the second plane created). Use **Intersection Curve**
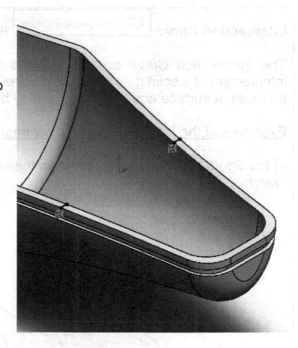 to create the 2 lines shown. Do this by selecting the top surface of the boat. (Note: You may have to select several different locations before the top is actually selected.) Convert these lines to **Construction Geometry** . (See the informational block on *Intersection Curves*.)

7) Draw a **Line** between the 2 short lines and then **Exit Sketch**.

Intersection Curve 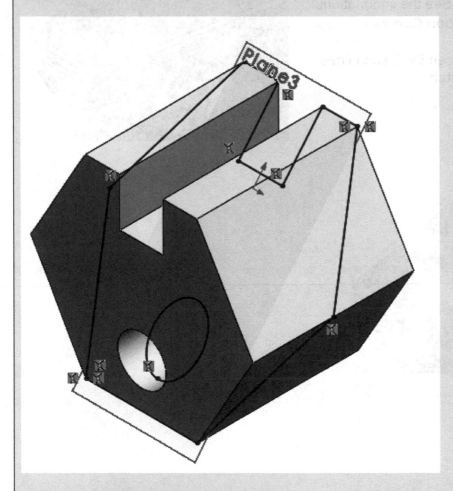 (Located in the *Sketch* ribbon)

The *Intersection Curve* command allows you to create a sketch based off of the intersection of a solid geometry and a plane. Other intersections, such as between two surfaces, a surface and a model face may be used.

Examples of the *Intersection Curve* command

In the figure the intersection between the solid part and the plane is used to create a sketch.

Using the *Intersection Curve* command

1) Sketch on the plane or face where the sketch will be supported.
2) Select the **Intersection Curve** command.
3) Select the faces or edges that will used to create the intersecting sketch.
4) Select OK.

8) **Rib** 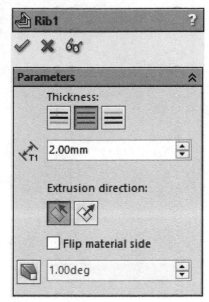 the line with **2 mm** of material on both sides. Then **Mirror** the **Rib** using the **Right Plane** as the mirror face.

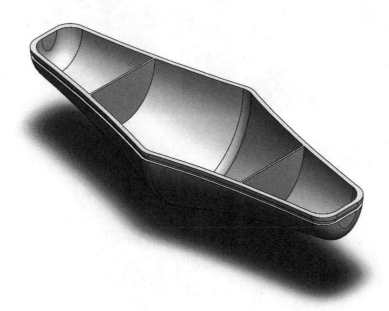

Rib1

Parameters

Thickness:

2.00mm

Extrusion direction:

☐ Flip material side

1.00deg

NOTES:

BOAT PROJECT PROBLEMS

P12-1) Use SOLIDWORKS® to create a solid model of one of the following object.

    a) Carabiner – Use at least one SWEEP command.

    b) Desk lamp – Use at least one SWEEP command and one LOFT command.

    c) A hanger

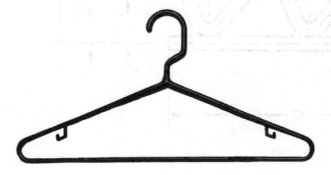

BOAT PROJECT QUIZ PROBLEMS

Q12-1) Use SOLIDWORKS® to create a solid model of the following 1045 Steel *Cotter Pin*. Dimensions are in millimeters and calculate the mass. Use the SWEEP command to construct the part.

Mass = _____ grams

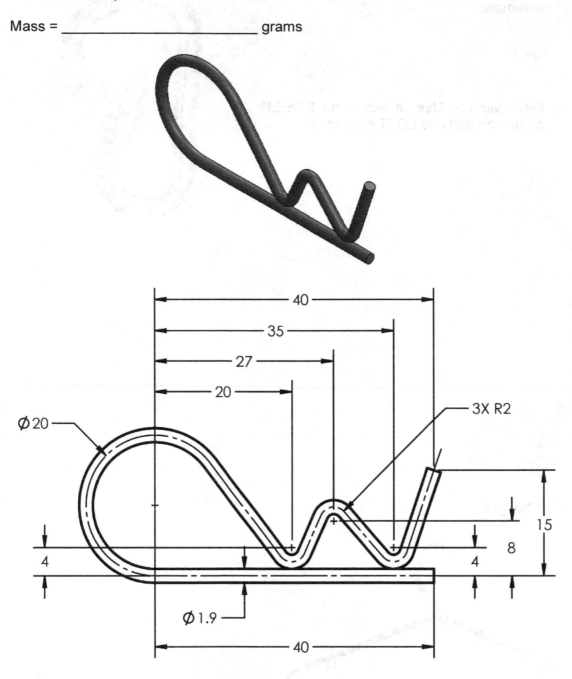

CHAPTER 13

VISE PROJECT
Tolerancing

CHAPTER OUTLINE

13.1) PREREQUISITES

Before starting this tutorial you should complete the following tutorials.

- Connecting rod project – Part model
- Flanged coupling project – Coupling

You should also have the following knowledge.

- Familiarity with threads and fasteners
- Creating threaded holes using the *Hole Wizard*
- Familiarity with tolerancing

13.2) WHAT YOU WILL LEARN

The objective of this tutorial is to introduce you to realistic part models that have toleranced dimensions. You will be modeling some of the parts that comprise the *Vise* assembly shown in Figure 13.2-1. Specifically, you will be learning the following commands and concepts.

Sketching

- Applying tolerances

Features

- Cosmetic Threads
- Applying tolerances

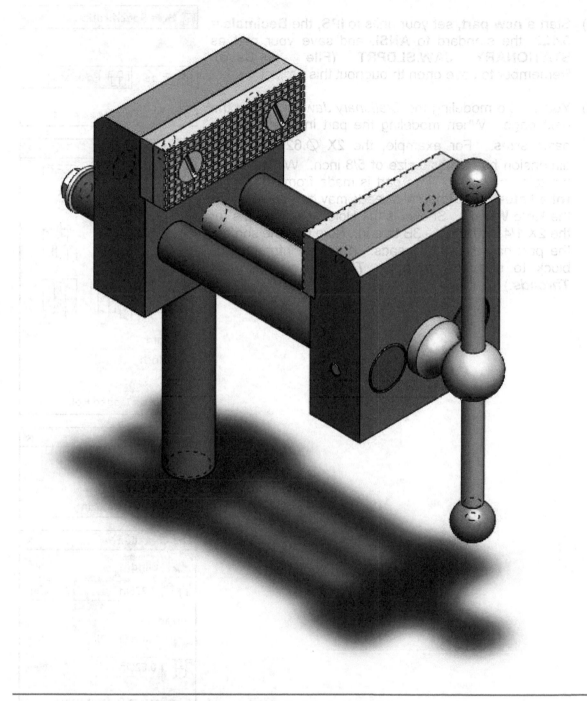

Figure 13.2-1: Vise assembly

13.3) STATIONARY JAW

1) Start a **new part,** set your units to **IPS,** the **Decimals = 0.123**, the standard to **ANSI**, and save your part as **STATIONARY JAW.SLDPRT (File – Save)**. Remember to save often throughout this project.

2) You will be modeling the *Stationary Jaw* shown on the next page. When modeling the part initially, use the basic sizes. For example, the 2X ∅.6250 - .6278 dimension has a basic size of 5/8 inch. We will apply the tolerance later. This part is made from **1020 cold rolled steel**. The internal threads may be applied using the **Hole Wizard**. Shown is the Hole Specifications for the 2X 1/4 - 20 UNC – 3B thread. Note that the shaft of the part has external threads. (See the informational block to see how to apply *Threads* or *Cosmetic Threads*.)

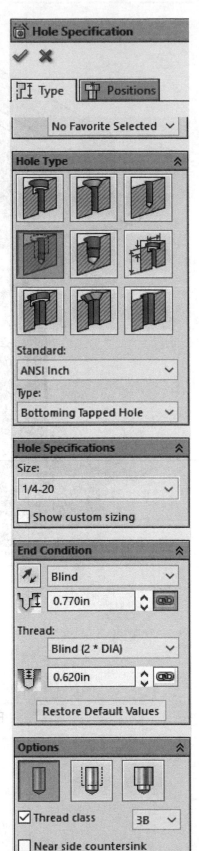

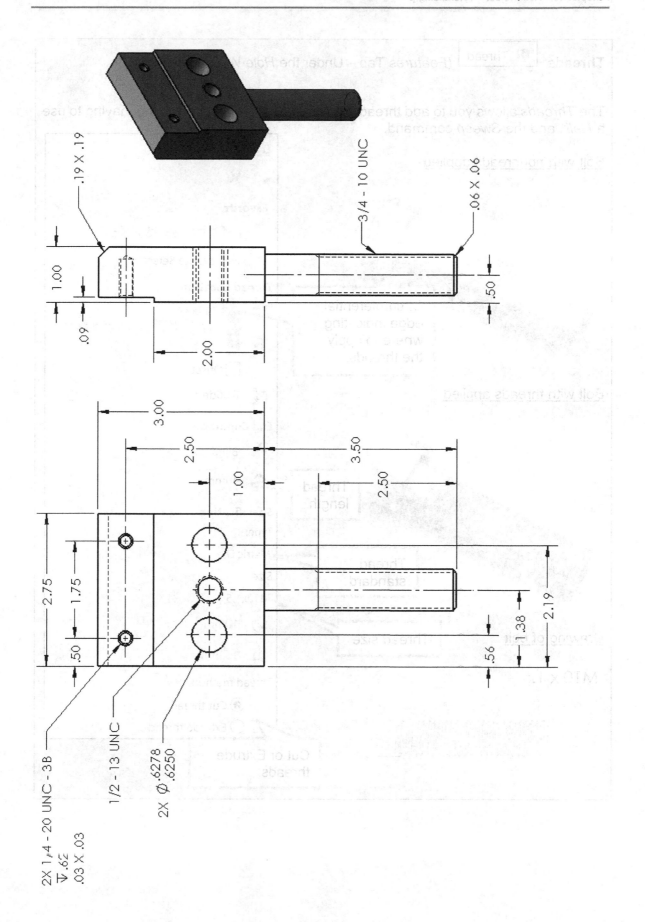

.19 X .19

1.00

.09

2.00

3/4 - 10 UNC

.06 X .06

.50

3.00

2.50

1.00

3.50

2.50

2.75

1.75

.50

2.19

1.38

.56

2X 1/4 - 20 UNC - 3B
▽ .62
.03 X .03

1/2 - 13 UNC

2X Ø .6278
.6250

Threads 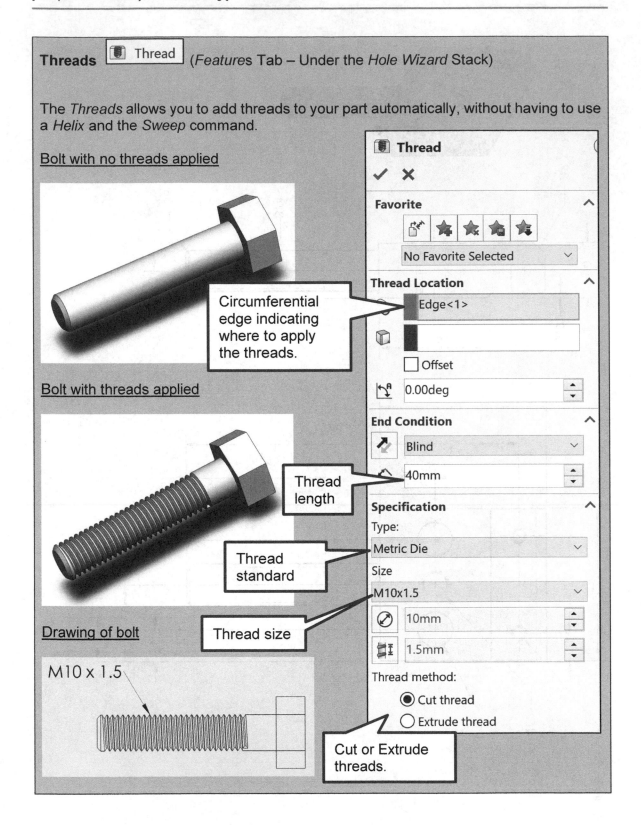 Thread (*Features* Tab – Under the *Hole Wizard* Stack)

The *Threads* allows you to add threads to your part automatically, without having to use a *Helix* and the *Sweep* command.

<u>Bolt with no threads applied</u>

Circumferential edge indicating where to apply the threads.

<u>Bolt with threads applied</u>

Thread length

Thread standard

Thread size

<u>Drawing of bolt</u>

M10 x 1.5

Thread

Favorite

No Favorite Selected

Thread Location

Edge<1>

☐ Offset

0.00deg

End Condition

Blind

40mm

Specification

Type:

Metric Die

Size

M10x1.5

10mm

1.5mm

Thread method:

● Cut thread

○ Extrude thread

Cut or Extrude threads.

Cosmetic Threads 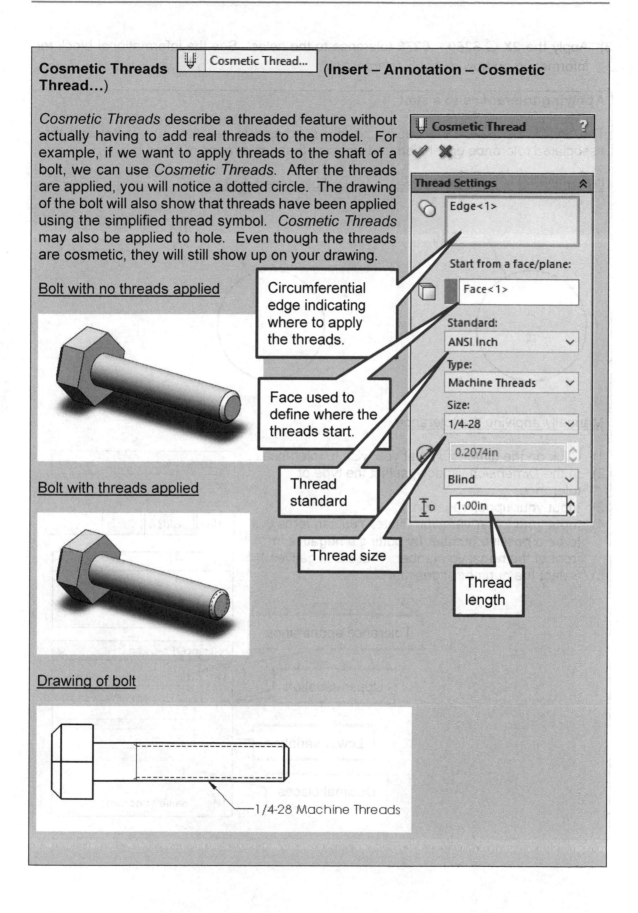 Cosmetic Thread... (Insert – Annotation – Cosmetic Thread...)

Cosmetic Threads describe a threaded feature without actually having to add real threads to the model. For example, if we want to apply threads to the shaft of a bolt, we can use *Cosmetic Threads*. After the threads are applied, you will notice a dotted circle. The drawing of the bolt will also show that threads have been applied using the simplified thread symbol. *Cosmetic Threads* may also be applied to hole. Even though the threads are cosmetic, they will still show up on your drawing.

Bolt with no threads applied

Circumferential edge indicating where to apply the threads.

Face used to define where the threads start.

Bolt with threads applied

Thread standard

Thread size

Thread length

Drawing of bolt

1/4-28 Machine Threads

Cosmetic Thread

Thread Settings

Edge<1>

Start from a face/plane:

Face<1>

Standard:

ANSI Inch

Type:

Machine Threads

Size:

1/4-28

0.2074in

Blind

1.00in

3) Apply the **2X** ⌀**.6250 - .6278** tolerance to the holes. See the informational block for information on how to *Apply tolerances*.

Applying tolerances to a sketch

The figures below show a basic size (the size used to calculate the limits) and the associated tolerance dimension (a dimension that has a range of sizes.)

Dimensioned using a basic size   Toleranced dimension

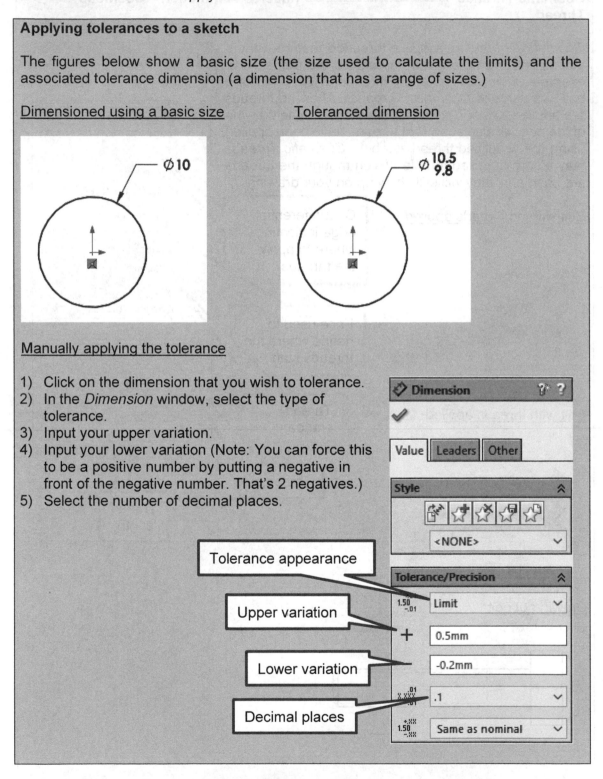

Manually applying the tolerance

1) Click on the dimension that you wish to tolerance.
2) In the *Dimension* window, select the type of tolerance.
3) Input your upper variation.
4) Input your lower variation (Note: You can force this to be a positive number by putting a negative in front of the negative number. That's 2 negatives.)
5) Select the number of decimal places.

Tolerance appearance

Upper variation

Lower variation

Decimal places

Applying tolerances to a *Hole*

1) Apply the **Hole**.
2) Click on the *Hole Sketch* that controls the size of the hole.
3) Click on the diameter dimension.
4) Apply the tolerance as you would apply it to a sketch.

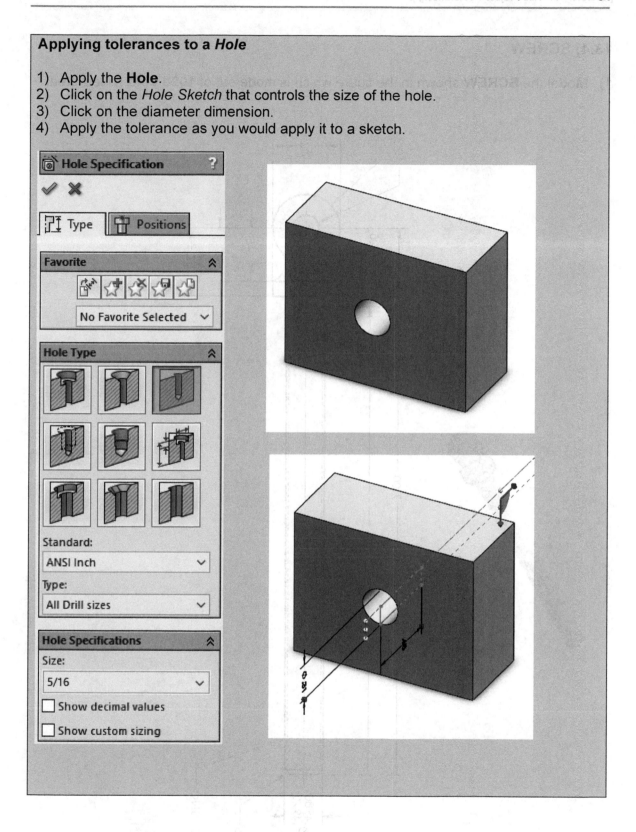

13.4) SCREW

1) Model the **SCREW** shown in the figure which is made out of **1020 cold rolled steel**.

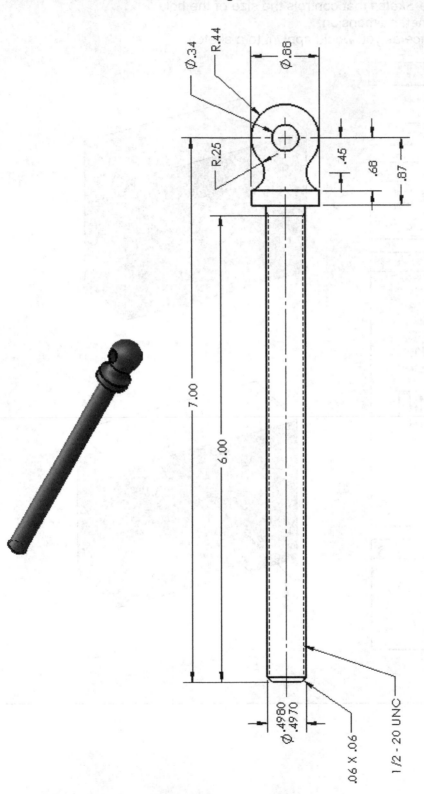

VISE PROJECT (TOLERANCING) PROBLEMS

P13-1) Model the following Cast Iron *Base*. Apply the appropriate tolerances. If you have not been taught how to calculate tolerances yet, ask your instructor for the appropriate values.

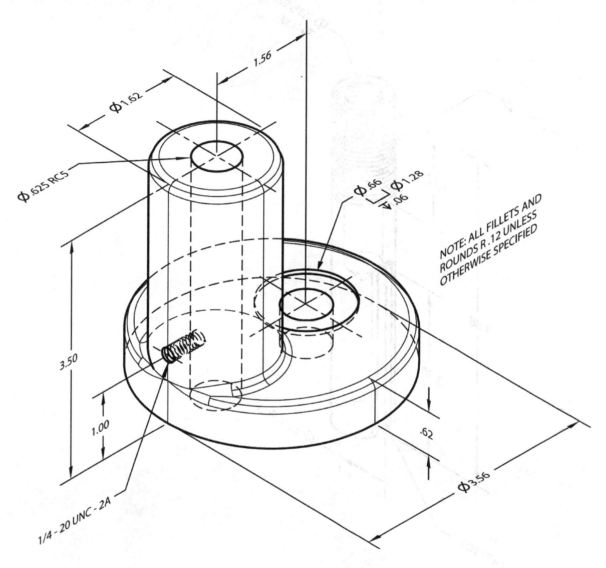

P13-2) Model the following 1045 Steel *Screw*. Apply the appropriate tolerances. If you have not been taught how to calculate tolerances yet, ask your instructor for the appropriate values.

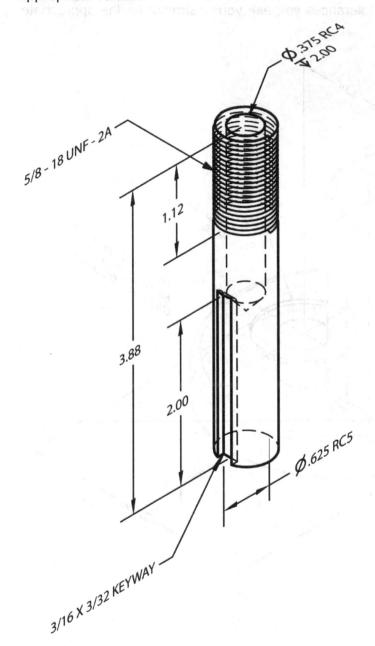

P13-3) Model the following 1045 Steel *V-Anvil*. Apply the appropriate tolerances. If you have not been taught how to calculate tolerances yet, ask your instructor for the appropriate values.

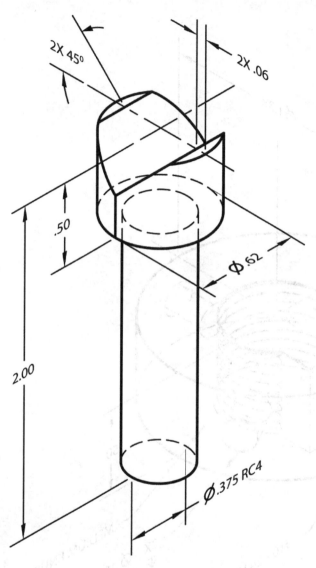

P13-4) Model the following 1045 Steel *Knurled Nut*. Apply the appropriate tolerances. If you have not been taught how to calculate tolerances yet, ask your instructor for the appropriate values.

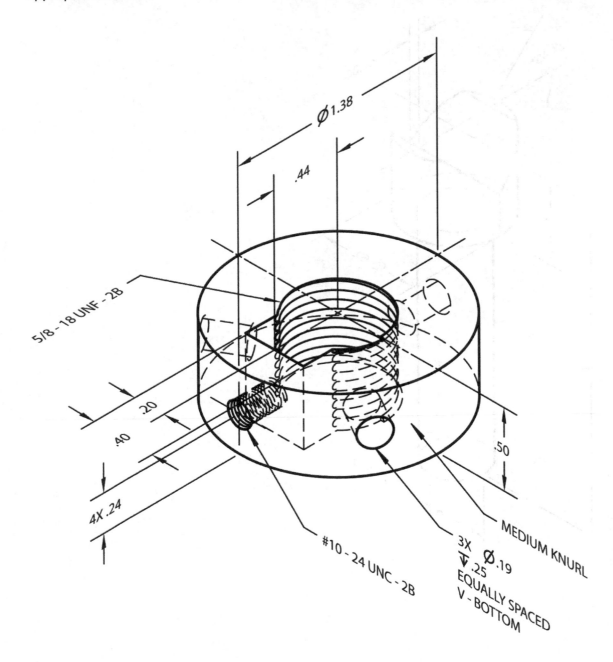

Ø1.38

.44

5/8 - 18 UNF - 2B

.20

.40

4X .24

#10 - 24 UNC - 2B

3X Ø.19
.25
EQUALLY SPACED
V - BOTTOM

MEDIUM KNURL

.50

VISE PROJECT (TOLERANCING) QUIZ PROBLEMS

Q13-1) Model the following 1020 Steel *Screw*. Apply the appropriate tolerances and threads. Dimensions are in millimeters. Calculate the mass and create a drawing dimensioning the toleranced hole and threads.

Mass (using *Threads* command) = _____ grams

Mass (using *Cosmetic Threads* command) = _____ grams

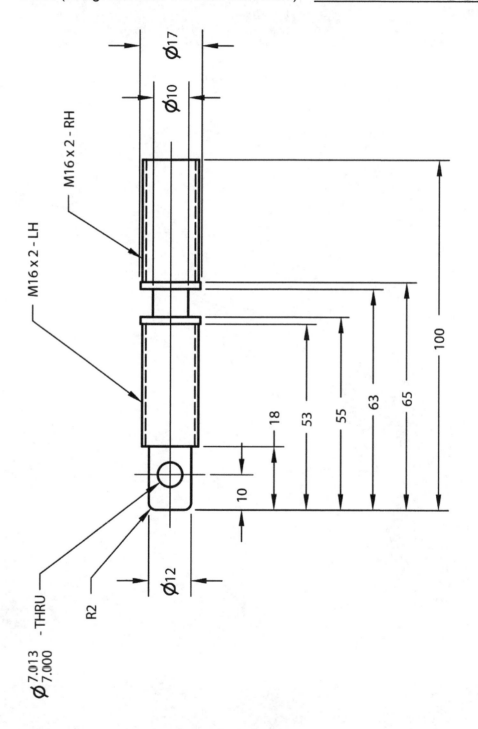

<u>NOTES:</u>

CHAPTER 14

VISE PROJECT
Design Intent / Parametric Modeling

CHAPTER OUTLINE

14.1) PREREQUISITES

Before starting this tutorial you should complete the following tutorials.

- Connecting rod project – Part model
- Flanged coupling project – Coupling

It will help if you have the following knowledge.

- Familiarity with threads and fasteners

14.2) WHAT YOU WILL LEARN

The objective of this tutorial is to introduce you to part models that have built-in design intent using parametric modeling. You will be modeling some of the parts that comprise the *Vise* assembly shown in Figure 14.2-1. Specifically, you will be learning the following commands and concepts.

Sketching

- Dimension names
- Equations

Features

- Dimension names
- Viewing feature dimensions
- Equations
- Feature suppression
- If statement

14.3) DESIGN INTENT AND PARAMETRIC MODELING

When you model a part with built-in design intent, you define how your part will change when parameters are modified. In general, you want to design a part for change and flexibility. This can be accomplished using parametric modeling. Parametric modeling allows you to relate two or more feature dimension together so that when one changes they all change, according to the design intent.

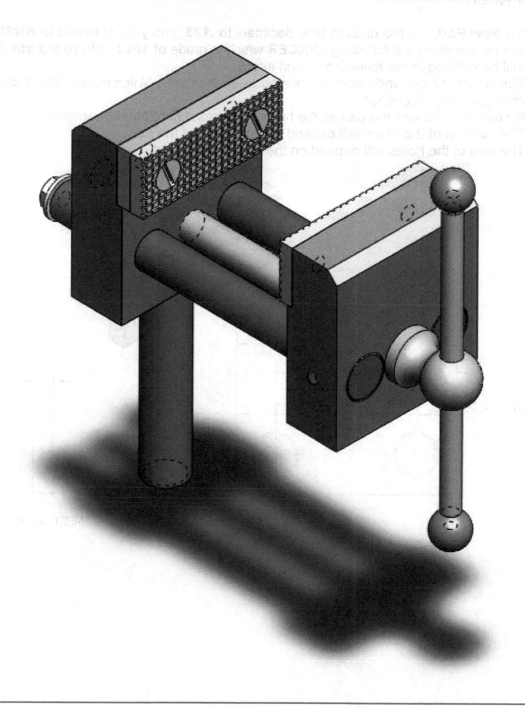

Figure 14.2-1: Vise assembly

14.4) SPACER

1) Start a **New Part**, set the units to **IPS**, decimals to **.123**, and your standard to **ANSI**. We will be modeling the following **SPACER** which is made of **1020 cold rolled steel**. We will be building in the following design intent.
   a) The length, height and depth are related to each other. Which means that if one changes, they all change.
   b) No matter what size the part is, the holes will remain horizontally centered.
   c) The location of the holes will depend on the length of the part.
   d) The size of the holes will depend on the height of the part.

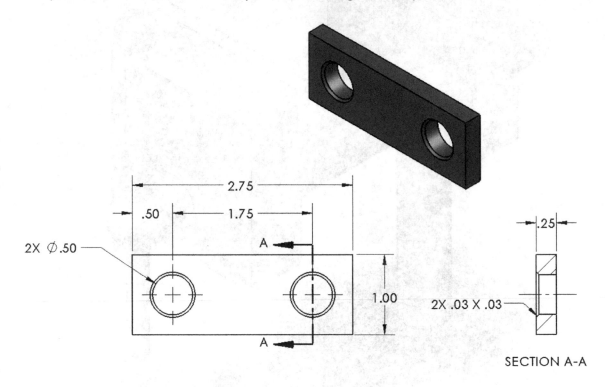

SECTION A-A

2) Start by drawing the following **Rectangle** `□ Corner Rectangle` with the dimensions shown on the **Front plane**. Name the dimensions as shown and then view them (**View – Hide/Show - Dimension Names**). See the informational block on **Naming Dimensions**.

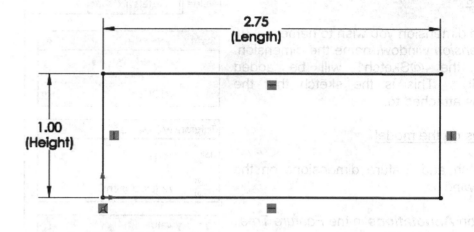

3) **Extrude** `Extruded Boss/Base` the sketch to **0.25 inches**. Name the *Extrude*, **Base**. (Remember, to name features, single click on the feature name in the *Feature Design Tree*.)

Naming Dimensions

Dimensions may be named so that they can easily be identified while applying equations.

Naming dimensions

1) Click on the dimension you wish to name.
2) In the *Dimension* window, name the dimension. Note that the @Sketch1 will be added automatically. This is the sketch that the dimension is attached to.

Viewing dimensions on the model

To view your sketch and feature dimensions on the model, do the following.

1) Right click on **Annotations** in the *Feature Tree*.
2) Select **Show Feature Dimensions**.

Viewing dimension names

1) **View – Hide/Show - Dimension Names**

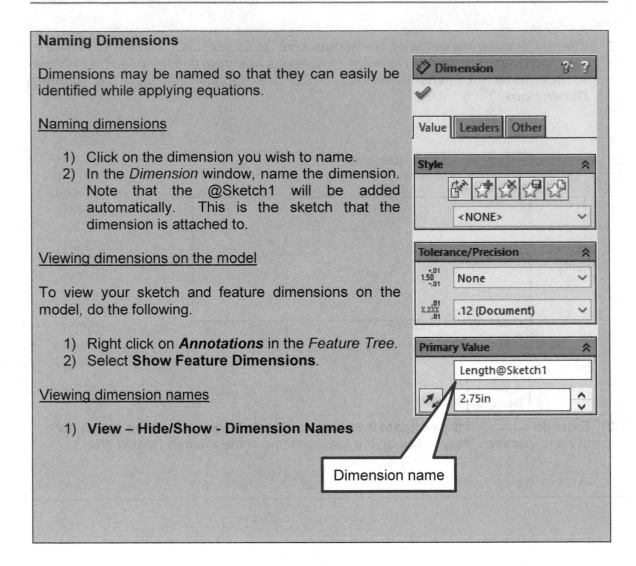

Dimension name

4) Right click on **Annotations** in the *Feature Design Tree* and select **Show Feature Dimensions**. If the dimensions don't appear, click on the *Base* extrude. Click on the 0.25 dimension and name it **Depth**. Add the following relationships between the dimensions. See the informational block on **Applying Equations** and **Adding Dimension Equations**.

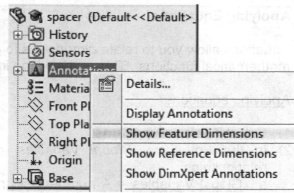

□ Dimensions		
Length@Sketch1	2.75in	2.75in
Height@Sketch1	= (4 / 11) * "Length@Sketch1"	1in
Depth@Base	= (1 / 11) * "Length@Sketch1"	0.25in

You may either select the actual dimension or type the text.

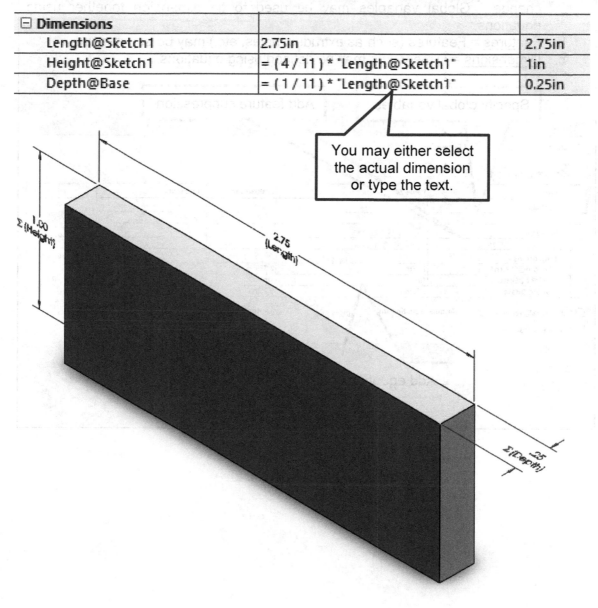

Applying Equations

Equations allow you to relate dimensions to global variables or other dimensions using mathematical functions. This can be done in both parts and assemblies.

Applying equations

1) Select **Tools – Equations**
2) In the *Equations, Global Variables, and Dimensions* window, you can add relationships.
   a. Global Variables = A number assigned to a variable that, in general, will not change. Global variables may be used to tie dimension together using equations.
   b. Features = Features (such as extrudes, holes, etc.) may be suppressed.
   c. Dimensions = Dimensions may be defined using equations.

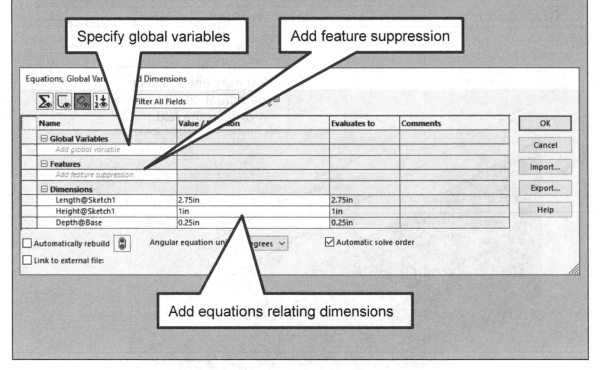

Specify global variables

Add feature suppression

Add equations relating dimensions

Adding Dimension Equations

1) The *Name* column under the *Dimensions* field should show all of the dimensions used to create your part. If the dimensions don't appear, click on the **Dimension View** icon [icon] at the top. Click in the cell next to the dimension you wish to define (under the *Value/Equation* column) and start with an "=". This will prompt selections that allow you to enter *Functions*, *File Properties* or *Measure...*

2) Follow the "=" with your desired equation. SolidWorks® generally follows the equation rules and syntax of EXCEL®. Variables/Dimension names need to be enclosed in double quotes and will turn blue if acceptable. You may also, just click on the dimension attached to the part and the name will automatically be added. A green check next to the equation will appear if the equation is valid.

`=(4/11)*"Length@Sketch1"` ✓

3) The calculated value of the equation will be shown in the cell to the right of the equation under the *Evaluates to* column.

⊟ Dimensions		
Length@Sketch1	=	✓
Height@Sketch1	Functions >	
Depth@Base	File Properties >	
	Measure...	

⊟ Dimensions		
Length@Sketch1	2.75in	2.75in
Height@Sketch1	=(4/11)*"Length@Sketch1" ✓	1in

4) If an error occurs that tells you that the equations are out of order, activate the **Automatic solve order** toggle.

⚠ Hole separation 1/2@Sketch2	= .5 * "Hole separation@Sketch2"	0.875in
⚠ Hole separation@Sketch2	= "Length@Sketch1" - 2 * "Hole DIA@Sketch2"	1.75in

☐ Automatically rebuild [icon]   Angular equation units: Degrees ⌄   ☐ Automatic solve order
☐ Link to external file:

1.00
Σ (Height)

5) After applying equations, the dimensions should have a Σ symbol next to them.

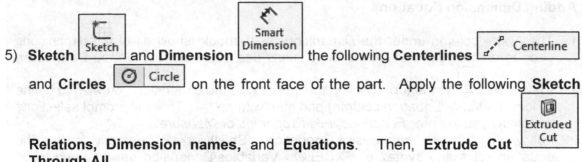

5) **Sketch** [Sketch] and **Dimension** [Smart Dimension] the following **Centerlines** [Centerline] and **Circles** [Circle] on the front face of the part. Apply the following **Sketch**

Relations, Dimension names, and **Equations**. Then, **Extrude Cut** [Extruded Cut] **Through All**.

a. The **Centerlines** start and end on the **Midpoint** of the sides.
b. The **Circle centers** are aligned on the horizontal **Centerline**.
c. The two **Circles** are **Equal**.

⊟ Dimensions		
Length@Sketch1	2.75in	2.75in
Height@Sketch1	= (4 / 11) * "Length@Sketch1"	1in
Depth@Base	= (1 / 11) * "Length@Sketch1"	0.25in
Hole DIA@Sketch2	= .5 * "Height@Sketch1"	0.5in
Hole separation 1/2@Sketch2	= .5 * "Hole separation@Sketch2"	0.875in
Hole separation@Sketch2	= "Length@Sketch1" - 2 * "Hole DIA@Sketch2"	1.75in

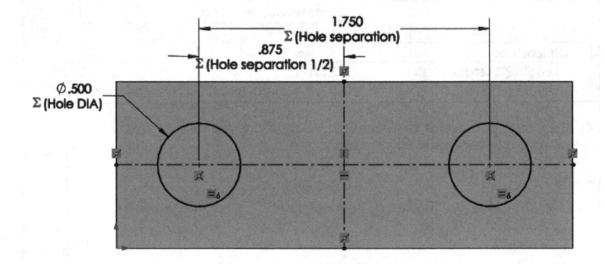

6) Change **Length** to **4 inches**. Your dimensions should change automatically in accordance with the applied equations. You may have to update ⬚ for the changes to take effect. Try changing **Length** to **1 inch** and then change it back to **2.75 inches**.

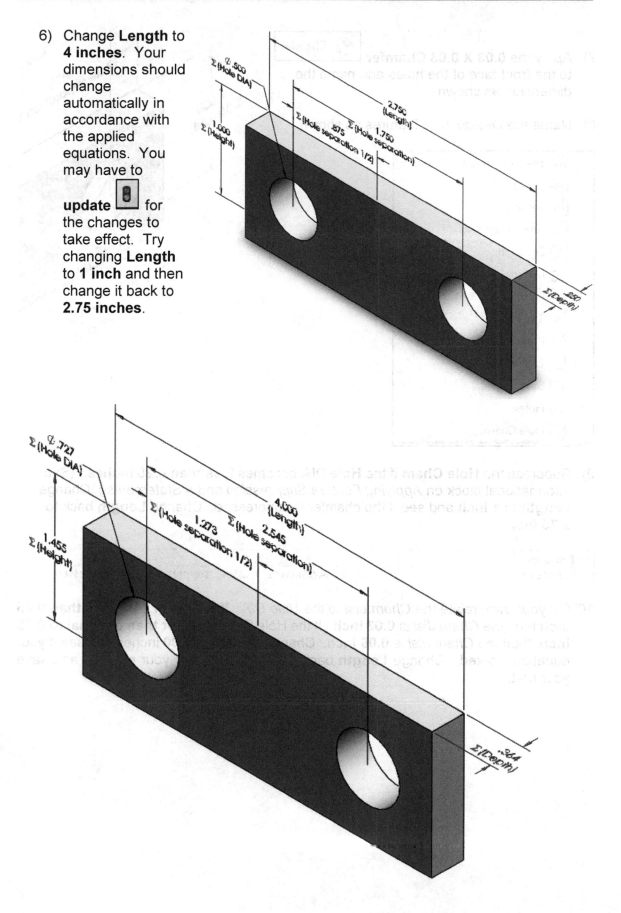

7) Apply the **0.03 X 0.03 Chamfer** 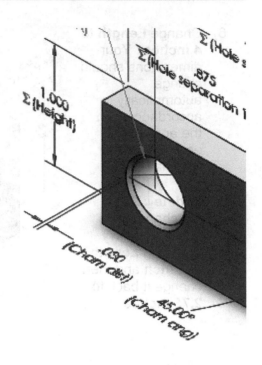 to the front face of the holes and name the dimension as shown.

8) Name the *Design Tree* features as shown.

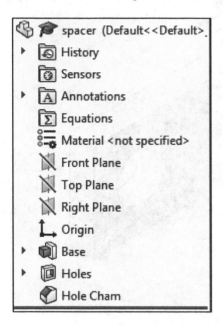

9) Suppress the **Hole Cham** if the **Hole DIA** becomes **less than 0.25 inches**. (See informational block on *Applying Feature Suppression* and *If Statements*.) Change **Length** to **1 inch** and see if the chamfer is suppressed. Change **Length** back to **2.75 inch**.

⊟ Features	
"Hole Cham"	= if ("Hole DIA@Sketch2" < .25in , "suppressed" , "unsuppressed")

10) On your own, relate the *Cham dist* to the *Hole DIA*. If the *Hole DIA* is **less than 0.75 inch** then the *Cham dist* is **0.03 inch**. If the Hole DIA is **greater than or equal to 0.75 inch**, then the *Cham dist* is **0.06 inch**. Change **Length** to **5.00** inches and see if your equation worked. Change **Length** back to **2.75** inches, set your material and save your part.

Adding Feature Suppression

1) **Tools – Equations**
2) Click on ***Add feature suppression*** in the *Equations, Global Variables, and Dimensions* window and then select the feature in the *Feature Design Tree* or enter or click on the feature name in the *Feature Design Tree*.
3) Click in the cell to the right of the feature (under the *Value/Equations* column). A list of options will appear. To simply suppress a feature, select **Global Variables** and then **suppress**. The **suppress** command is usually applied within an if statement. See below.
4) Functions may be used to indicate conditions for suppression.

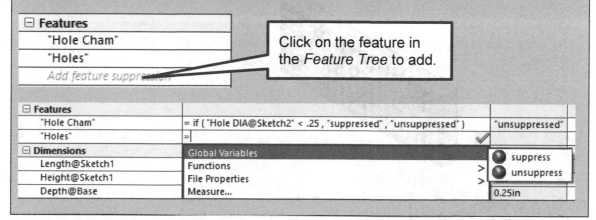

If Statements

The syntax for the **if** statement is as follows.

Hole DIA@Sketch2	=if("Length@Sketch1" > 2, 0.5, 0.25)

The above equations states that the *Hole DIA* is 0.5 units if the *Length* is greater than 2 units and 0.25 units if the *Length* is less than or equal to 2.

Hole Cham	=if("Hole DIA@Sketch2" < .25 in, "suppressed", "unsuppressed")

The above equation states that if the *Hole DIA* becomes less than .25 inches, the *Hole Cham* is suppressed. If the *Hole DIA* becomes equal to or greater than .25, the feature is unsuppressed.

Mathematical symbols (=, <, >) may be used.

14.5) JAW INSERT

1) Start a **New Part** and set your units to **IPS**, your decimals to **.123** and your standard to **ANSI**. We will be modeling the following **JAW INSERT** which is made of **Alloy steel**. We will be building in the following design intent.
    a) The number of countersunk holes will depend on the length of the part with equal spacing between them.
    b) No matter what size the part is, the holes will remain vertically centered.
    c) The grooves will cover the entire face of the part no matter what size it is.

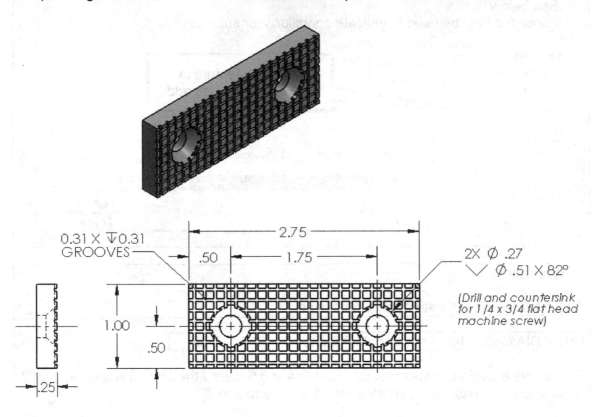

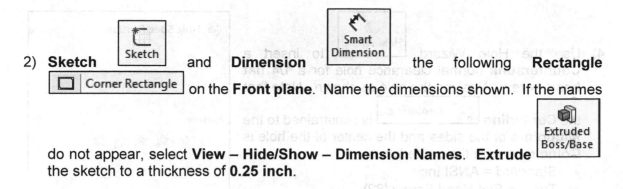

2) **Sketch** and **Dimension** the following **Rectangle** on the **Front plane**. Name the dimensions shown. If the names do not appear, select **View – Hide/Show – Dimension Names**. **Extrude** the sketch to a thickness of **0.25 inch**.

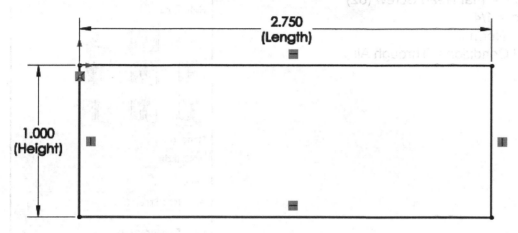

3) Apply the material **Alloy Steel** and save your part as **JAW INSERT**.

4) Use the Hole Wizard 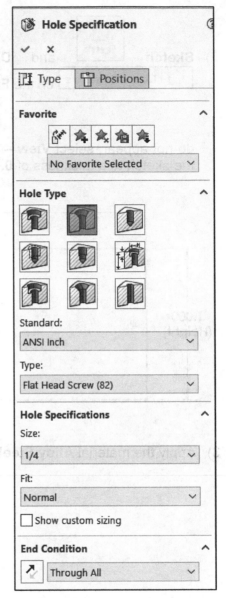 to insert a **Countersunk** normal clearance hole for a **1/4 flat head screw**. Position the hole as shown. Note that the **Centerline** is constrained to the **Midpoints** of the sides and the center of the hole is **Coincident** with the centerline.

- Standard = ANSI Inch
- Type: = Flat Head Screw (82)
- Size = 1/4
- Fit = Normal
- End Condition = Through All

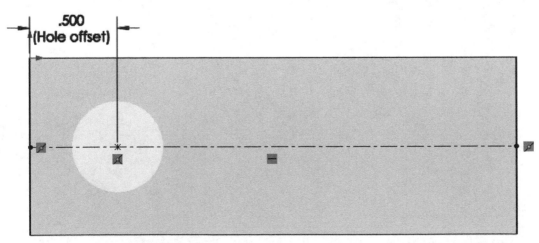

5) Create a vertical groove using a **Rectangle** ☐ Corner Rectangle on the front face of the part. Name the dimensions as shown.

Extrude Cut [Extruded Cut] the rectangle **0.031 inch**.

6) Name the *Extrude-Cut* depth dimension **Groove depth**.

7) Create a horizontal groove using a **Rectangle** ☐ Corner Rectangle on the front face of the part. Set these dimensions equal to the vertical groove dimensions. This can be done in the dimension *Modify* window.

Extrude Cut [Extruded Cut] the rectangle **0.031 inch**.

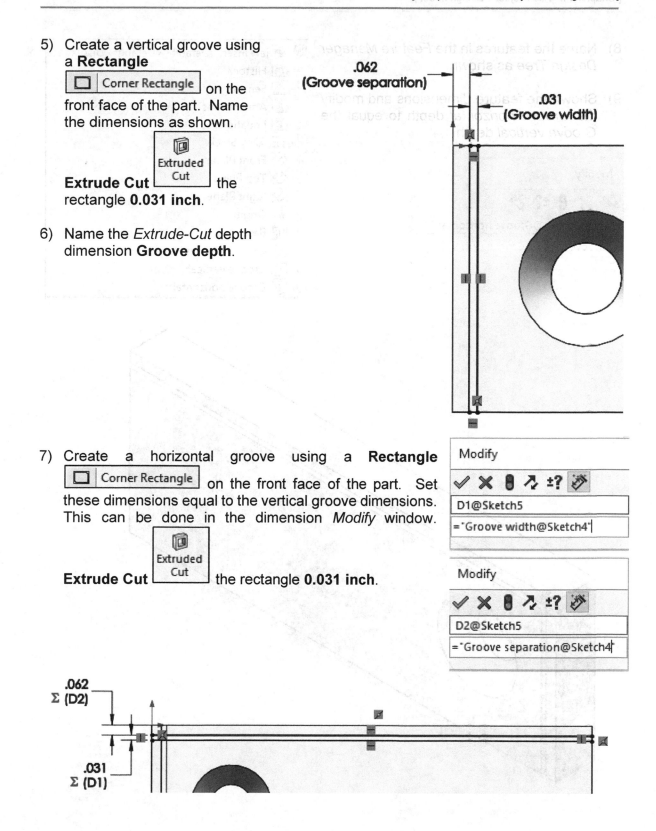

8) Name the features in the *Feature Manager Design Tree* as shown.

9) Shown the feature dimensions and modify the *Groove horizontal* depth to equal the *Groove vertical* depth.

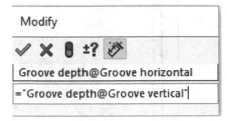

Modify

Groove depth@Groove horizontal

="Groove depth@Groove vertical"

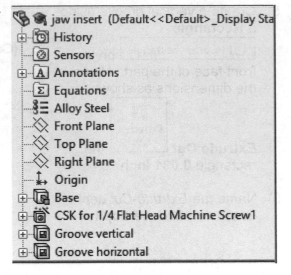

jaw insert (Default<<Default>_Display Sta
- History
- Sensors
- Annotations
- Equations
- Alloy Steel
- Front Plane
- Top Plane
- Right Plane
- Origin
- Base
- CSK for 1/4 Flat Head Machine Screw1
- Groove vertical
- Groove horizontal

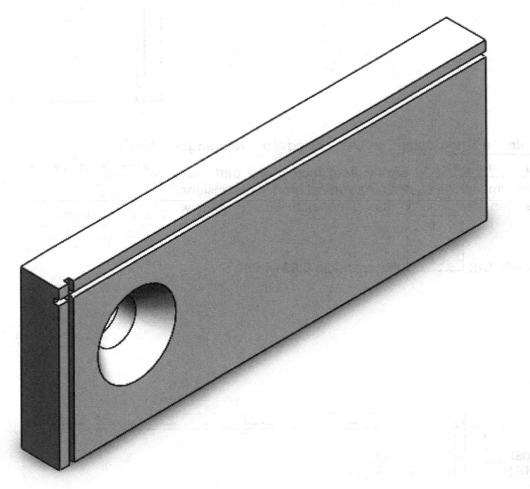

10) **Pattern** Linear Pattern the countersunk hole **1.75 in** apart using the following equations to control the number of holes (**=int("Length@Sketch1"/1.75 + 0.5)**). The int() function returns an integer.

11) **Pattern** Linear Pattern *Groove vertical* using the following equations to control the number of grooves (**=int("Length@Sketch1"/0.093)**). Set the distance between the groove equal to **=3*"Groove width@Sketch4"**.

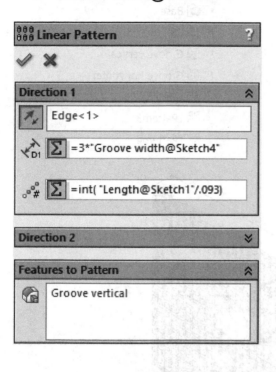

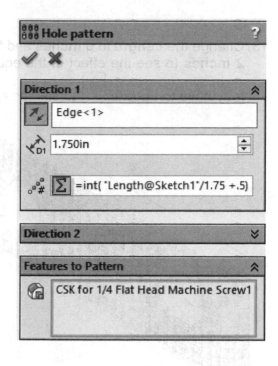

12) **Pattern** Linear Pattern *Groove horizontal* using the following equations to control the number of grooves (**=int("Height@Sketch1"/0.093)**). Set the distance between the groove equal to **=3*"Groove width@Sketch4"**.

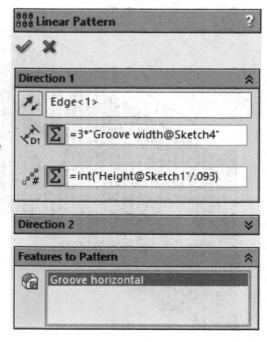

13) Change the **Length** to **5 inches** and the **Height** to **2 inches** to see the effect of the equations. You may have to **update** 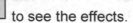 to see the effects.

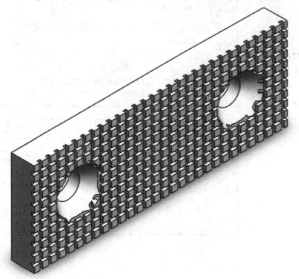

jaw insert (Default<<Default>_Dis

- ▸ History
-     Sensors
- ▸ Annotations
-     Equations
-     Alloy Steel
-     Front Plane
-     Top Plane
-     Right Plane
-     Origin
- ▸ Base
- ▸ CSK for 1/4 Flat Head Machine Scre
- ▸ Groove vertical
- ▸ Groove horizontal
-     LPattern2
-     LPattern3
-     LPattern4

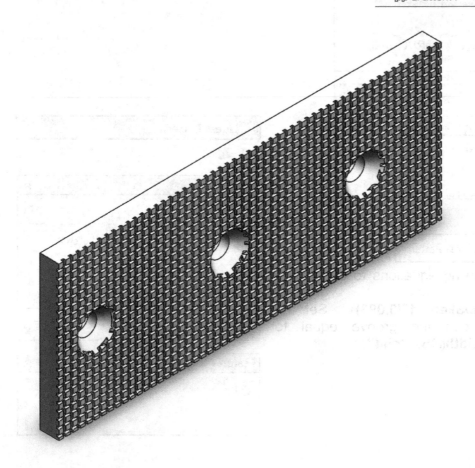

VISE PROJECT (DESIGN INTENT) PROBLEMS

P14-1) Use SolidWorks® to create the following part using the stated design intent requirements.
1) The holes always remain centered with respect to the width (50 mm).
2) The diameters of the 3 holes are proportional to the width of the part.
3) The thickness of the part (10 mm, all the way around the part) is proportional to the length of the part (110).
4) Challenge: The toleranced hole changes appropriately as the nominal diameter of the hole changes.

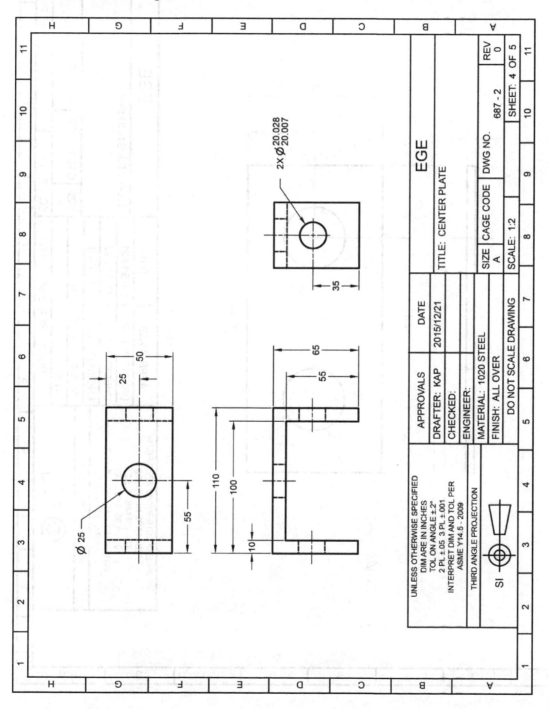

P14-2) Use SolidWorks® to create the following part using the stated design intent requirements.
1) The holes remain centered with respect to the height of the part (2.00 in).
2) The number of holes increase as the length (4.50 in) allows. The distance between each successive hole should remain the same.

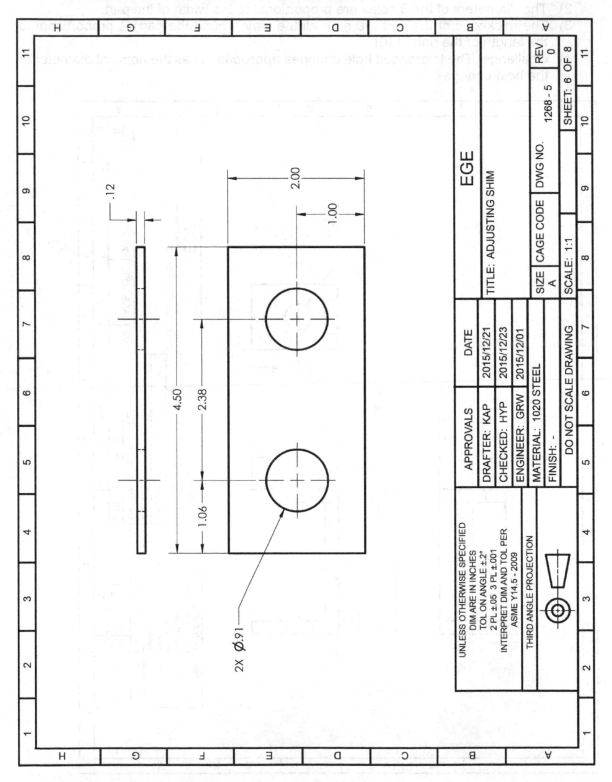

VISE PROJECT (DESIGN INTENT) QUIZ PROBLEMS

Q14-1) Open up **Childs block - Student.SLDPRT**. Apply the following design intent. By just changing one dimension (i.e. the dimension for the overall size of the block 50 mm) the following should occur.

1. The block remains a cube (i.e. all sides equal).
2. The fillets change size with the size of the block (i.e. Fillet radius = Size/10)
3. The shapes change size with the size of the block (i.e. Shape size main dimension = Size/2). Also, change all other sizes of the shape as the main dimension changes.
4. Make sure each shape stays centered. This should happen automatically for each shape except the triangle. Apply the appropriate equations/constraints to make sure the triangle remains centered.
5. The amount each shape is raised changes with the size of the block (i.e. height = Size/25)

Q14-2) Open up **Fan - Student.SLDPRT**. Apply the following design intent. By just changing one dimension (i.e. the dimension for the hub diameter 2 inches) the following should happen.

1. All fan components should scale at the same proportion as the hub diameter.
2. When the hub diameter is less than 1.00 inch, the fillets should be suppressed.
3. Note the weights for the following conditions to an accuracy of 4 decimal places.
4. Show your model to your instructor when completed.

Weight (Hub DIA = 2.00 inches) = _____ lb

Weight (Hub DIA = 4.00 inches) = _____ lb

Weight (Hub DIA = 0.75 inches) = _____ lb

CHAPTER 15

VISE PROJECT
Assembly

CHAPTER OUTLINE

15.1) PREREQUISITES

Before starting this tutorial you should complete the following tutorials.

- Vise Project – Tolerancing
- Vise Project – Design Intent / Parametric Modeling
- Flanged coupling project – Assembly
- Linear bearing

15.2) WHAT YOU WILL LEARN

The objective of this tutorial is to introduce you to *Advanced* and *Mechanical Mates*. You will assemble the parts that comprise the *Vise* assembly shown in Figure 15.2-1. Specifically, you will be learning the following commands and concepts.

Assembly

- Insert Component
- Mechanical Mates

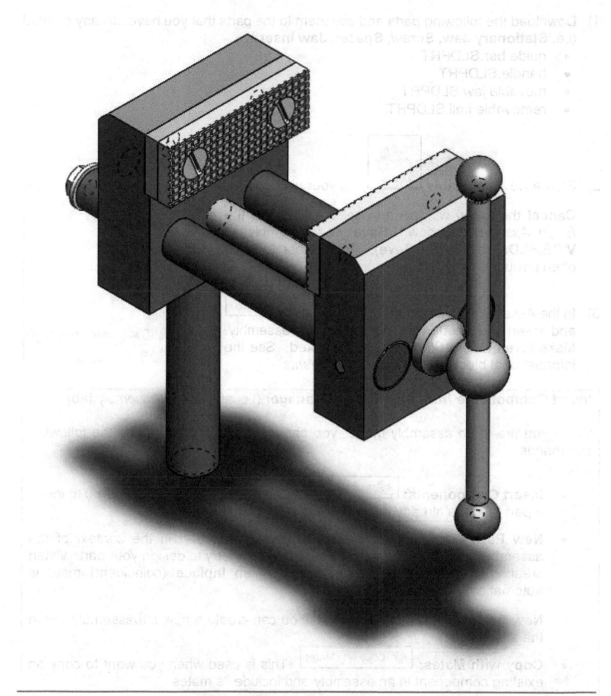

Figure 15.2-1: Vise assembly

15.3) INSERTING COMPONENTS

1) Download the following parts and add them to the parts that you have already created (i.e. **Stationary Jaw, Screw, Spacer, Jaw Insert**).
   - guide bar.SLDPRT
   - handle.SLDPRT
   - movable jaw.SLDPRT
   - removable ball.SLDPRT

2) Start a **New assembly** [Assembly], set your units to **IPS**.

   Cancel the *Open* window and select **ok** ☑ in the *Begin Assembly* window. **Save** your assembly as **VISE.SLDASM (File – Save)**. Remember to save often throughout this project.

3) In the *Assembly* tab select **Insert** [Insert Components] and insert the **Stationary Jaw** into your assembly. Make sure that the *Stationary Jaw* is **Fixed**. See the informational block on *Inserting Components*.

   - 🔲🔩 VISE (Default<Display State-
     - ⊞ 🕐 History
     - 🔘 Sensors
     - ⊞ 🅰 Annotations
     - ◇ Front Plane
     - ◇ Top Plane
     - ◇ Right Plane
     - ↳ Origin
     - ⊞ 🔩 (f) stationary jaw<1> (D₍
     - 🔲 Mates

Insert Components from the Property Manager (Located in the *Assembly* tab)

When you are in an assembly model, you can insert components using the following commands.

- **Insert Components:** [Insert Components] This command enables you to insert a part that has already been created.
- **New Part:** [New Part] You can create a new part in the context of the assembly. This allows you to use existing geometry to design your part. When creating a new part within an assembly an **Inplace** (coincident) mate is automatically created.
- **New Assembly:** [New Assembly] You can create a new subassembly within the assembly.
- **Copy with Mates:** [Copy with Mates] This is used when you want to copy an existing component in an assembly and include its mates.

---

4) **Insert** 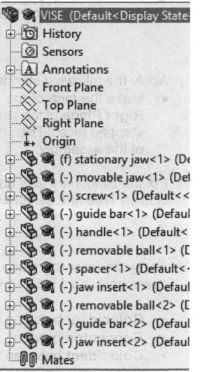 the following parts.
   - movable jaw
   - stationary jaw
   - screw
   - guide bar
   - handle
   - removable ball
   - spacer
   - jaw insert

5) Make a **copy** of the following parts (**Ctrl + click + drag**).
   - guide bar
   - removable ball
   - jaw insert

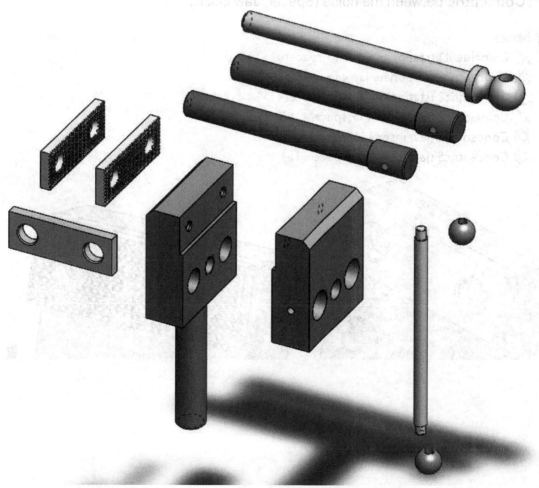

15.4) STANDARD MATES

1) Apply the following standard **Mate** 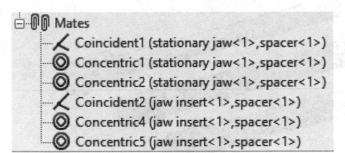 to the **Stationary Jaw**.
   - Make the face of the *Stationary Jaw* that contains the holes **Coincident** with the **Right Plane** of the assembly. Flip the alignment if need be so that you can see the stepped face. Then make the perpendicular face **Coincident** to the **Front Plane** of the assembly.

2) **Fix** the *Stationary Jaw* and **Float** the other parts (right click on the part in the *Feature Design Tree* and select either Fix or Float).

3) Apply the following standard **Mates** to achieve the following. The *Spacer* and *Jaw insert* should align with the holes in the *Stationary Jaw*.

   - **Coincident** between faces (Stationary jaw, Spacer)
   - **Concentric** between the holes (Stationary jaw, Spacer)
   - **Coincident** between faces (Spacer, Jaw insert)
   - **Concentric** between the holes (Spacer, Jaw insert)

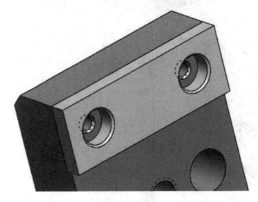

```
⊟ 🔘🔘 Mates
     ∠ Coincident1 (stationary jaw<1>,spacer<1>)
     ◎ Concentric1 (stationary jaw<1>,spacer<1>)
     ◎ Concentric2 (stationary jaw<1>,spacer<1>)
     ∠ Coincident2 (jaw insert<1>,spacer<1>)
     ◎ Concentric4 (jaw insert<1>,spacer<1>)
     ◎ Concentric5 (jaw insert<1>,spacer<1>)
```

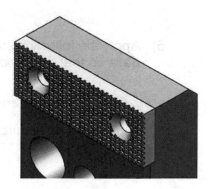

4) Apply the following standard **Mates** 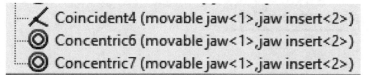 to achieve similar results between the **Movable jaw** and the other **Jaw insert**. You will most likely have to use **Mate Alignment** to get the part flipped in the correct direction.

   ∠ Coincident4 (movable jaw<1>,jaw insert<2>)
   ◎ Concentric6 (movable jaw<1>,jaw insert<2>)
   ◎ Concentric7 (movable jaw<1>,jaw insert<2>)

5) Apply the following standard **Mates** between the **Movable jaw** and the **Guide bars** so that the *Guide bars* fit into the holes and the holes for the *Pin* align.

   ◎ Concentric7 (movable jaw<1>,guide bar<2>)

   ◎ Concentric8 (guide bar<1>,movable jaw<1>)

   ◎ Concentric9 (guide bar<1>,movable jaw<1>)

   ◎ Concentric10 (movable jaw<1>,guide bar<2>)

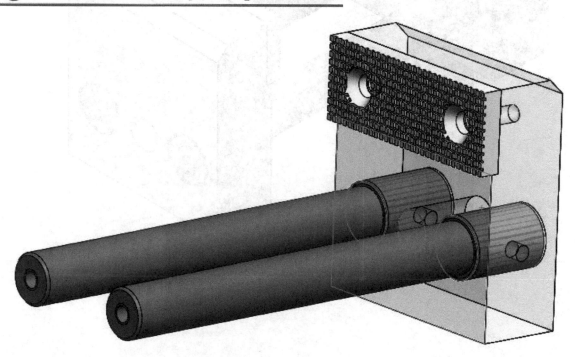

6) Apply the following standard **Mates** 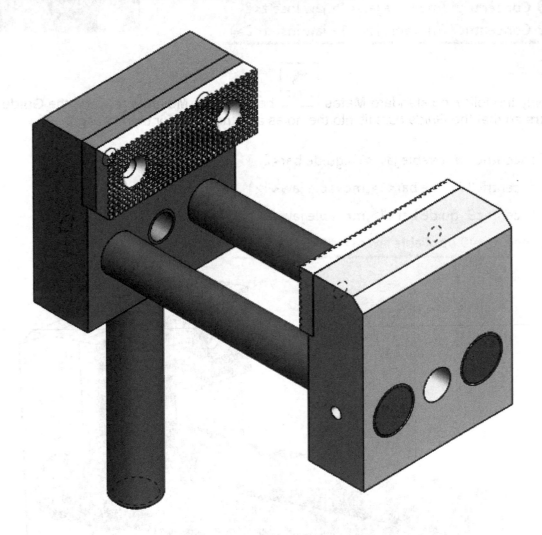 between the **Stationary jaw** and the **Guide bars** so that the *Guide bars* fit into the holes.

   ◎ Concentric12 (stationary jaw<1>,guide bar<2>)

   ◎ Concentric13 (guide bar<1>,stationary jaw<1>)

7) Apply the following standard **Mates** 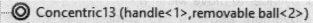 between the **Handle** and the **Removable** balls. Note that the **Coincident** mates are between the rim of the hole on the *Ball* and the stepped surface on the *Handle*. You will most likely have to use **Mate Alignment** to get one of the balls to be flipped in the correct direction.

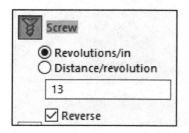

- ⊙ Concentric13 (handle<1>,removable ball<2>)
- ∠ Coincident7 (handle<1>,removable ball<2>)
- ⊙ Concentric14 (handle<1>,removable ball<1>)
- ∠ Coincident8 (handle<1>,removable ball<1>)

15.5) MECHANICAL MATES

1) Apply a **Screw Mate** between the **Screw** and **Stationary Jaw**. (See the informational block on **Mechanical Mates**.)

a. Select the **Mate** command.
b. Open up the **Mechanical Mates**.
c. Select the shaft of the *Screw* and the inner surface of the center threaded hole of the *Stationary Jaw*.
d. Select the **Screw** mate.
e. Select the **Revolutions/in** radio button. Since the threads are 1/2 – 13, the Screw will advance 1 inch per every 13 revolutions.
f. <u>Note:</u> When the assembly is complete and you rotate the screw, you may need to edit the mate and click the reverse on or off if it is rotating in the wrong direction.

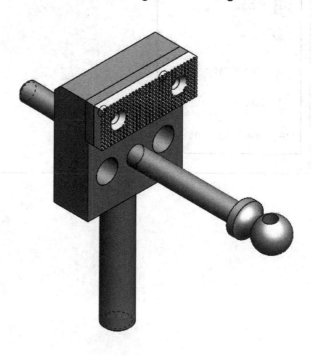

Mechanical Mates

SOLIDWORKS® gives you a variety of *Mechanical Mates* to choose from. These mates are associated with certain machine elements. The available *Mechanical Mates* are

- **Cam:** This mate is a type of coincident mate. It allows you to mate a cylinder, plane, or point to a surface that is closed and does not have any discontinuities.
- **Slot:** This mate forces an axis or cylinder to move within a slot.
- **Hinge:**   This mate limits the movement between two components to one rotational degree of freedom. You may also limit the angular movement between the two components.
- **Gear:** This mate forces two components to rotate relative to one another about selected axes.
- **Rack Pinion:**   This mate forces one component to rotate when another translates or vice versa.
- **Screw:** This mate constrains two components to be concentric and also adds a pitch relationship. This means that the translation of one component along the axis causes rotation of the other component according to the pitch relationship or vice versa.
- **Universal Joint:** With this mate the rotation of one component about its axis is driven by the rotation of another component about its axis. The axes are usually different.

15.6) TOOL BOX COMPONENTS

1) Use the **Tool Box** to insert the following components.
   - 4X 1/4 – 20 UNC Countersunk Flat Head Screw that is 1.00 inch long with a thread length of 0.75 inch.
   - 2X 1/4 – 20 UNC Hex Head Bolt that is 0.875 inch long with a thread length of 0.75 inch.
   - 2X 3/8 - Type A Plain Washer. This will produce a 0.406 ID and 0.812 OD.
   - 2X 3/16 Spring Pin Slotted that is 0.875 inch long.

2) Apply the appropriate **Mates** [Mate] to the tool box components to achieve the results shown. Use the assembly drawing shown on the next page to guide you on the placement of the tool box components.

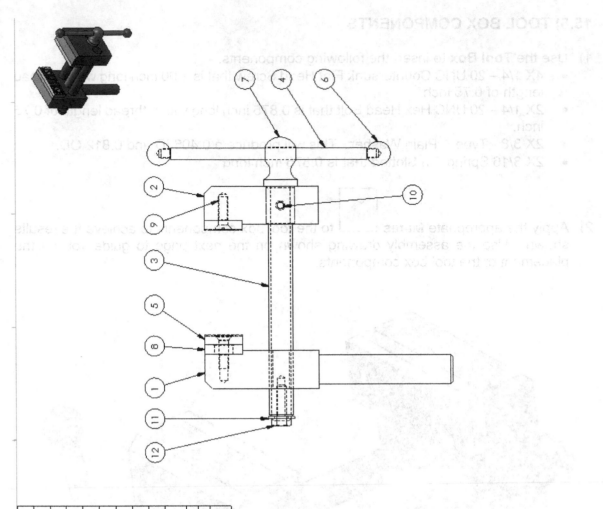

ITEM NO.	PART NUMBER	DESCRIPTION	QTY.
1	STATIONARY JAW		1
2	MOVABLE JAW		1
3	GUIDE BAR		2
4	HANDLE		1
5	JAW INSERT		2
6	REMOVABLE BALL		2
7	SCREW		1
8	SPACER		1
9	1/4 - 20 UNC FLAT HEAD SCREW		4
10	3/16 PIN		2
11	FLAT WASHER		2
12	1/4 - 20 UNC HEX HEAD BOLT		2

15.7) ADVANCED MATES

1) Apply the following standard **Mates** 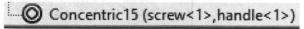 between the **Handle** and the **Screw** so that the *Handle* fits through the hole in the *Screw*.

> ◎ Concentric15 (screw<1>,handle<1>)

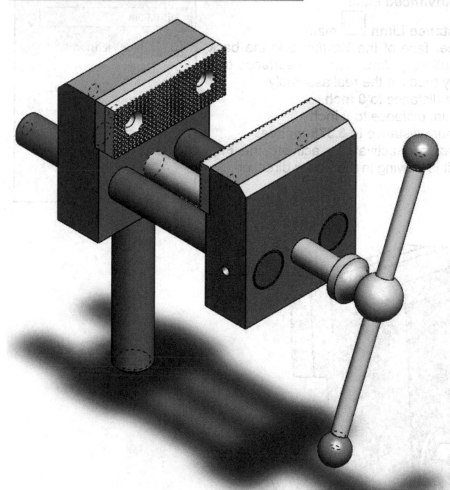

2) Pull on the *Movable Jaw, Handle,* and *Screw* and see how they move in unrealistic ways. Parts will pass right though each other. This should not happen in a real assembly. We will fix these problems with *Advanced Mates.*

3) Apply a **Distance Limit Mate** to the **Guide Bar Washers** so that they don't go through the **Stationary Jaw**. After applying the mate, pull on the *Movable Jaw* to see if the mate works properly. The *Washers* should not go through the *Stationary Jaw*.

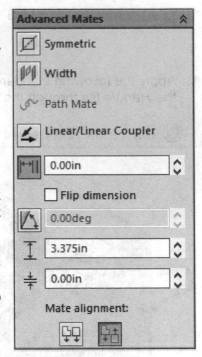

a. Select the **Mate** command.
b. Open up the **Advanced Mates**.

c. Select the **Distance Limit** mate.
d. Select the inner face of the *Washer* and the back face of the *Stationary Jaw*. The two surfaces that would normally touch in the real assembly.
e. Set the default distance to **0 inch**.
f. Set the minimum distance to **0 inch**.
g. Set the maximum distance to **3.375 inches**.
h. You may have to deactivate or activate the **Flip dimension** if it is moving in the wrong direction.

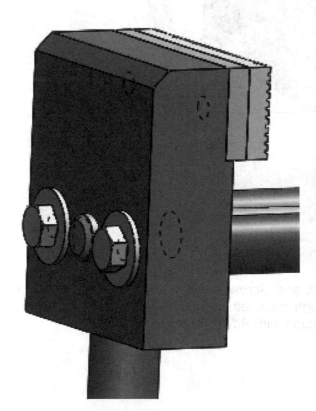

4) Apply other **Distance Limit Mate** 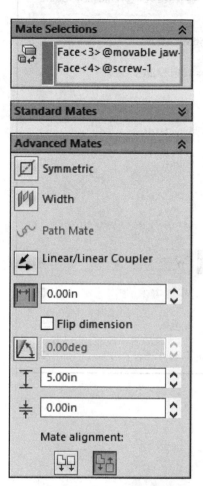 to the **Screw** so that it does not go through the **Movable Jaw**. Use a default distance of **0** inches, a minimum distance of **0** inches, and a maximum distance of **5** inches.

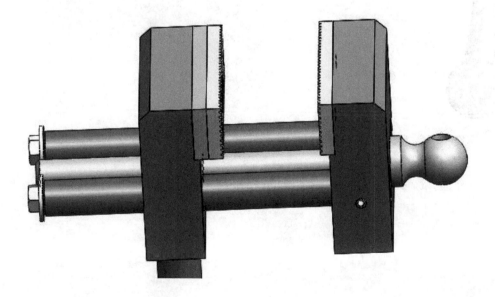

5) On your own, apply a **Distance Limit Mate** between the *Handle* and *Screw*.

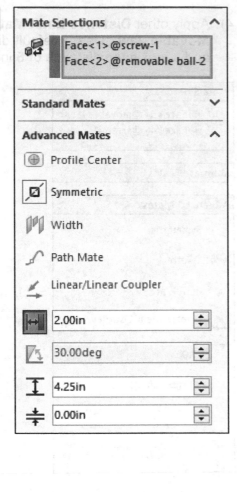

VISE PROJECT (ASSEMBLY) PROBLEMS

P15-1) Use SOLIDWORKS® to create an assembly model of the *Milling Jack* shown. Use the appropriate tolerances and mates.

<u>Milling Jack</u>

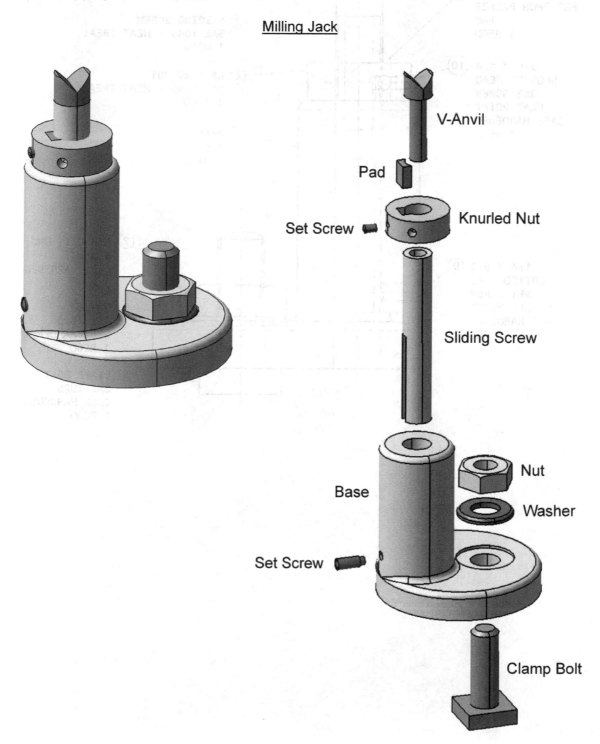

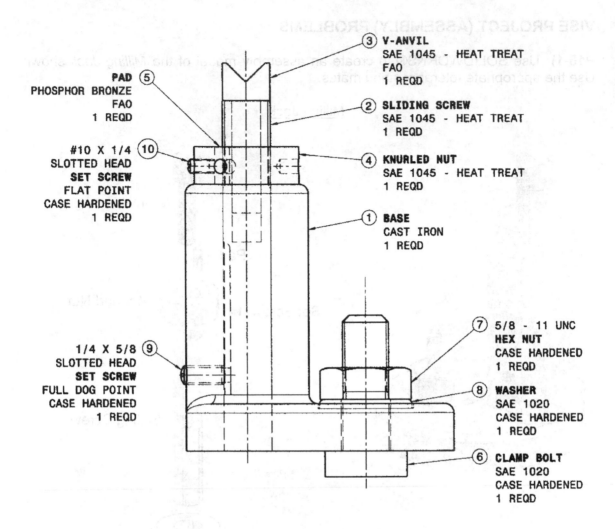

PAD (5)
PHOSPHOR BRONZE
FAO
1 REQD

#10 X 1/4 (10)
SLOTTED HEAD
SET SCREW
FLAT POINT
CASE HARDENED
1 REQD

1/4 X 5/8 (9)
SLOTTED HEAD
SET SCREW
FULL DOG POINT
CASE HARDENED
1 REQD

(3) **V-ANVIL**
SAE 1045 - HEAT TREAT
FAO
1 REQD

(2) **SLIDING SCREW**
SAE 1045 - HEAT TREAT
1 REQD

(4) **KNURLED NUT**
SAE 1045 - HEAT TREAT
1 REQD

(1) **BASE**
CAST IRON
1 REQD

(7) 5/8 - 11 UNC
HEX NUT
CASE HARDENED
1 REQD

(8) **WASHER**
SAE 1020
CASE HARDENED
1 REQD

(6) **CLAMP BOLT**
SAE 1020
CASE HARDENED
1 REQD

Base

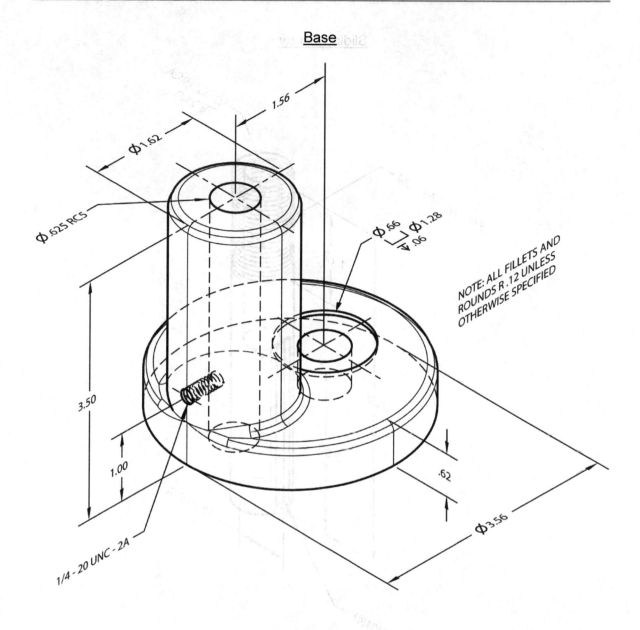

1.56

Ø1.62

Ø.625 RC5

Ø.66 Ø1.28
.06

NOTE: ALL FILLETS AND
ROUNDS R .12 UNLESS
OTHERWISE SPECIFIED

3.50

1.00

.62

Ø3.56

1/4 - 20 UNC - 2A

Sliding Screw

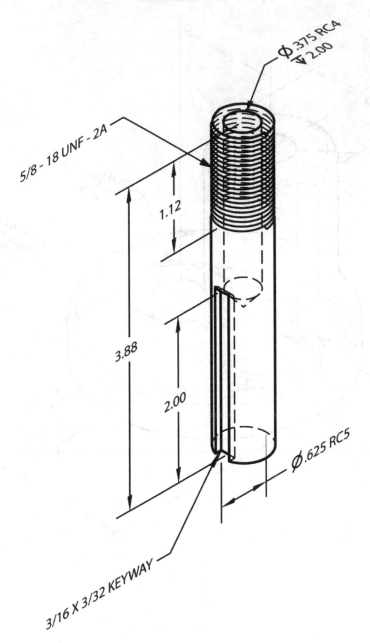

V-Anvil

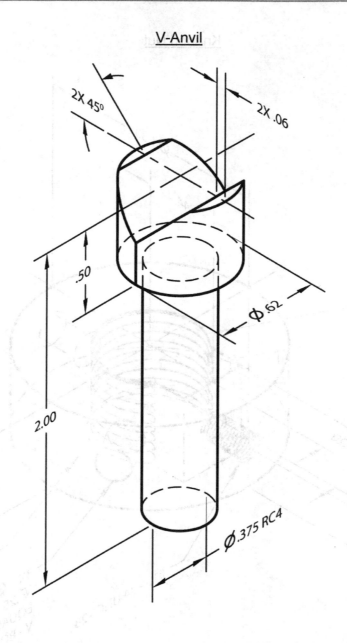

Knurled Nut

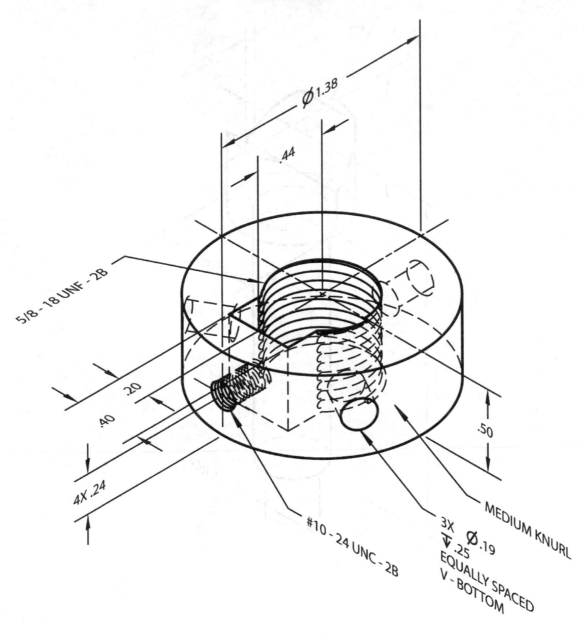

Ø1.38

.44

5/8 - 18 UNF - 2B

.20

.40

4X .24

#10 - 24 UNC - 2B

3X   Ø.19
⊽ .25
EQUALLY SPACED
V - BOTTOM

MEDIUM KNURL

.50

Pad

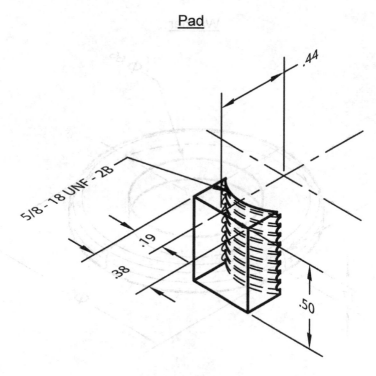

Clamp Bolt

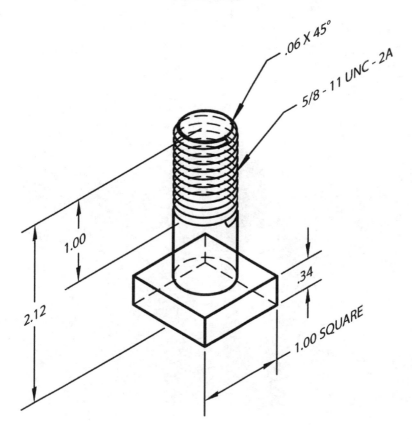

Washer

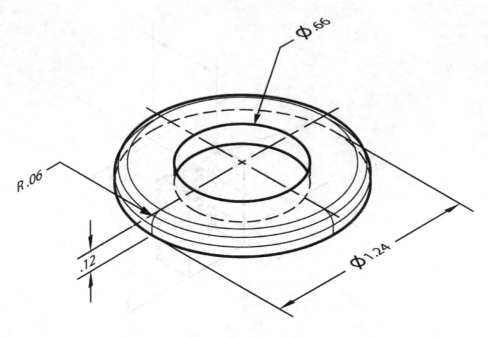

VISE PROJECT (ASSEMBLY) QUIZ PROBLEMS

Q15-1) Use SOLIDWORKS® to create an assembly model of the *Dowel Fixture* shown. Use the appropriate mates.

1) Download the following files and insert them into a new Assembly.
   - **Center Block.SLDPRT**
   - **Custom Snap Washer.SLDPRT**
   - **Guide Bar.SLDRT**
   - **Handle.SLDRT**
   - **Left Clamp.SLDRT**
   - **Right Clamp.SLDRT**
   - **Right-Left Hand Screw.SLDRT**

2) Make one **copy** of the *Guide Bar*.

3) Assemble the *Dowel Fixture* using the assembly drawing and posted video as a guide.

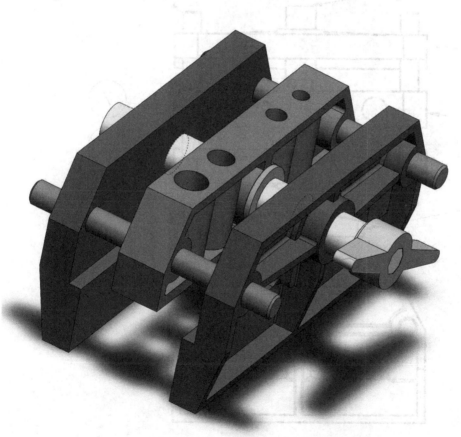

ITEM NO.	PART NAME	QTY.
1	Center Block	1
2	Guide Bar	2
3	Handle	1
4	Left Clamp	1
5	Right Clamp	1
6	Right-Left Hand Screw	1
7	Custom Snap Washer	1

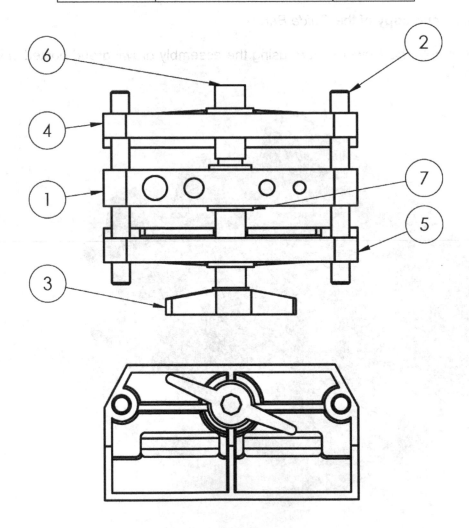

CHAPTER 16

BICYCLE HANDLEBAR PROJECT
3D Sketch

CHAPTER OUTLINE

16.1) PREREQUISITES

Before starting this tutorial, you should complete the listed tutorial.

- Chapter 2 – Connecting Rod Project– Part model tutorial
- Chapter 10 – Microphone Project – Base
- Chapter 11 – Microphone Project - Arm
- Chapter 12 – Boat Project

16.2) WHAT YOU WILL LEARN

The objective of this tutorial is to introduce you to SOLIDWORKS' 3D Sketching capabilities. You will be modeling the *Drop-Down Bicycle Handlebar* shown in Figure 16.2-1. Specifically, you will be learning the following commands and concepts.

View

- Adding commands to the Command Manager

Sketch

- 3D Sketch
- Spline

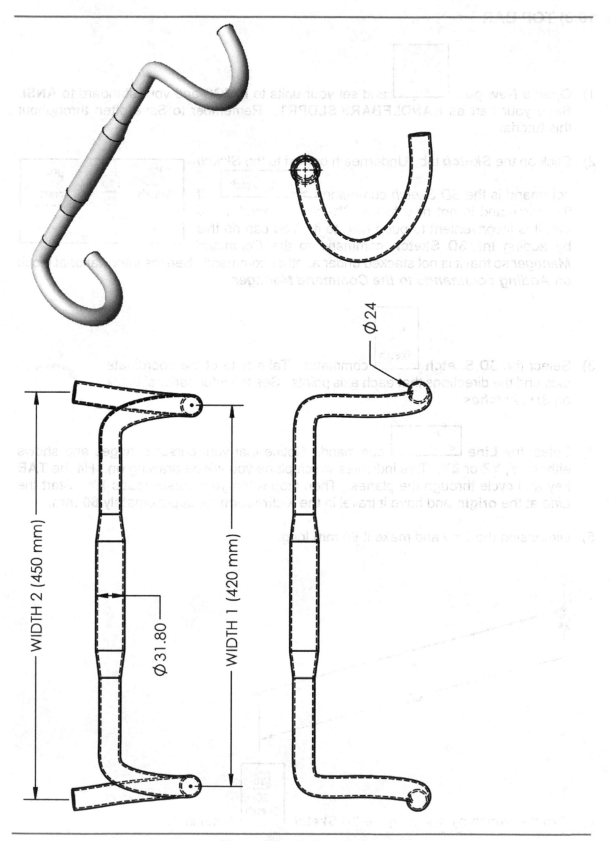

Figure 16.2-1: Handlebar

16.3) TOP BAR

1) Open a **New part** 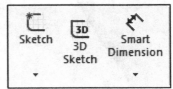 and set your units to **MMGS** and your standard to **ANSI**. **Save** your part as **HANDLEBARS.SLDPRT**. Remember to Save often throughout this tutorial.

2) Click on the **Sketch** tab. Underneath or next to the *Sketch* command is the *3D Sketch* command. If the command is not next to the *Sketch* command, I find that it is inconvenient to put it next to it. You can do this by adding the **3D Sketch** command to the *Command Manager* so that it is not stacked under another command. See the informational block on **Adding commands to the Command Manager**.

3) Select the **3D Sketch** command. Take note of the coordinate axis and the directions that each axis points. See the informational block on **3D sketches**.

4) Select the **Line** command. Notice that your cursor changes and shows either **XY, YZ** or **ZX**. This indicates which plane you will be drawing on. Hit the **TAB** key and cycle through the planes. Then stop when your cursor reads **XY**. Start the *Line* at the **origin** and have it travel in the **X-direction** for approximately **60 mm**.

5) Dimension the *Line* and make it **60 mm** long.

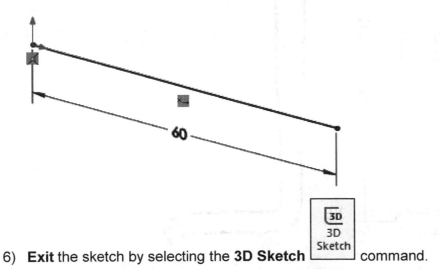

6) **Exit** the sketch by selecting the **3D Sketch** command.

Adding commands to the *Command Manager*

The *Command Manager* may be customized to hold any command that you find useful. To add or remove commands, follow these steps.

1) **Right click** on the *Command Manager* in an open area (an area with no commands) and select **Customize**.
2) In the *Customize* window, select the **Commands** tab.
3) Select the *Category* in which the command resides. A set of *Buttons* will appear on the right side.
4) **Click and drag** the desired command to the *Command Manager*.

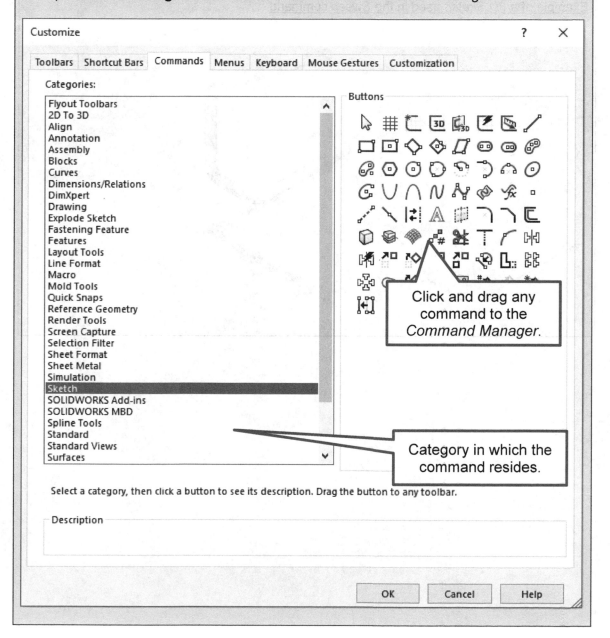

3D Sketch 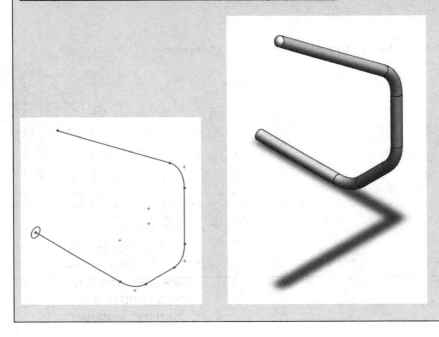 (Located in the *Sketch* tab)

A **3D Sketch** is a non-planar sketch that may be used as a guide curve in the *Sweep* or *Loft* commands. A *3D Sketch* may be drawn on the **XY, YZ** or **ZX** plane. You can even switch between the planes within a single sketch. For example, you can start drawing on the **XY** plane and then switch to drawing on the **YZ** plane. To switch between planes, select the **TAB** key.

Example of a *3D Sketch* used in the *Sweep* command

7) **Sketch** 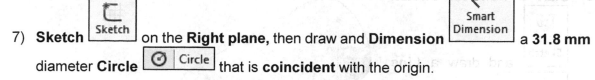 on the **Right plane,** then draw and **Dimension** a **31.8 mm** diameter **Circle** that is **coincident** with the origin.

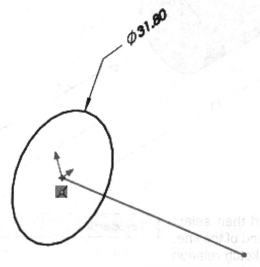

8) **Sweep Boss/Base** 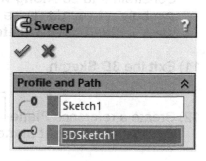 the *Circle* along the *Line.* If the *Sweep* command is grayed out, **Rebuild** .

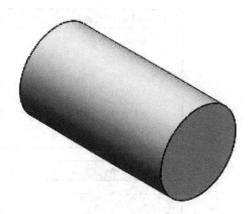

9) Start a new **3D Sketch**
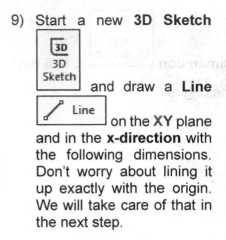
and draw a **Line**
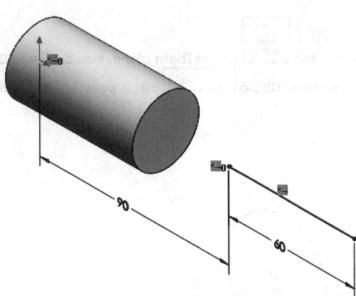
on the **XY** plane and in the **x-direction** with the following dimensions. Don't worry about lining it up exactly with the origin. We will take care of that in the next step.

10) **Exit** the *Smart Dimension* command and then select the origin, hold the **Ctrl** key and then the end of the line. Constrain it to be **Along X**. Notice the sketch relation symbols. If you don't see any sketch relations, select **View – Hide/Show – Sketch Relations**.

11) **Exit** the **3D Sketch**.

12) Create a reference **Plane** [Plane] that is **90 mm** to the right of the **Right plane**.

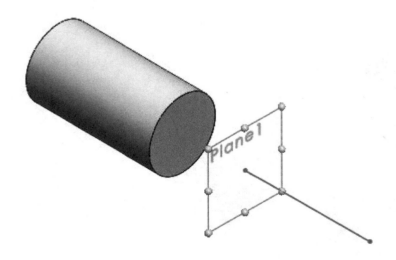

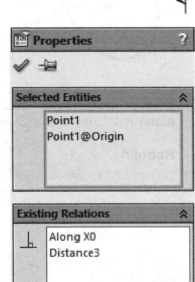

Properties ?

Selected Entities
> Point1
> Point1@Origin

Existing Relations
> Along X0
> Distance3

ⓘ Fully Defined

Add Relations
> ⤒X Along X
> ⤒Y Along Y
> ⤒Z Along Z
> ⟋ Coincident

13) On the new plane, draw a **24 mm** diameter **Circle** 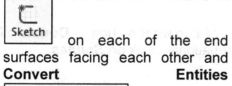 that is **coincident** with the origin.

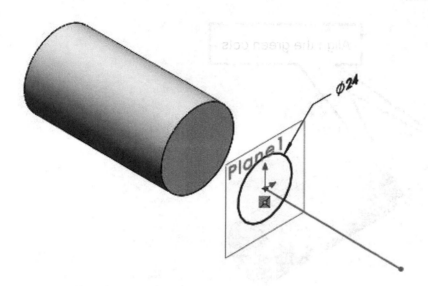

14) **Sweep Boss/Base**

 Swept Boss/Base   each *Circle* along each *Line*.

15) We want to connect the gaps to make one single bar. **Sketch**

 Sketch   on each of the end surfaces facing each other and **Convert** **Entities**

 Convert Entities   the ends into sketches. You should have two circles when you are done.

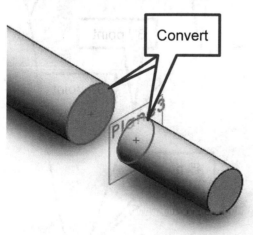

16) **Loft Boss/Base** 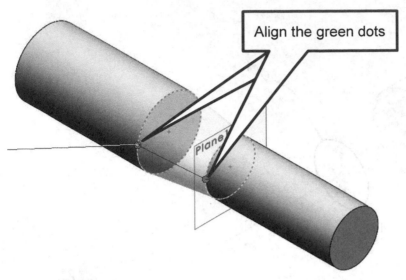 between each pair of circles. If the *Loft* is twisted, move the green dots so that they lineup. (A description of the *Loft* command is given in the *Microphone Project*.)

16.4) SPLINE

1) View your part from the **Top**. The **Shift + arrow** key will rotate the part so that you can get it into the position shown. Start a new **3D Sketch** and draw a 6-point **Spline** on the **ZX** plane that looks similar to what is shown. **Double click** on the last point to end the *Spline*. See the informational block on *Splines*.

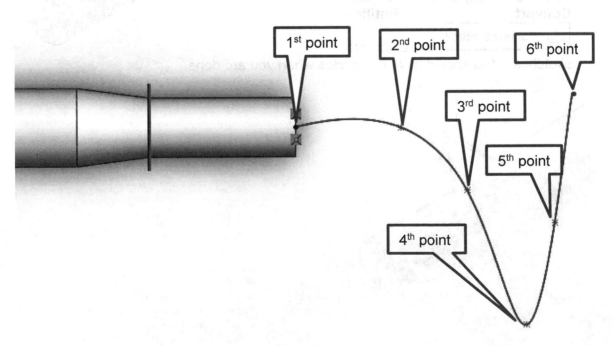

2) Set the coordinates of the *Spline* points to the following. After you adjust the coordinates of the points, your sketch will look like the figure.
   a. First point = 150,0,0
   b. Second point = 180,0,0
   c. Third point = 210,-19,65
   d. Fourth point = 210,-60,89
   e. Fifth point = 217,-127,15
   f. Sixth point = 225,-127,-40

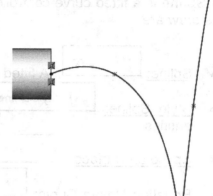

3) Show the isometric view (**Ctrl + 7**). This is now the general shape of the drop-down part of the handlebar, but we need to tweak the tangencies.

4) **View** the handlebar from the **top** and click on the **first point**. Notice that a spline handle appears. Drag the end of the arrow so that it is horizontal. Then, adjust the tangency of the **second point** to create an approximate straight line between the first and second points.

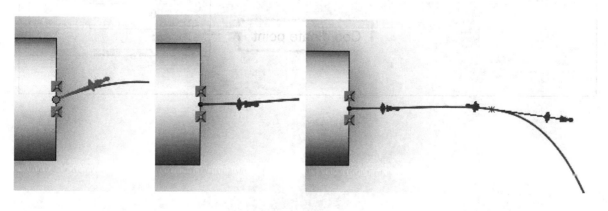

Spline 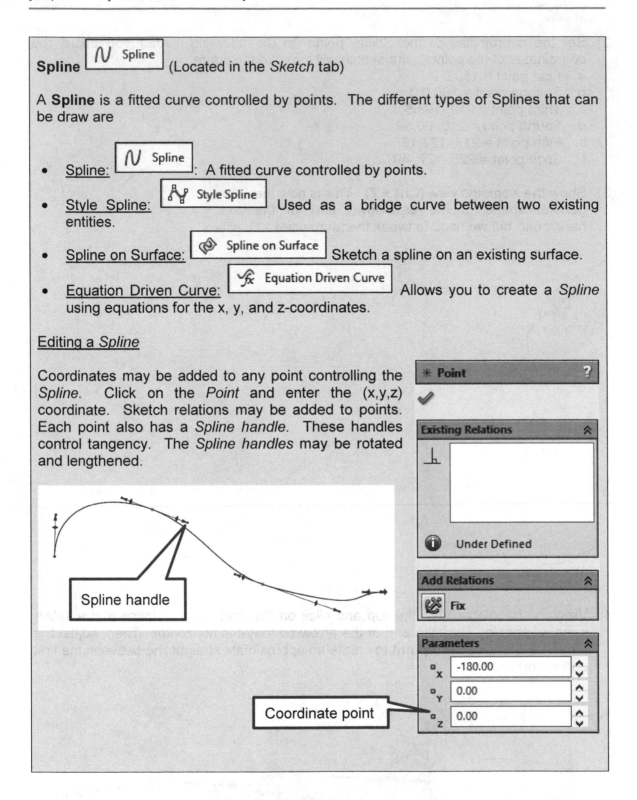 (Located in the *Sketch* tab)

A **Spline** is a fitted curve controlled by points. The different types of Splines that can be draw are

- Spline: : A fitted curve controlled by points.

- Style Spline: Used as a bridge curve between two existing entities.

- Spline on Surface: Sketch a spline on an existing surface.

- Equation Driven Curve: Allows you to create a *Spline* using equations for the x, y, and z-coordinates.

Editing a *Spline*

Coordinates may be added to any point controlling the *Spline*. Click on the *Point* and enter the (x,y,z) coordinate. Sketch relations may be added to points. Each point also has a *Spline handle*. These handles control tangency. The *Spline handles* may be rotated and lengthened.

Spline handle

Coordinate point

5) In the same view, adjust the tangency of the **sixth point** to create an approximately straight line between the fifth and sixth point.

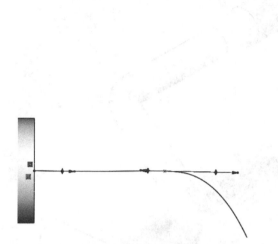

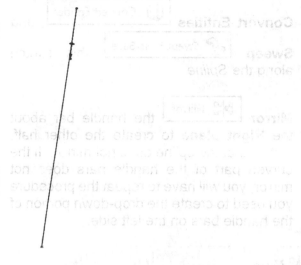

6) **View** the handlebar from the **right side**. Adjust the tangency of the **sixth point** to create an approximatly straight line between the fifth and sixth point.

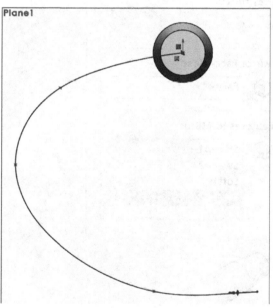

7) When you are done, you should have a shape similar to what is shown. **Exit** the **3D Sketch**.

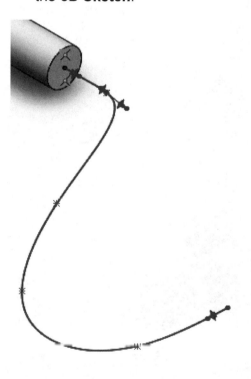

16.5) DROP DOWN BAR

1) **Sketch** on the right end of the top bar, **Convert Entities** 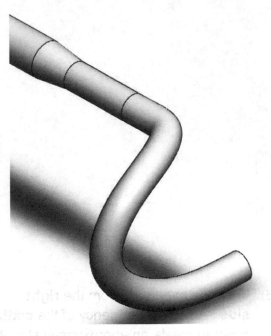 , and **Sweep** [Swept Boss/Base] this sketch along the *Spline*.

2) **Mirror** [Mirror] the handle bar about the **Right plane** to create the other half. Notice that the spline does not mirror. If the curved part of the handle bars does not mirror, you will have to repeat the procedure you used to create the drop-down portion of the handle bars on the left side.

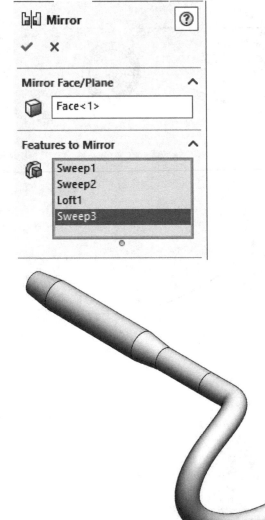

3) **Shell** 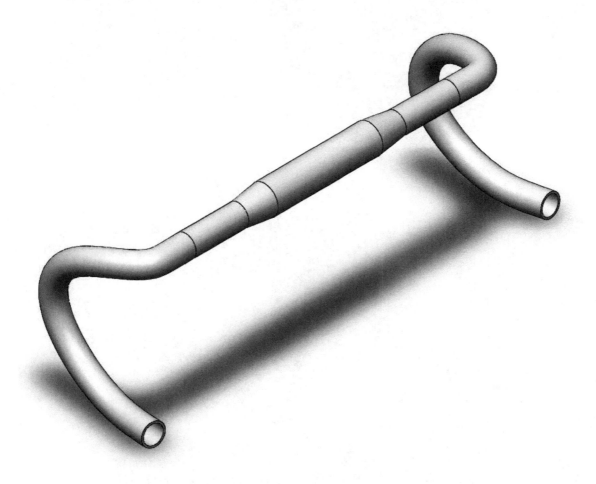 the part to **2 mm** eliminating the two end faces. (The *Shell* command is described in *Microphone Project*.)

NOTES:

BICYCLE HANDLEBAR (3D SKETCH) - PROBLEMS

P16-1) Model one of the following objects.

a) A whisk

b) Spring – Use at least one SWEEP command.

c) An exhaust pipe

d) A fluorescent light bulb

e) An oven rack

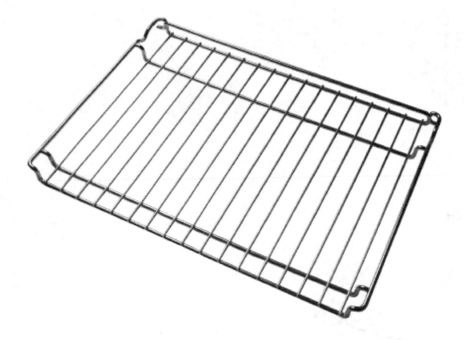

BICYCLE HANDLEBAR (3D SKETCH) – QUIZ PROBLEMS

Q16-1) Model the frame of the following chair and then calculate your mass. Dimensions are given in millimeters.

Mass = _____ g

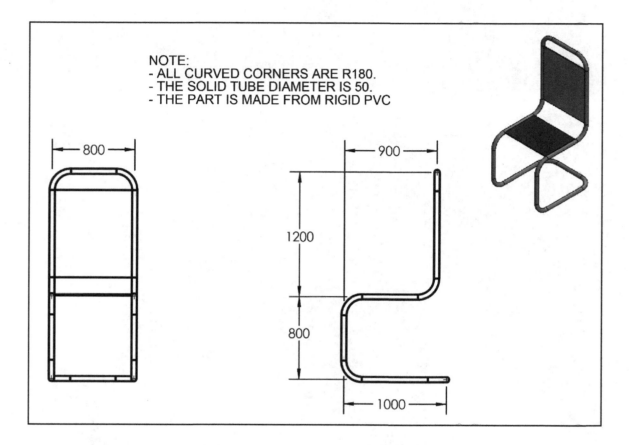

NOTE:
- ALL CURVED CORNERS ARE R180.
- THE SOLID TUBE DIAMETER IS 50.
- THE PART IS MADE FROM RIGID PVC

NOTES:

NOTES: